Éloi Ficquet, Wolbert G. C. Smidt (Eds.)

The Life and Times of *Lïj* Iyasu of Ethiopia

Northeast African History, Orality and Heritage

edited by

Dirk Bustorf and Wolbert G. C. Smidt

Volume 3

LIT

The Life and Times of *Lïj* Iyasu of Ethiopia

New Insights

edited by

Éloi Ficquet and Wolbert G. C. Smidt

LIT

This book is dedicated to the memory of
Professor Hussein Ahmed (1952 – 2009)

Cover picture: *Lïj* Iyasu, ca. 1912, watching a horse race in Addis Abeba, sitting on the seat of his grand-father Emperor Mïnilïk II, and dressed like him. Detail from the exhibition "Lights and Shadows: Insights in the photographic heritage of Lij Iyasu (1898 – 1935)", Addis Abeba, National Museum of Ethiopia, and Museum of Dessie, curated by Estelle Sohier during the Lij Iyasu Workshop, November2009, with courtesy of IsIAO, Rome (Collection Bertolani).

This book is published with the financial support of: the French Center for Ethiopian Studies (CFEE) in Addis Ababa, the French National Center for Scientific Research (CNRS), Paris, and the Austrian Embassy in Ethiopia.

This book is printed on acid-free paper.

Bibliographic information published by the Deutsche Nationalbibliothek
The Deutsche Nationalbibliothek lists this publication in the Deutsche Nationalbibliografie; detailed bibliographic data are available in the Internet at http://dnb.d-nb.de.

ISBN 978-3-643-90476-8

A catalogue record for this book is available from the British Library

Klosbachstr. 107
CH-8032 Zürich
Tel. +41 (0) 44-251 75 05
Fax +41 (0) 44-251 75 06
E-Mail: zuerich@lit-verlag.ch
http://www.lit-verlag.ch

LIT VERLAG Dr. W. Hopf
Berlin 2014
Fresnostr. 2
D-48159 Münster
Tel. +49 (0) 2 51-62 03 20
Fax +49 (0) 2 51-23 19 72
E-Mail: lit@lit-verlag.de
http://www.lit-verlag.de

Distribution:
In Germany: LIT Verlag Fresnostr. 2, D-48159 Münster
Tel. +49 (0) 2 51-620 32 22, Fax +49 (0) 2 51-922 60 99, E-mail: vertrieb@lit-verlag.de

In Austria: Medienlogistik Pichler-ÖBZ, e-mail: mlo@medien-logistik.at
In the UK: Global Book Marketing, e-mail: mo@centralbooks.com
In North America: International Specialized Book Services, e-mail: orders@isbs.com
e-books are available at www.litwebshop.de

Table of Contents

Part III: *Lïj* Iyasu's Foreign Relations

Part IV: The Long End of His Reign

List of Figures and Pictures

Final picture:

Note on the transliteration

The system for the transliteration of Ethio-Semitic languages used in this book does not employ any special diacritics and is therefore practical. It is close to the transliteration established by the *Acta Aethiopica* and is the closest to the simplified spelling habits used by educated Ethiopians when they use the Latin alphabet instead of the much more exact Geez script.

If words in non-Ethiosemitic languages appear which do not use the Geez script, the already established local orthography in Latin script is followed. Arabic words, in Arabic context, are transliterated following the standard system of the Deutsche Morgenländische Gesellschaft.

Vowels

The seven vowels, following the order of the traditional *fidel*-table:

1st order	2nd order	3rd order	4th order	5th order	6th order	7th order
ለ	ሉ	ሊ	ላ	ሌ	ል	ሎ
le	lu	li	la	lé	l(ï)	lo

Note on the 6th order (shwa): The shwa is sometimes pronounced, sometimes not. Accordingly it is noted (ï) only when pronounced.

Consonants

a. Consonants typical for Ethiopian languages:

Plosive-ejectives: ቀ = q | ቐ = q̲ | ጠ = t’ | ጨ = ch’ | ጰ = p’ | ጸ / ፀ= ts

Fricatives: ሐ = h̲ | ኸ = k̲ |

Laryngals: ዐ = ‘ *(ayn)* | አ = ’ *(alif) (can be left away if a word starts with this vowel)*

NB1: *ts* can also be transliterated as s’, but *ts* is closer to the local usage. **NB2:** the differences are noted for fricatives and laryngals if there are differences in pronounciation, e.g. in Tigrinya, not in Amharic. **NB3:** Gemination is shown by double writing of a consonant, e.g. *abyot* / *Abbo.*

b. Other consonants (pronunciation mostly as in English):

| ሀ/ኀ *h* | ለ *l* | መ *m* | ሠ/ሰ *s* | ረ *r* | ሸ *sh* | በ *b* | ተ *t* | ቸ *ch* | ነ *n* | ኘ *ñ* | ከ *k* |

| ወ *w* | ዘ *z* | ዠ *zh* | የ *y* | ደ *d* | ጀ *j* | ገ *g* | ፈ *f* | ፐ *p* |

Examples

Addis Abeba | *Atsé* | *Lïj* Iyasu | *Dejjazmach* | Hayle Sïllasé | Gï‘ïz | Ïch’egé | Ïnt’ott’o | Mika’él | Mammedoch | Mïnilïk II | *Nïgus* | *Qeññazmach* | Shewa | Tïgray | T’aytu | *Tseh̲afé tï’ïzaz* | Wello | Yoh̲annïs IV |

Placenames of ETHIOPIA
relevant to the understanding
of the LÏJ IYASU years - ca. 1909 -1921
Italian Colony of
Eritrea
Red Sea
Mitsiwwa
Asmara
Anglo-Egyptian
Sudan
200 km
Shiré
Aksum
'Agamé
Ïndïrta
Welqayt
Tembén
Meqele
Wegera
Sïmén
Tïgray
Gonder
Wag
Maych'ew
Dembïya
Zobïl
Lasta
Mokha
Asab
Aden
French Coast of
the Somalis
Gulf of Aden
Qwara
Begémdïr
Yejju
Awsa
Obock
Tadjourah
Djibouti
Zayla
Gayïnt
Wadla
Aysaita
Mecch'a
Tenta
Desé
Gojjam
Wello
Kombolcha
Beni
Shangul
Agawmïdïr
Damot
Werre Ilu
Senbeté
Berbera
Guduru
Railway
Fiché
Ankober
British Colony of
Somaliland
Wallaggaa
Shewa
Segelé
Dirré Dawa
Naqamtee
Addis Alem
Addis Abeba
Awash
Mi'éso
Harer
Jigjiga
Gara Muleta
Leeqa
Harergé
Gimbi
Gimirra
Guma
Guragé
Kambata
Jimmaa
Arsi
Jimmaa
Kefa
Konta
Kullo
Welamo
Balee
Ogaden
Sidamo
Bonga
Booranaa
Italian Colony of
Somalia
British Colony of
Eastern Africa
Mogadiscio
boundary of Somalia before the transfer
of Jubaland in 1925.
Indian Ocean

Foreword

Éloi Ficquet – Wolbert G.C. Smidt

One hundred years ago, the young Shewan[1] prince *Lïj* Iyasu assumed power as the uncrowned emperor of Ethiopia. In 1909 Emperor Mïnilïk II had declared to his notables that *Lïj* Iyasu, his grandson, will be his successor, and in 1910 – after a short interim under Empress T'aytu as the de-facto-regent of Ethiopia – *Lïj* Iyasu was effectively nominated ruler of Ethiopia, replacing T'aytu and his ailing grandfather. Iyasu's short reign from 1910 to 1916 was marked by uncertainties and great challenges both internally and externally, and constituted a crucial period of transition. These uncertainties were amplified by the international context of World War I, which broke out only a few years after *Lïj* Iyasu had assumed power. Remarkably, even if this period was an important turning point of modern Ethiopian history, many questions remain unanswered. The aim of this book is not to celebrate *Lïj* Iyasu's centenary jubilee, but to ask new questions and look for new answers. The period of *Lïj* Iyasu's reign, which lasted only six years, remains obscure and widely unknown, even to specialized researchers. This is, on the one hand, due to a great lack of sources and, on the other hand, due to an oversimplified condemnation of his rule, initiated by his successor Hayle Sïllassé, whose legitimacy depended to some degree on the de-legitimization of *Lïj* Iyasu. Both factors helped to discourage research until recently. During the past two decades, however, new sources started to come up[2] and they allow some new insights in this crucial period of modern Ethiopia during World War I, making a more differentiated analysis of *Lïj* Iyasu's controversial reign possible.

Lïj Iyasu implemented a series of reforms within the process of construction of a modern state in Ethiopia that remain to be assessed. He also attempted the reconciliation of the most diverse princedoms, provinces and submitted territories under the "crown" – the concept of crown being of particular ambiguity under his rule. On his shoulders there was the weight of international diplomacy and relationships, on the one hand, with colonial powers and, on the other hand, with resisting anti-colonial chiefdoms and power

1 Politically he was raised as a prince of Shewa, but through direct descent he belonged to the Wello Muslim dynasty – this plurality of origins reflects the characteristic ambiguity of his reign.

2 After 1991 for example two important texts were published, which marked a change of perspective, the Chronicle of Zewditu and Iyasu (edited by Molvaer in 1994), and the historical essay by Gobezé T'affet'e (published in Amharic by the French Centre for Ethiopian Studies in 1996), followed by the publication of further sources.

networks in the Horn of Africa. At a time of conflicting colonial empires this task was most delicate, a truly burning issue, while Ethiopia had no choice but find and define her role as an independent nation between both camps. As any Ethiopian king, but under the new conditions of a recently expanded and modernized empire, *Lïj* Iyasu was torn between two different political models, the dream of a central Christian state and the customary autonomy of local entities and powers. In his case, both Ethiopian realities were most symbolically represented by his two ancestral lineages, the Christian Solomonic dynasty and the pseudo-Sharifian ancestry of Wollo (see the article by Gori), from whom he descended through two kings, his grandfather *Atsé* Mïnilïk II, and his father, *Nïgus* Mika'él. This double ascendency placed *Lïj* Iyasu also in the heart of a conflicting encounter between the two most important religions of Ethiopia, Christianity and Islam, historically strongly interlinked, but officially in total contradiction with each other – a conflict which he attempted to smoothen in his own idiosyncratic and syncretic way, often interpreted as awkward, and an expression of his lack of experience and art of rulership.

The dilemmas and challenges of Ethiopian politics – and their solutions – are traditionally strongly linked with historical discourses and publicized memories. While for example the kings of kings Téwodros II, Mïnilïk II and Hayle Sïllassé I and to a some degree also Empress Zewditu and Yoḥannïs IV, play well-established roles in the public historical memory, each of them representing central *topoi* of Ethiopian identity and state art (or problems linked with it), *Lïj* Iyasu remains neglected. The role he played is largely either a matter of disagreement, or – even more – an object of ignorance and oblivion, and with him central topics of his reign. Some of these, as sketched above and discussed in detail in this book, are crucial, however, for the understanding of the complexities of the Ethiopian state, such as the regional and religious diversities and the need for solutions of coexistence without forced unification.

This book is the outcome of an international workshop, which took place at Wollo University in Desé, Ethiopia, in November 2009, whose aim was to assemble different perspectives on *Lïj* Iyasu's politics and life. It includes discussions on his international relations (Agstner, Erlich, Smidt), his 'pluralistic' local politics (Ahmed Hassen, Pankhurst), religious inclinations (Gori, Ficquet, Erlich) and politically important family connections (Ficquet, Augustyniak). Further contributions discuss the construction of his image as a heir and as a sovereign (Sohier, Semenova), his complex marriage relations (Augustyniak), and finally his downfall (Shiferaw Bekele, Aramis Houmed Soulé, Asfa-Wossen Asserate). The diverse articles presented here reflect discussions and researches undertaken during the last years to bring at least some light into this obscure period of modern Ethiopian history. We are grateful to the French Center of Ethiopian Studies in Addis Ababa and to the Austrian Embassy in Addis Ababa for their active and generous support of this publication.

Addis Ababa, May 2013

Part I - The Background: Family, Marriages and Alleged Origins

Understanding *Lïj* Iyasu through his Forefathers: The Mammedoch *Imam*-s of Wello*

Éloi Ficquet

In 1916, when a league of oligarchs worked for the dismissal of the royal prince *Abéto* or *Lïj* Iyasu, one of the principal objections against him — in addition to his inexperience and his offhand way of governing — was that he was descended from a dynasty of Muslim Oromo lords of Wello, allegedly linked to the lineage of the Prophet of Islam,[1] known as the Mammedoch *Imam*-s. His father, indeed, had been one of the two last *Imam*-s of this dynasty, under the name of Muhammad Ali, until he was baptized with the name of Mika'él, and made *Ras* in 1878, after his submission to King of Kings Yoḥannïs IV. *Ras* Mika'él then concluded an alliance with Mïnilïk and married (in 1892) his daughter, Shewaregga, who gave birth to Iyasu in 1897.

Although he was born Christian and educated as such under the supervision of Mïnilïk,[2] Iyasu was blamed by his opponents to be ill-suited for taking on the role of guardian of the Christian faith held by the dynasty of the Ethiopian Solomonic kings. The most virulent charges of his detractors thus reproached him for continuing to maintain ambiguous relationships with Islam, the religion of his ancestors, not only through signs of sympathy but also through acts interpreted as denials of the Christian faith.

The degree of truth or propaganda behind these accusations of apostasy has been a subject of controversy between historians, which has remained unsettled despite their work of gathering and confronting facts. The chapter by Haggai Erlich in this volume follows an interpretation for the prosecution corresponding to the mainstream version of Iyasu's "return to Islam" as a sufficient reason to account for his overthrow. This charge was made and widely disseminated by the rivals of Iyasu as a justification of the 1916 coup d'état and it was later erected to the status of official history by Hayle Sïllasé I himself in his autobiography. Contrary to Erlich who argues that "*we have no reason to dispute*" Hayle Sïllasé's account, I believe that the huge sum of interests behind the construction of this historical episode as an undisputable truth and its

* The author thanks Shiferaw Bekele, Marie Miran-Guyon, Benjamin Soares, Bethlehem Dejene, Leila Qashu and Luc Journé for their remarks on preliminary versions of this text.

1 See the next chapter by Alessandro Gori for more details on this Sharifian genealogy of *Lïj* Iyasu.

2 See the chapter by Estelle Sohier in this volume on the childhood of Iyasu and his education.

lasting effect on the official silencing of Iyasu's reign is the reason for which we should at least give the benefit of the doubt. For the rivals of Iyasu — made of a coalition of the Shewan aristocracy and colonial powers —, accommodation with Islam was the most treacherous act that could be done against the Ethiopian crown. The charge of apostasy was therefore the most handy to disqualify a competitor who had to be eliminated for many other reasons including personal humiliations and diverging political views (as shown by the account of Avedis Terzian given by Richard Pankhurst in this volume). In a period of international conflict that was conducive to the collision of dual categories, the rather confusing manner of Iyasu's interreligious policy and international strategy was curtailed as a treacherous duplicity rather than an attempt of safeguarding Ethiopia through an association with the Muslim leaders of its border territories.

The purpose of this paper is to trace back the genealogy of the Mammedoch forefathers of *Lïj* Iyasu to show that a certain amount of ambivalence in religious adherence was an almost structural characteristic of this dynasty. At nearly each generation, these Muslim rulers of Wello, who were very strongly engaged in the defence and diffusion of Islam, nevertheless had close ties with Christianity, generally through matrimonial alliances with neighboring Christian polities. Eventually, this insight on the patrilineal background of *Lïj* Iyasu will allow to shed light on the conception of power and religious policy that the young sovereign may have partly inherited from his father and his paternal entourage.

Chronology

In the most restricted sense, the Mammedoch dynasty designates the succession of chiefs carrying the title of *Imam*, who governed the territory of Werre Himeno as well as other dependences in the north of what formed the area of Wello, bounded at that time in the north by the course of the Beshlo River. They exerted power as Muslim *Imam*-s from the last quarter of the 18th century until the last quarter of 19th century, when, as mentioned above, the Mammedoch Imamate was subjugated by the Christian kingdom, entailing the conversion to Christianity of *Imam* Muhammed Ali (renamed Mika'él), and his rival *Imam* Amedé Abba Wat'ew (renamed Hayle Maryam). The dynasty survived, however, this denominational switch. In particular Mikael's offspring flourished until reaching its climax under the short reign of *Lïj* Iyasu, before their downfall marked by the defeat of Segelé (October 1916) leading to the capture of *Nïgus* Mikael (who died two years later) and the escape of Iyasu (until his capture in 1921 and his death in custody in 1935).

Another preliminary note should be added on ethnic designations. Categorizing the Mammedoch as Oromo, as it is generally stated, is a bit simplistic since historical and cultural dynamics show that this dynasty was at the core of interactions between Oromo and Amhara societies, as well as between Islam and Christianity, that resulted in mixed and transitional identities characterizing, until today, the whole social environment in Wello. The distinctive position of the Mammedoch in the Ethiopian political arena was asserted through religious and political differentiation rather than secular ethnic identities.

Our focus will be on the interreligious marriages contracted by the first *Imam*-s of the dynasty, under the period of the Ethiopian history known as *Zemene mesafint* or "Era of the princes", from the second half of the 18th century to the mid-19th century. This period was characterized by the weakening of the coordinating (rather than central) authority of the royal Solomonic dynasty established in Gonder since the 17th century.

The assassination of the King of Kings *Atsé* Iyo'as in 1769 marked the collapse of the monarchy of Gonder. This event was the result of an accumulation of tensions between established regional ruling families. Each of them "*attempted to maximize their holdings within the bounds allowed by their own military and political prowess vis-a-vis their peers*" (Crummey 1975a: 270). To consolidate their power, they needed alliances with outsiders, to get access to the resources of peripheral territories and to secure protections against external aggressions. Alliances were concluded through marriages. These political matrimonial strategies led to the interweaving of wide transterritorial bonds between ruling families. Following this process, peripheral Oromo (so-called "Galla") lineages were assimilated into the political game centered on Gonder, provoking situations of tension when old families eventually realized they were superseded by newcomers whose "genealogical capital" was low and who were still considered as foreign intruders. This is the same kind of crisis that would later cause the downfall of *Lïj* Iyasu.

Iyo'as' reign was the outcome of the rise to power of an Oromo family from Wello.[3] His father, King of Kings *Atsé* Iyasu II (r. 1730-1755), had married Webit, the daughter of Amit'o. The latter was the chief of a territory in southeast Wello, probably around nowadays Kombolcha (according to Zergaw 1973: 24). He had been an ally of *Atsé* Bekaffa (r. 1721-1730). Webit was baptized as Bersabéh at the time of her marriage. She gave birth to Iyo'as, who would become king of kings in 1755, at the early age of about fifteen. He was backed by four of his uncles who managed to reach important positions by adopting the manners of the court of Gonder, including probably their conversion to Christianism, but they did not give up their Oromo identity. "*In an instant, nothing was heard in the palace but Galla* [Oromiffa]. *The king* [Joas] *himself affected to speak nothing else. He had entirely intrusted the care of his person to his two uncles; and, both being men of intrigue, they thought themselves sufficiently capable to make a party, support it, and place the king at the head of it*". (Bruce 1790: 274-75). These clashes of cultural identities were exacerbated by struggles between armed factions that led to the

3 For an analysis of the penetration of the Gonderian political arena by Oromo groups, see Ficquet 2000; Toubkis 2010.

deposition of Iyo'as and his assassination. He was survided by two of his uncles, Lubo and Birallé who kept influential positions in the agitated period that followed.

Despite the loss of its authority, Gonder continued to play a central role on the messed up chessboard. It remained the seat of two high symbolic figures, the Archibishop (*Abun*) and the King (*Atsé*). The latter position was occupied by aged and powerless representatives of the Solomonic dynasty who were placed under the executive authority of regional rulers conferred with the title of *Ras Bitwedded*.

This paramount role was held during 67 years by a dynasty of Muslim Oromo origin, the Werre-Shékoch (literally: "the house of the *shaykh-s*"), who came from the territory of Yejju, to the north-east of Wello. They took power in Gonder in the last decades of the 18th century, by assimilating the norms of the Christian Amhara monarchy and converting to Christianity, after having concluded an alliance-through-marriage with the ruling family of Lasta. This mixed Yejju-Lasta lineage reached the highest political functions in Gonder in 1786 when Ali Gwangul was named *Ras* and *Ïnderasé* by *Atsé* Tekle Giyorgis (Weld Blundell 1922: 342). *Ras* Ali governed only two years. His position was taken over by his brothers and subsequently by their descendants despite strong internal feud between them.[4]

We will see below that the Mammedoch had a very similar background to the Werre-Shékoch and that they intermingled with them. They followed, however, a different political strategy by sticking to their adherence to Islam as a way of resisting against their incorporation into the Christian kingdom.[5]

Sources

The historical understanding of this agitated period relies on a variety of sources that provide rich, albeit tortuous, information. The Ethiopian Gï'ïz chronicle of this period was published by Conti Rossini (1916), then by Weld Blundell (1922).[6] This text provides essential information on confrontations, alliances and reorganizations of local powers between the 1770s and the 1840s, but it remains focused on the deeds of the lords established in Gonder. This internal source is supplemented by the accounts of European travellers. Starting from the 1810s (with the travels of the British subjects Salt and Pearce) a growing number of scholars and missionaries travelled and stayed in different regions of Ethiopia from where they reported a great number of factual elements on local politics, as understood from the point of view of the entourage of influential oligarchs under the protection of whom they were sheltered.

---

4 On the dynasty of Yejju, see Molla Tikuye 1994 and Shiferaw Bekele 1990.

5 This view was already defended by Mohammed Hassen 1992. More historical details are discussed here.

6 The text edited by Conti-Rossini is based on a manuscript collected by Antoine d'Abbadie (Abb 118 of the French National Library in Paris) including some variations from the version collected by Rüppel (Frankfurt Or. 38). The edition by Weld Blundell is based on the ms. Or 821 of the British Museum in London. See Kropp 1987: 103-105.

Our focus being the territory of Wello, we will make use of extracts from unpublished handwritten notes by the French traveler Arnauld d'Abbadie (the brother of Antoine) from his archives kept at the Vatican Library. During his twelve-year stay in Ethiopia in the 1840s he recorded about sixty pages of notes from an oral account on the history of the Mammedoch *Imam-s* since Amedé Kollasé. This text offers an original and detailed vision of the regional conflicts from the point of view of Wello protagonists.[7]

Other data from the oral history of Wello were collected and treated more than one century later. On the one hand, Domenico Brielli, who was in charge of the Italian Consulate in Desé in the 1930's, collected historical information on the regional history of Wello, which was published and abundantly commented on by the Ethiopianist scholar Carlo Conti-Rossini in a collection of studies published in 1945. On the other hand, in his 1973 B.A. thesis, Zergaw Asfera compared the available sources with information he collected himself in the city of Desé from seven Welloyyé learned informants and other information gathered in an unpublished manuscript by Mr. Abbebe Ayïchéh, a scholar of Desé, who was the author of several novels.

Hypotheses on the foundation of the Mammedoch dynasty

Three etymological hypotheses are usually mentioned in oral traditions to account for the origin of this dynasty, whose name is built with the Amharic suffix "*-och*", indicating the plural form. The most frequent assumption points to the locality of Mammed, in the territory of Gerfa, not far from the current town of Bati. It is there that the founding ancestor of the dynasty, Babbo Nuraddin, is supposed to have settled in the middle of the 18th century. This figure is described as a Muslim religious dignitary, of Oromo culture, who had come from Arsi with a group of disciples and a large herd (Zergaw 1973: 19).

The two other etymologies, which are not incompatible with the first, interpret the name Mammedoch as the contraction of Muhammedoch, "those of Muhammed". One etymology connects the dynasty with the Sharifian descendance of the prophet of Islam through the famous *shaykh* Nur Husayn, holy founder of the sanctuary of Anajina in Balé, which attracts huge crowds of pilgrims twice a year. This assumption certainly corresponds to a later reconstruction elaborated for purposes of prestige, but it remains coherent with the assumption of an Arsi origin and a connection to the brotherhood of Islam, reactivated in Ethiopia at the end of the 18th century,[8] in particular with the reinvestment in the sanctuary of Shaykh Husayn by the Emirate of Harer in the 1780's.[9]

7 Biblioteca Apostolica Vaticana, chart d'Abbadie № 18. This text is in the process of being edited and published by Eloi Ficquet and Shiferaw Bekele. We thank Michel Perret for having provided us a copy of this text.

8 This process of spreading of the networks of mystical Islam in Ethiopia is discussed by Hussein Ahmed (2001: 71-83).

9 The mausoleum dedicated to Abd el Qader Al-Jilani, founder of the Qadiriyya order, was built on the instructions of the *Amir* of Harär Abd-Al Shakur (1783-1794).

The third etymology, also derived from the eponym Muhammed, points to the great-grandson of Babbo Nuraddin, Muhammed Ali, known by the warrior name of Abba Jïbo. He is considered as the true founder of the dynasty for having settled his stronghold in Werre Himeno, and for having founded the town of Tenta, on a strategic location at the end of a plateau overhanging the valley of Beshlo, protected by impregnable *amba*-s (natural fortresses) such as Meqdela and Lïgot. He was also probably the first to have claimed the title of *Imam* to show that his authority rested on the observance of Islam.[10]

Although these etymological assumptions do not constitute a factual answer to the question of the origin of this group of power, they converge to support the hypothesis of a group of Islamized Oromo migrants led by missionary motivations.

In three generations, between Babbo Nuraddin and Muhammed Abba Jïbo, the process of political and territorial expansion of the Mammedoch was fast. It only took them a few decades to subjugate the Oromo chiefdoms of Wello, which were divided and in conflict with one another. Their descendants managed to control and unify this territory using Islam as the medium of a common identity, standing up to the neighbouring Christian areas while at the same time entering into temporary alliances with them.

The characteristic of the Mammedoch was to associate their religious authority with a political project which was partly inspired by the egalitarian ethos promoted by the Sufi currents of Islam. The traditions collected by Zergaw suggest that the first leaders of Mammedoch fought against the local authorities who had preceded them by promoting greater social justice through the reduction of tax levies and by making favourable gestures towards the tributary peasants, which enabled them to gain their support (Zergaw 1973: 19-21).

The first intermarriages of the Mammedoch with Christian families

Since their emergence as regional magnates, the Mammedoch *Imam-s* had consolidated and expanded their power by entering into matrimonial alliances with the Christian polities which surrounded them. Marrying women of Christian origin (without systematically expecting from them to convert to Islam) was practiced by almost every *Imam* at each generation. This implied that most of them received a Christian education in their maternal environment during their childhood.

10 It is what several local traditions affirm; those I collected confirm those collected by Zergaw. However Hussein Ahmed (2001: 123, n. 31), basing his argument on Brielli (1945: 101), questions the idea that Abba Jïbo was the first to carry the title of *Imam*, instead proposing Amedé Kollasé. The notes of Arnauld d' Abbadie seem to confirm this, stating that Amedé Kollasé preferred the title of *Imam* rather than *Ras,* which his entourage proposed for him to take after his first victories against Christian rivals.

This policy of interreligious alliances started at a very early stage in the foundation of the dynasty. When Ali Godana (grandson of Babbo Nuraddin, the first migrant and initiator of the dynasty) moved into the interior of the highlands to reinforce his power base, he married a Christian woman, Lïbbïyat, daughter of a lord of the territory of Wadla Delanta.[11] This territory, located to the north of the Beshlo River, represented a strategic zone of circulation between Wello, Yejju, Begémeder and Lasta.

Muhammed Abba Jïbo was born from the interreligious and intercultural union, the first of a series in the history of this family. As mentioned above this leader gave a strong impetus to the development of the dynasty. He used the same interreligious alliances as his predecessors to expand his base of power on a larger territory and protect its borders.

According to different local traditions, Abba Jïbo married two Christian women, who gave birth to two rival lines of descendants. Concerning the first line, we only have the information collected by Brielli (1945: 95) that is not corroborated by other sources. Two sons, Yïmeré and Kesimé, were born from a certain Ïjjïg Ayyehu, who was originated from Ambassel. These descendants were suspected of attempting a plot with the assistance of their uncles. They were imprisoned in Meqdela and then eliminated by their half-brothers. The dynasty was continued by the offspring of the other marriage of Abba Jïbo with a certain Alko. She was descended from several generations of governors of the Christian fortified strongholds of the area (Lïgot, Ambassel). The detailed ancestry of Alko given by Zergaw (1973: 70) is an indication that ancient networks of matrimonial exchanges were binding these polities that became, through intermarriage, the shield of the Mammedoch against their Christian challengers. Alko gave birth to at least three sons, of whom the youngest, Amedé Kollasé, would be the continuator of the dynasty.

Dejjazmach Bett'o: the strategy of conversion

Before examining the career of *Imam* Amedé Kollasé, let us consider briefly his elder brother, Bett'o. The latter appears in the Gïʿïz chronicle of the period, in the passage which reports the military campaign of *Atsé* Tekle Giyorgis against Wello in 1783-84 (Weld Blundell 1922: 269-292). This Gonderine King tried to reaffirm the supremacy of the Solomonic dynasty against the independent regional powers.[12] At this time, Muhammed Abba Jïbo still controlled Werre Himeno and the surroundings. According to oral accounts collected by Zergaw (1973: 23), he delegated some power to his elder sons, Bett'o and Adem, the former controlling Meqdela and territories in the north of Werre Himeno, the latter being in charge of the territories in the east of Werre Himeno. The Gïʿïz chronicle of the period reports that Bett'o paid allegiance to

11 According to Brielli (1945: 91).

12 By taking his army to Wello, Tekle Giyorgis pursued several goals. He sought to take control of this rebellious territory, to convert its population to Christianity in order to restore the old territory of the Amhara in the bosom of Christian monarchy, and to reestablish a territorial continuity with Shewa.

King Tekle Giyorgis immediately after the King crossed the borders of Wello. As a reward, Bett'o obtained the title of *Dejjazmach* in conjunction with the responsibility of the entire territory of Wello and Wuch'alé (Weld Blundell 1922: 273).

According to traditions collected by Brielli, Bett'o inherited the power of Abba Jïbo and exerted it for five years. He was baptized in Gonder, where he received the title of *Ras*. He could not, however, take the benefit of his conversion because he died of smallpox on his journey back to Wello (Brielli 1945: 96). The circumstances of his death is not confirmed by the Gï'ïz chronicle, for which Bett'o continued to show his loyalty to the King and was confirmed in his position of *Dejjazmach*. He was blamed, however, by the King because he refused to convert his captives to Christianity (Weld Blundell 1922: 283), an indication that his conversion was more a lip-service than a genuine "new start". Shortly after this verbal sanction he was imprisoned for the same reason of not being zealous in converting local population and for having protected his brother Adem and his men who were fighting against the King (*ibid.*). This is another indication that Bett'o could have played a double game.

Bett'o reappears shortly in the chronicle, for the last time, in 1788, four years after the above-mentioned events. He had kept his title of *Dejjazmach* and he brought his support to *Ras* Ali who was marching on Meqdela to catch the rebel called Yusufé. The end of his career cannot be established with certainty. For Zergaw, Bett'o has been cancelled from local traditions because "*his being taken to Gondar and Christianized had disqualified him for being considered as an* imam *of the Māmadoch*" (1973: 37). We can only speculate about the motivations of his half-hearted conversion. As his mother was Christian, the opportunist strategy behind his conversion may have been supported by his maternal side. Furthermore, he may have been encouraged by the political context of the time that opened the door for the integration of Oromo factions into the military hierarchies and matrimonial networks of the Christian royalty, as seen above about the rise to power of Iyo'as' maternal lineage and the seizure of Gonder by the Werre-Shékoch of Yejju. This is confirmed by the fact Bett'o was in relation with Lubo, one of the uncles of Iyo'as and by his acquaintance with *Ras* Ali. These alliances with men who shared the same kind of background may have encouraged him to follow the same kind of career that involved fake acts of conversion and occasional demonstrations of loyalty.

As other Oromo groups settled on the fringes of the Christian kingdom, the Mammedoch were taken in the sphere of attraction of the political center of Gonder. The conversion of Bett'o and his intrigues in local politics could have led to an early absorption of Wello into the Christian kingdom. This was not, however, an inescapable scenario.

The defeat of Adem the giant

Unlike Bett'o, the other Mammedoch leaders (Muhammed Abba Jïbo and his son Adem) fought against the Christian royal army (Weld Blundell 1922: 289). It is even stated in the Gï'ïz chronicle that Adem, who is described as a giant, was the first to reject the option of submitting and converting as well as high-rank position that was offered by the Christian King who intended "*to bring him up as a son*" (Weld Blundell 1922: 289). We have seen that Bett'o made the opposite choice. It seems, however, that Adem maintained some relations with Bett'o, for the latter was accused to have protected him and let him flee at night.

Adem was eventually killed and decapitated in a fight described as a major victory of the Christian army. The lengthy narration of this exploit, compared to passages from the Bible and described as "*a wonder and great blessing for seven years to this day*" (*ibid.*) is an indication that Adem was considered as a strong and feared rival who could have been in position to challenge the strategy of reestablishing Christian rule over the region.

After the death of Adem, Mammed Abba Jïbo died shortly after the expedition of *Atsé* Tekle Giyorgis probably in a fight against rival Oromo groups in the south-east. This could have been the end of the Mammedoch who would have been lost in oblivion.

Imam Amedé Kollasé: the reaffirmation of Islam

Amedé Kollasé, the youngest son of Abba Jïbo, reoriented the declining course of the familial destiny towards greater ambitions. The name of Amedé is not mentioned in this episode of the chronicle. The notes of Arnauld d'Abbadie, taken from a local informant, start with the recounting of the campaign of Tekle Giyorgis, providing details that match those given in the chronicle. According to this account, Amedé joined his brother Adem in the fight. He fled when Adem was killed and he took refuge for some years in the central highlands of Wello, where he engaged in banditry (*shifta*), before he returned to Werre Himeno and took the control of it, the year of the death of *Ras* Ali I, in 1788. We do not know if Amedé actually fought against his elder Bett'o, but we can notice from the Christian chronicle that by 1790 he was recognized as the only ruler of the area with his warrior-name of Kollasé.[13]

Before he became *Imam* and used the affirmation of Islam as his distinctive political trademark, as we will see below, Amedé had ambiguous relations with the Christian faith. As his brothers Bett'o and Adem he was born in the 1850's of a Christian mother, Alko. According to d'Abbadie's informant, he grew up as a shepherd in the entourage of his father, where he probably received an Islamic education. When he became a

13 The meaning of *kolaasee* in Oromo language "castrated horse, gelding".

young adult, he shifted for some years to an alliance with Christian neighbours:

"*When he was twenty,* Ras *Goshu* [governor of Amhara Sayïnt, Christian territory] *took a liking him, baptized him and gave him for a wife, Sïhin, the daughter of his paternal aunt.*[14] *The name Ahmedé was changed to Welde Gebre'él. He joined the service of Goshu where he remained for approximately nine years. After the death of the latter he abandoned his wife who had refused to follow him to Muslim country.*" (d'Abbadie, nd: 21).

If we follow this local account, recorded forty years only after Amedé's death, the latter lived several years in a Christian environment, was baptized and married a high-ranking Christian woman. We can infer that he probably followed this trajectory of assimilation because he was the youngest son and there was little chance of him succeeding his father. He was not without scruples, however. According to the same source, he reconverted to Islam and abandoned his wife and son when he joined his father and brother to fight against the invasion of Wello by *Atsé* Tekle Giyorgis.

We have already mentioned that the circumstances under which he took over Werre Himeno. His first mention in the chronicle is dated to 1790, when *Ras* Aligaz tried to win Amedé Kollasé on his side, by offering him to marry the sister of his daughter (Weld Blundell 1922: 414). This is corroborated by d'Abbadie's notes that add Amedé refused to submit himself and to bargain his title of *Imam* against a position in the Christian hierarchy.

The Islamic orientation of Amedé Kollasé is underlined by the Christian chronicle that specifies that he is named with the title of *Imam* (*Yïmam*) (Weld Blundell 1922: 168, 442). Eight lines below Amedé is qualified as "*tenbelatawi*" (ibid: 443), an expression that is derived from the Gï'ïz verb *tenebele* - "to intercede", and that designates a Muslim ("coming from the idea of Muhammad being the messenger of Allah") (Leslau 1987: 576).

These precise indications on Kollasé's Islamic faith may refer to the audacious act he had performed when he seized Gonder in January 1799 to show his strength. Oral traditions of Wello recount that he performed the Muslim call for prayer (*aḏān*) from the top of the highest tower of the royal castle of Gonder. Zergaw Asferra thus reports on how this satirical event has been preserved in the memory of Muslims of Wello in the 1970s:

"Most Muslim leaders in Wallo, proudly and at the same time inhibited by fear, further claim that Kollase had turned the tower platform of the Gondar castle into a minaret and compelled Christians and their priests to respond to the muezzin's cry. This could be a later fabrication; but it is what they feel and tenaciously believe about their own past." (Zergaw 1973: 50)

14 Zergaw (1973: 70) gives the extended and detailed genealogy of Sïhin, who descended from King Dawit II by his matrilateral ascent that links her with the local authorities of Amhara, Wadla and Gojjam.

Zergaw is right to use some precaution in his analysis, by supposing a possible fabrication of the collective memory. The same story was recorded by d'Abbadie, one hundred forty years before Zergaw, a proof of the amazing longevity of some oral traditions:

"After the victory of Kai Afer [won against *Ras* Ali Gaz in 1799], *Ahemedié pushed on as far as Gondar and called the muezzin from the top of the highest tower of the imperial castle."* (d'Abbadie, nd: 24)

One can interpret this episode as a provocation addressed to the Werre-Shékoch lords from Yejju established in Gonder. By calling the Muslim prayer in this highly emblematic place of Christian sovereignty, Kollasé may have had the intention to show his rivals that he disapproved of their apostasy and that he was challenging them for this reason.

There is no report of this humiliating event in the Christian chronicle of the period, but another facet of Amedé's personality is disclosed by relating that during his stay in Gonder he met with the two leaders of the Church, the *Abun* and the *Ïch'egé* and that he had "*much useless debate*" with them. Though he was castigated as a heathen by the Patriach, he reacted in a gentle manner to prove the contrary (Weld Blundell 1922: 464). In this line of thought, Zergaw indicates that:

"The Wallo Muslims still admire Kollasé for not having been seduced by any of the Amhara sunna while he was at Gondar (the Wallo Muslims use the term 'sunna' to mean simply practice and custom; Amhara meant 'Christian')." (Zergaw 1973: 50)

Amedé Kollasé did not try to settle in Gonder. The chronicle and d'Abbadie's notes agree on the fact that he stayed there no more than six weeks. Then the *Imam* returned to Wello, without being forced by his opponents. He used this advantageous situation at the top of the ladder of regional power to make some nominations of high-rank officers, including his son Liben, as we will see below. He refused, however, to take for himself the title of *Ras* or to install himself in the position of king maker. He kept his title of *Imam* and imposed his men on territories bordering Wello in order to create a protecting buffer zone.

After having secured the boundaries between the Muslim imamate of Werre Himeno with northern Christian polities, *Imam* Amedé expanded southwards the realm of his power by fighting against Oromo groups of central Wello (particularly Lege Hida, Lege Gora and Jamma). He died during one of these battlefields in September 1803.[15]

15 Conti Rossini 1916: 873; Weld Blundell 1922: 474.

Liben: Something of "kafir" about him

Liben was the only son of Amedé Kollasé. His mother, Sïhin was an Amhara Christian from high-ranking noble lineage, who was married by Amedé when he became Christian for some years. Liben grew up with his mother in a Christian environment. After the struggle against *Atsé* Tekle Giyorgis, which determined Amedé's return to Islam, the latter "*demanded that his wife return to him, which her parents refused under pretext of religion. Besides, she had* [re]*married. She fled to Begemder with her* [new] *husband and her son Liben She died three years later* ». Five years later, "*After the battle of Gouna* [in 1788], *Ahemedié met again with Liben, his son, whose mother had died. He was Christian and refused* to "selemer"[16] [to become Moslem], *but he became Moslem after his father had tricked him into eating Muslim*[17] *sheep meat.*" (d'Abbbadie ms: 23-24).

Thus, through a cunning use of food taboos,[18] Liben had been reinstated into the dynasty. Ten years later, in 1799, when Amedé Kollasé entered Gonder victoriously, an episode which marked the apogee of his power, he assigned Liben to the governorship of the territories north and west of the Beshlo (Gayïnt, Wadla, Dawïnt), which were mainly populated with Christians, by conferring him with the title of *Dejjazmach*, which belonged to the Christian military hierarchy. The notes of d'Abbadie (ms: 24) attribute these words to Amedé: "*Liben, this bastard who has something* kafir [infidel] *about him, can take the title of Dedjazmac. I give him the countries beyond the Nile.*"

This episode, transmitted through an oral source of Wello collected in the 1840's, reveals the high level of paradox with which the Mammedoch played in order to constitute their base of power. First paradox: Amedé, who was born from a woman of Christian ancestry, and who lived part of his youth as a Christian, considers that his son, also born from a Christian woman and who grew up in a Christian milieu but reconverted to Islam, kept "*something* kafir *about him*", ie. something of his Christian background. Second paradox: the identification as *kafir*, which in this sentence obviously seems to be a defect, since it is associated with the term "bastard", is turned into a quality because it confers sufficient legitimacy upon him to control Christian territories with a Christian title. We can also notice that Amedé Kollasé granted to his son the position and the title that his brother and rival Bett'o had obtained a few years before, when he submitted to *Atsé* Tekle Giyorgis.

---

16 In this sentence, Arnauld d'Abbadie francizes an Amharic verb, *täsallämä*, "to bow low", which also means, in the dialectical use of Wällo, "to convert to Islam".

17 i.e. meat of an animal butchered by a Muslim, see more comments in the next note.

18 To eat meat, even inadvertently, of an animal that was not slaughtered in the name of one's religion is considered as an act of apostasy, abandonment of one's religious faith, that can lead to conversion to repair the breaking of the taboo. During the 19th century, meat consumption, in a forced or disguised way, was often used as a means of conversion by both Christians and Moslems, particularly in Wello. For a further discussion on this question see Ficquet, 2006.

Like his father, Liben was engaged in the defense and expansion of his family's territory. After his conversion, he became a fervent supporter of Islam understood as a distinctive ideological feature in the regional political game. He was portrayed by his rivals as a fanatic Muslim. For instance, the Gïʿïz chronicle has recorded that in June 1800, before Amedé Kollasé's death, Liben "*started laying waste three sanctuaries* [...] *and after massacring a great number of monks* [...] *entered his province*".[19] This frightening reputation could be turned into a strategic advantage for it could deter actual or potential rivals to enter into conflict.

The same kind of information regarding the deeds of *Imam* Liben Amedé is reported by the British sailor and intelligence officer, Nathanael Pearce, who had been residing at the court of *Ras* Welde Sïllasé of Tïgray from 1806 to 1819. In the first volume of his memoirs, Liben is mentioned as a friend and an ally of the ruler of Tïgray against the authority of the Werre-Shékoch family, then exercised by *Ras* Gugsa. This "friendship" was only of convenience, however. In March 1811, Pearce noted the news item of a victorious fight of Liben's army against Gugsa's, whereupon Liben is said to have "*burnt and destroyed all Daunt* [Dawïnt], *Wadler* [Wadla], *and Begemder. The old Ras was far from pleased on hearing of his friend's burning Christian churches*" (Pearce 1831: 80).

Some years later, Liben shifted his alliance and sided with Gugsa. Bonds of friendship were broken and it may have had consequences on representations that switched from conciliatory to negative.

When the news of the death of Liben reached the headquarters of Welde Sïllasé in Ch'eleqot on May 8, 1815 "*every one expressed great joy, on account of the barbarous acts he had committed 12 days before he died*". According to Pearce's report on this event, the *Imam*, shortly before his death, had gathered monks and "*poor people*" under the pretext of celebrating a memorial ceremony (*tezkar*) in honour of his father Kollasé. He ordered that meat and cloths should be distributed to them. However, this was in fact a trap conceived to attract and slaughter them by the hundreds. In the eyes of Liben, Pearce asserts, their offence was the support they had given to the marriage between his principal rival, Goji (the leader of the territory of Yejju, son of *Ras* Aligaz, the former Werre-Shékoch lord of Gonder) and Serku Sïllasié, the daughter of Wesen Seged, the ruler of Shewa. The local Christians of Wello [an indication that there were Christians in Wello at that time] had helped this princess to camouflage herself among a group of pilgrims returning from Debre Libanos [another interesting piece of information]. Pearce also explains that Goji was already married to a Christian woman, daughter of *Ras* Ilo [Haylu] of Lasta, and that he had already converted three times before to Christianity for the same purpose. This time, the fourth, he had promised the lord of Shewa that he would not betray his Christian faith anymore. However, he did not keep his word.

19 Weld Blundell 1922: 466. See also Conti Rossini 1916: 865.

This story reported by Pearce contains several intertwined layers of information, which may appear contradictory at times. The religious affiliations are presented as very dividing, with mass murders being committed for this reason. At the same time, they are very blurred, as interreligious marriage can exist, thus necessitating conversions which can be reversed. The fact that all these facts are considered credible is indicative of the rather unstable state of interreligious relations during this period. However, are these diverse accounts veracious?

The notes of Arnauld d'Abbadie reveal other facts which allow us to question the truth of the massacre described by Pearce. According to these notes, a few months before his death, *Imam* Liben Amedé had fought very hard against Oromo groups of the central highlands of Wello (ie in the area of Leggambo). He was aiming to recover the remains of his father that were buried in this area and that the inhabitants refused to return, as these relics represented to them a guarantee for good rains. Having won this fight and having unearthed the remains of his father, Liben erected a tomb which, according to d'Abbadie, remained a very respected *gedam* (sanctuary). In this context, it is extremely probable that celebrations honouring the memory of the late *Imam* Amedé Kollasé did take place. According to the notes of d'Abbadie, these events happened nine months before the death of Liben. However, Pearce claims that the ceremony which turned into the massacre had taken place twelve days before Liben's death. The chronological precision which Pearce attaches to the events he heard about is in contradiction with the oral testimony recorded by d'Abbadie which asserts that Liben suffered from a serious abdominal hernia which caused him to be confined to bed for several weeks before his death. This information seems rather reliable since one can suppose that it was told by a direct witness of the death of the *Imam*. Indeed, d'Abbadie specifies that there were six servants around Liben when he was agonizing and adds in the margin: "*one of them was Haylo*". We may infer this man named Haylo is the narrator hidden behind the notes of the French traveller. This hypothesis is confirmed in the second volume of the travel account of Arnauld d'Abbadie, in which he recalls the long and instructive discussions he had with a certain Haylu T'emru (transcribed Teumro Haïlo), an independent soldier who was the son of *Dejjazmach* T'emru of Amhara Sayïnt, in western Wello: "*He knew all about everybody's genealogy, the history of each province. His information on current political and military events was accepted as authoritative*" (d'Abbadie 1980b: 84). If one accepts that d'Abbadie's informer, Haylo, was an eye-witness of *Imam* Liben's death some twenty-five years before telling the story, consequently, one can doubt that *Imam* Liben actually took part in a massacre of Christians a few days before his death.

The point here is not to exonerate murders which could have been committed by a Muslim ruler against Christians, but to relativize the value of the information passed on by Pearce, which could be a fabrication inspired by actual events such as the celebration of the reburial of the bones of Kolasé, which had followed a violent conflict to recover them.

To a large extent, the reputation of Muslim fanaticism borne by Liben was a stereotype reflecting the fear of Christian rulers against the development of a Muslim regional power. This fear was supported by some acts of destruction of churches which were not, however, systematically undertaken but were acts of war aimed at securing boundaries on contested areas. The testimony recorded by d'Abbadie from an insider, who had a direct knowledge of Liben and his entourage, confirms that Liben's personality was violent, severe and uncompromising against all of his rivals, notwithstanding their religious affiliations. Under his leadership the troops of Werre Himeno spent more time and had more hardship in fighting against the Oromo chiefdoms of the central highlands of Wello, which were Muslim or non-monotheist. There were also heavy fights against Gojji, the Muslim potentate of Yejju, member of the Werre-Shékoch who was defying the authority of his Christianized cognates based in Gonder. Fighting against Christian armies was not Liben's main concern. His interest was to keep them at large through demonstrations of strength and through diplomacy. He waged some attacks on border zones with Christian territories to reaffirm the military capacity and the territorial extent of his authority. Once it was done, he kept a stabilizing position in the regional balance of power by setting up agreements with Christian allies. Before the above-mentioned pact of non-aggression and mutual support with Welde Sïllasé of Tïgray against Gugsa, Liben had concluded a peace agreement with Gugsa. Despite it was short-lived, this agreement had been a determinant step in the political evolution of the Mammedoch dynasty since it involved the marriage of Liben's daughter, Menen, with Gugsa's son, Alula. This marriage was the starting point of Menen's political career that, after Liben's death, would drag the next generation of Mammedoch leaders into the Gonderine political game.

Absorption into Gonderine politics: Empress Menen and her brothers

Liben had several wives and concubines,[20] but only three lines of his descendants are known through the sources. The first of these lines consisted of Menen and her brother Amedé. Their mother was named T'uma Gaddisa, a name which indicates an Oromo origin. She was Christian according to Pearce for whom: "*it was the particular wish of the Ras Welled Selasse, Guxo, and the other formidable chiefs of the country, that* Homoda [Amedé] *should succeed, as he was the son of a Christian woman.*" (Pearce 1831, vol. 2: 49). This information is contradicted by the fact that another wife of Liben, whose name was Sïnïddu, was also a Christian from Begémdïr descending from a line of high-ranking nobles, like Liben's mother.[21] Her only known child was Ali, known as Abba Bulla, representing the second line of Liben's offspring. He fought against his half-brother

20 D'Abbadie's informant counted eight of them.

21 Her detailed genealogy is given by Zergaw (1973: 71-72), showing that she descended from a long series of marriages between members of the royal Solomid line and local ruling families of theBäshïlo area.

Amedé for the succession at the head of the dynasty. According to d'Abbadie's informant, Liben's last will was that Ali should succeed him, but Amedé was named as a result of internal intrigues (d'Abbadie, ms: 41-42). The third line of Liben's descendants consisted of Beshir whose mother was named Wïddït, whose religion has not been recorded. He did not compete for the succession, but he was on the side of Ali Abba Bulla.

While they competed to take over the leadership on Werre Himeno and its dependencies, the two sons of *Imam* Liben, Amedé and Ali, continued the strategy of their predecessors to preserve their independence and distinctiveness as Muslim rulers through opportunistic relations with their Christian counterparts. But this strategy gradually drifted away from its initial goals. Instead of being a shelter these alliances turned out to be a net in which the Mammedoch rival *Imam-s* were caught, becoming pawns of the political calculations of the Gondarine ruling elite.

A significant role in this process of absorption of the Mammedoch into the Gonderine sphere of power was played by Menen, the daughter of Liben and the uterine sister of Amedé. As stated above, she had been married, at the age of seven, to Alula, son of *Ras* Gugsa, as part of the peace agreement concluded between *Imam* Liben and *Ras* Gugsa. After the death of Alula, in 1822, Menen married his brother, Welé,[22] further reinforcing the bonds between the Werre-Shékoc family and the Mammedoch. Her son, Ali Alula, alias Ali Tïkku, was declared *Ras* in 1831, at the age of 13, being the last male representative of Gugsa's line after the death of *Ras* Marïyyé. According to Arnauld d'Abbadie in the first volume of his travel account (1980a: 183), the young ruler "*was subjected to a regency council under the leadership of Dedjaj Ahmedé, Governor of Wora-himano and relative of the Waïzoro, but the latter knew, by her manoeuvring, how to disunite the council and assume the sovereign authority on behalf her son.*" The dominant position of Menen was reinforced when she married Yohannes, a scion of the Solomonic line whom she placed on the throne as *Atsé* Yohannes III (Crummey 2007). With the title of *Ïtégé* she continued to act as a regent queen and became the most influential figure of Gonderine politics throughout the 1830s and 1840s.

During his youth, Amedé was the captive of *Ras* Gugsa, the ruler of the Werre-Shékoch in Gonder. The reasons for this detention are not known. Amedé was released on the occasion of an exchange of prisoners resulting from the peace agreement between *Ras* Gugsa and *Imam* Liben (d'Abbadie, ms: 36). He was then entrusted to *Dejjach* Tumro, who was in charge of a part of Amhara Sayïnt, a Christian territory located between Werre Himeno, Begémïdïr and Gojjam. Two years later, Liben, his father, died, and Amedé was invested as *Imam* at the very early age of twelve (d'Abbadie, ms: 42). He had to face the rivals of his father who sought to benefit from the lack of military and political experience of the young *Imam*. After resisting a few months, Amedé lost a battle against *Ras* Gugsa and was made captive again for three years (d'Abbadie, ms: 46-47). He

---

22 See Crummey, 2007.

was sent to an estate in Fogera, on the eastern shores of T'ana lake, and kept watch on by local peasants. When the governor appointed by Gonder to Wello lost control of the region, *Ras* Gugsa sent the young *Imam* back to his country to restore calm.

During the following years, Amedé was mainly in conflict with his half-brother Ali, known as Abba Bulla, who wanted to seize Werre Himeno and the title of *Imam*. Amedé also fought very hard battles against other Muslim Oromo chiefdoms of interior Wello (Jarso, Qallu, Tehuladeré). These confrontations against Muslim and Oromo clearly stand out from d'Abbadie's notes on Amedé's rule, showing that he actively contributed to the subjugation of Wello under the control of the quasi-central authorities of Gonder and Debre Tabor, the headquarters of the Werre-Shékoc rulers. This collaborative role is not reported in the Gïïz chronicle, which continues to portray Amedé like his ancestors, as a fanatic and aggressive Muslim, blamed for having committed several offences against Christians. In a first case: "*Amadé entered the church, defiled it, had food and drink brought to it and invited to it all the Muhammedans. While they were there eating and drinking, a thunderbolt fell and terrified them, even as it had terrified Paul. However, he was not converted like Paul, but hardened his heart, like Pharaoh, for he belonged to the race of Gran. Before that he had set fire to many churches, and some of these he had turned mosques for the Musselmans* [sic.]." (Weld Blundell 1922: 487-488)

Furthermore, "*After a time, Amadé came bearing the books of the Musselmans and all their laws, to convert the Christians to Islam and deny Christ. While he was on the road and was trying to join the son of his sister* [*Ras* Ali II, son of Menen and Alula Gugsa], *he died on the march.*" (Weld Blundell 1922: 488)

These two events date back to 1831. His death is interpreted by the chronicler as a manifestation of Providence. At each occurrence, their description is preceded by the mention of the fact that Amedé was released from custody by order of *Ras* Ali II, his young nephew who had just succeeded to the head of the dynasty of Werre-Shékoch of Gonder. The first time, Amedé was guarded by the *Ras* Dori of Amhara Sayïnt, the second time by Ali Faris of Lasta. The acts of anti-Christian profanation and blasphemy could have been reported in detail in the chronicle in order to show that the favours granted by *Ras* Ali to his maternal uncle were wrong.

Less information is known on Ali Abba Bula, the half-brother and challenger of Amedé, but he would leave his imprint in the dynasty as the father of Muhammed Ali, the future *Nïgus* Mikaél. He relentlessly fought to get the title and office of *Imam*. To this end, he also consented to be manipulated in the political game of the Werre-Shékoch of Gonder by allying himself with the two brothers and successors of *Ras* Gugsa, *Ras* Yïmam (between 1825 and 1828) and then *Ras* Marïyyé (between 1828 and 1831). After the death of his half-brother, Amedé, in 1831, Ali obtained full control of Werre Himeno for a few years, before confronting the son of his rival, his nephew, Liben Amedé.

These developments show that the Mammedoch leaders of Werre Himeno were on the edge of being incorporated into the machinery of the Gonderian state that had been run for forty years by two generations of Werre-Shékoch rulers from Yejju. The two families were characterized by their Oromo Muslim origins and by their intermarriages with local Christian aristocracies. They were merging into one another through the figure of the young *Ras* Ali II, the son of Alula and Menen, the latter acting as the regent-queen, as seen above. The portrait of *Ras* Ali drawn by Arnauld d'Abbadie in his travel account (1980a: 184) is based on the common opinions he heard in Gonder in 1840 before he met the *Ras* in person in his camp at Debre Tabor: "*It was feared that he leaned towards Islamism: there were several Muslims among his relatives, he rarely went to church and he was fond of the turns of phrase and the style of Wora Himano, where the religion and the manners of Muslims prevailed. However there was still hope in him* (...) *the oppressed, especially the farmers, considered he was accessible to their complaints.*"

The long-standing and self-sustaining supremacy of Yejju and Wello dynasties at the highest position of the country worried the other regional overlords who considered that the ascension of outsiders and recent converts at the top of the political ladder was perverting the ancestral legacy of the Christian kingdom of Ethiopia and threatening the independence of the country. In the popular opinion, this political dissent was expressed in religious terms by the expectation of a messianic king, named Téwodros, who will restore peace through the reunification and the reconciliation of the Christian territories into one kingdom. This role was eventually taken by a rebel petty lord from the western region of Qwara, *Dejjazmach* Kassa. His defiance of Menen's rule in the 1840's had been tempered through an attempt of winning his loyalty by marrying him to Tewabech, the daughter of *Ras* Ali II. His stubbornness and ambition, however, were stronger and he turned against his in-laws. He defeated *Ras* Ali in 1853 and thereafter laid down the principles of a new political order, considering that reforms and modernization could be achieved only through the restoration of a strong royal authority, hence his coronation as King of Kings *As'é* Téwodros II in 1855.

Resistance, submission and conversion, 1855-1878

The policy designed by Téwodros was aimed at building a powerful and unified Christian kingdom put an end to the previous situation of loose and unstable coalition of interests between regional lords. In the first years of his reign, Téwodros II carried out several very violent military campaigns against Wello in order to reduce this Muslim enclave in the highlands that was epitomizing the political (dis)order he was determined to remove.[23] Another strategic reason for conquering Wello was to reconnect the southern territory of Shewa to the rest of the Christian kingdom. The fact that the *amba* Meqdela, that used to be the seat of the Mammedoch power, became the last stronghold of Tewodros II is

23 See Crummey, 1971.

revealing the central importance of this area in the configuration of the struggles of the time. These conflicts, worsened by attempts at forced conversion of Wello Muslims to Christianity, hardened the "otherness" of the Wello people by reactivating their opposition against the Christian monarchy in which they had been slowly integrated.

In front of this major political turn, which meant the collapse of the system in which the Mammedoch had emerged and prospered, the continuators of the dynasty continued to appear as the main force of political and military leadership in Wello. They gathered around them the other local authorities with the aim of organizing resistance against the rule of Téwodros. The conflict of succession for the head of the imamate that opposed Amedé and Ali Abba Bulla did not stop with the death of the two rival *imam*-s (the former in 1831, the latter in 1852), but continued through their two wives, Mestewat, wife of Amedé, and Werqitu, wife of Ali. Both of these ladies fought to preserve the chances of succession for their young sons. For more than ten years, a rather singular mode of competition took place between the two regent women. While they continued to clash with each other, these two warlike women fought vigorously against the grasp of Téwodros over Wello.

After the death by suicide of Téwodros, in Meqdela[24], Wello was divided between the two most important regional powers, Shewa in the south (ruled by Mïnilïk), and Tïgray in the north (ruled by Kassa, who soon became King of Kings Yoḥannïs IV after 1872). These two sovereigns competed for the recognition of their territory as the new centre of the kingdom. Yoḥannïs eventually won and Mïnilïk agreed to recognize it, with the condition that he could maintain an entirely autonomous power over Shewa and its dependences, which included a part of Wello.

While this bargaining over Wello was going on, the Mammedoch family remained in the middle of the political game by alternating between rivalries and alliances with each of these two neighbouring potentates. Mestewat with her son, Amedé Liben, alias Abba Wat'ew, continued to defend the legitimacy of their line to rule. Werqitu was weakened by the fact that her son, Amedé Ali, who was made prisoner at Meqdela, was sentenced to death by Téwodros in 1865, as a punishment for the fact that she assisted in the escape of Mïnilïk, then young prince of Shewa, who was also imprisoned in Meqdela.[25] She benefited in return from the support of Mïnilïk, after he became the mighty ruler of Shewa. He needed her support to make Wello a dependent territory, useful as a buffer zone to protect the northern border of Shewa.

24 Téwodros II committed suicide on April 13, 1868, in Meqdela. He was defeated by a powerful British military expedition sent the only goal of releasing the European hostages held by the Ethiopian king since 1864 as a reaction of the ignorance of the European powers (in particular Britain and France) regarding his requests for reciprocal diplomatic relations.

25 Perhaps she initially wanted to "exchange" Menilek against the release of her son, but the fury of Téwodros did not leave her time for this.

At this time, Muhammed Ali entered the scene. He was the step-son of Werqitu, being the son of *Imam* Ali Abba Bulla and another of his wives. He too staked a claim over the imamate. He grew up in Sayïnt[26], a Christian territory, following the familial model which included a period of education in a Christian environment. After siding with Mïnilïk for a while, Muhammed Ali allied himself with Yoḥannïs, who recognized him as *Imam* and consecrated him as *Ras*, by converting him to Christianity with the name of Mika'él, after the religious council held in Boru Meda (north of Desé) in June 1878. His rival, Amedé Abba Watew, who went to the side of Menilek and was converted the same day, with the name of Hayle Maryam and the title of lower rank of *Dejjazmach*. Wello was thus completely absorbed into the Christian monarchy.

The end of the Mammedoch

The end of this dynasty as an autonomous Muslim political family was marked by the definitive conversion to Christianity of the two *Imam*-s. But this dynasty in the broad sense, as a family, did not become extinct with the conversion of two of its prominent members. It also includes all the descendants of the *Imam*-s who held offices of varying importance at local or higher levels in the aristocracy of the Christian kingdom of Ethiopia until its collapse. One can thus consider that the last important member of this dynasty was the heir to the throne (*Alga Werash*), Asfaw Wesen. Son of the King of Kings, *Atsé* Hayle Sïllassé I, Asfaw Wesen was descended from the Mammedoch family through his mother Menen. He was appointed governor of Wello in 1930 (at the age of 14). His maternal ancestry conferred a certain amount of legitimacy on him to hold this office, but his lack of charisma prevented him from appeasing the strong resentment against the central government that the inhabitants of Wello had been feeling since the overthrow of Mika'él and Iyasu and the placement of Wello under control of the imperial army (Asnake 1986).

Conclusion: a political model for Iyasu?

The first Muslim leaders of Werre Himeno and founders of the Mammedoch dynasty established their power by concluding interreligious matrimonial alliances that were instrumental in putting up and maintaining a protecting shelter against the incursions of rival armies from bordering Christian territories. Their interactions with Christian ruling families were thus based on confrontational relations balanced by temporary alliances. The affiliations to Islam or to Christianity marked distinct positions and ideological options in power relations on local, regional and international scales. There were, however, numerous possibilities of circulation, conversion, reconversion, alliance, or other kinds of arrangement, which created situations of in-betweenness, uncertainty and

26 According to Asnake Ali (1983: 7-8).

fluctuation. The Mammedoch *Imam*-s tried to play their advantages from these fuzzy areas between strong blocks. This may explain their success both in terms of territorial expansion and in terms of ascent of the hierarchical ladder of the Christian kingdom. As *Imam-s*, they behaved as fervent or even conquering Muslims (particularly against rival Oromo groups of interior Wello). But as they were surrounded by Christian powers, and as they controlled populations whose religious adhesions were either old but friable (Christianity or traditional Oromo religion), or recent but unstable (Islam), they could make strategic use of religious mobility.

This strategy of religious mobility was continued at each generation. On a first level it was implemented through marriages with women from more or less high-ranking Christian families (or, in a single case, a Mammedoch woman, Menen, married to very high-ranking dignitaries of Gonder). On a second level, these marriages had an impact on the life and personality of the future *Imam-s*, who were brought up in their maternal Christian environment during part of their childhood or their adolescence. This period in their education resulted in a certain level of complicity between the *Imam-s*, after their reconversion to Islam, and their Christian partners and adversaries. Thus, in only a few generations, the Mammedoch were able to weave a very tight network of alliances with the bordering Christian powers and, in spite of ongoing conflicts, to negotiate the conservation of their difference.

Many analogies can be drawn between the traces the Mammedoch had left in the pages of the history of Ethiopia and the "sketch of reign" that Iyasu begun to draw up. In particular the attempts made by the royal prince Iyasu to address interreligious issues by inventing a new form of multi-religious sovereignty might be thought in line with the history of his patrilineal forefathers who were characterized by the practice of more or less temporary adaptation of religious memberships in accordance with political strategies. As a royal prince who was trained to govern, Iyasu was exposed to several models of education. Not only did he receive the religious and military education of a Christian aristocrat, he was also exposed to the basics of modern European education. After the death of his regent *Ras* Tesemma, he drew closer to his father Mika'él and he openly expressed his pride in belonging to the dynasty of Mammedoch *Imam-s*. His awareness of the legacy of his paternal forefathers might have reinforced his conception of government that tended to be closer to the flexible, pluralistic and opportunistic political behaviour of the Mammedoch.

Bibliography

Abbadie, Arnauld d', 1980 a, *Douze ans de séjour dans la Haute Ethiopie*, Edition et notes par Jeanne-Marie Allier, tome 1 (original edition : Paris, 1868), Città del Vaticano: Biblioteca Apolostica Vaticana.

Abbadie, Arnauld d', 1980 b, *Douze ans de séjour dans la Haute Ethiopie*, Edition et notes par Jeanne-Marie Allier, tome 2 (inédit). Città del Vaticano: Biblioteca Apolostica Vaticana.

Abbadie, Arnauld d'., ms. n.d., "Recueil de renseignements juridiques, historiques et littéraires éthiopiens", Biblioteca Apostolica Vaticana : Carte d'Abbadie, 18.

Abir, Mordechai, 1968, *Ethiopia: The Era of the Princes. The Challenge of Islam and the Re-unification of the Christian Empire, 1769-1855.* Harlow, Longmans.

Abbink, Jon, 2008, "Muslim Monasteries? Some Aspects of Religious Culture in Northern Ethiopia", *Aethiopica*, 11, pp. 117-133.

Abbink, Jon, 1998, "An historical-anthropological approach to Islam in Ethiopia: issues of identity and politics", *Journal of African Cultural Studies*, 11 (2), pp. 109-24.

Asnake Ali, 1983, *Aspects of the Political History of Wallo: 1872-1916*", M.A. Thesis, Addis Ababa University, Department of History.

Asnake Ali, 1986, "The condition of the peasantry in Wallo, 1917-1935: A review of the traditions", *Proceedings of the 3rd Annual Seminar of the Department of History.* Addis Abeba University, pp. 1-8.

Berhanou Abebe, 2001, "Le coup d'Etat du 26 septembre 1916 ou le dénouement d'une décennie de crise", *Annales d'Ethiopie*, 17, pp. 309-359.

Brielli, Domenico, 1945, "Ricordi storici dei Uollo (con note di C. Conti Rossini) ", in C. Conti Rossini (raccolta da), *Studi Etiopici*, Roma, Istituto per l'Oriente, pp. 78-110.

Conti Rossini, Carlo, 1916, "La Cronaca Reale Abissina dall'anno 1800 all'anno 1840", *Rendiconti della Reale Accademia dei Lincei*, S5, 25.

Crummey, Donald, 1975a, "Society and Ethnicity in the Politics of Christian Ethiopia during the Zamana Masafent", *The International Journal of African Historical Studies*, 8(2), pp. 266-278.

Crummey, Donald, 1975b, "C'äc'äho and the politics of the northern Wällo-Bägémder border", *Journal of Ethiopian Studies*, 1975, 13 (1), pp. 1-9.

Crummey, Donald, 2007, "Mänän Libän Amäde", *Encyclopaedia Aethiopica*, vol. 3, pp. 721-722.

Ficquet, Eloi, 1999, "La traversée du Wällo par J.L. Krapf en mars 1842", in A. Rouaud, ed., *Les orientalistes sont des aventuriers. Guirlande pour Joseph Tubiana.* St Maur, Sépia, pp. 117-129.

Ficquet, Eloi, 2000, "L'intervention des Oromo-Wällo dans la dynastie éthiopienne salomonide sous les règnes de Bäkaffa, Iyyasu et Iyo'as, 1721 à 1769", *Annales d'Éthiopie*, 16, pp. 135-146.

Ficquet, Eloi, 2002, "Du barbare au mystique: Anthropologie historique des recompositions identitaires et religieuses dans le Wällo (Ethiopie centrale) ", Thèse de doctorat en sciences sociales, EHESS, Paris.

Ficquet, Eloi, 2006, "Flesh Soaked in Faith: Meat as a marker of the boundary between Christians and Muslims in Ethiopia", in B.F. Soares, ed., *Muslim-Christian Encounters in Africa*, Leiden/Boston, Brill, pp. 39-56.

Ficquet, Eloi, 2008, "Mammädoč dynasty", *Encyclopaedia Aethiopica*, vol. 3, pp. 715-717.

Ficquet, Eloi, 2010, "La mixité religieuse comme stratégie politique. La dynastie des Māmmadoč du Wallo (Éthiopie centrale), du milieu du XVIIIe siècle au début du XXe siècle", *Afriques* [on line], 01. URL : http://afriques.revues.org/533

Kropp, Manfred, 1987, "Les premières querelles théologique d'Abuna Salama III en Ethiopie", *Annales d'Éthiopie*, 14, pp. 101-116.

Leslau, Wolf, 1987, *Compartive Dictionary of Ge'ez (Classical Ethiopic)*, Wiesbaden, Harrassowitz.

Izarn, Reginald R., 1969, "Les documents Arnauld d'Abbadie" *Proceedings of the 3rd International Conference of Ethiopian Studies*, Addis Abeba, IES, vol. 1, p. 158.

Hussein Ahmed, 2001, *Islam in Nineteenth-Century Wallo, Ethiopia. Revival, Reform and Reaction*, Leiden, Brill.

Mohammed Hassen, 1992, "Islam as Resistance Ideology Among the Oromo of Ethiopia: The Wallo Case, 1700-1900" in S. Samatar, ed., *In the Shadow of Conquest: Islam in Colonial Northeast Africa*, Trenton, Red Sea Press, pp. 75-101.

Molla Tikuye, 1994, "The rise and fall of the Yajju Dynasty (1784-1980)", *Proceedings of the 11th International Conference of Ethiopian Studies*, Addis Ababa: IES, vol. 1, pp. 197-216.

Pearce, Nathaniel, 1831, *The Life and Adventures of Nathaniel Pearce, written by himself during a residence in Abyssinia, from the years 1810 to 1819. Together with Mr. Coffin's account of his visit to Gondar. Ed. by J.J. Halls*, London, H. Colburn and R. Bentley, 2 vols.

Rubenson, Sven, 2003, "Ali Alula", *Encyclopaedia Aethiopica*, vol. 1, p. 199.

Shiferaw Bekele, 1990, "Reflections on the power elite of the Wärä Seh Mäsfenate (1786-1853)", *Annales d'Ethiopie*, 15, pp. 157-176.

Toubkis, Dimitri, 2010, "Les Oromo à la conquête du trône du roi des rois (XVIe-XVIIIe siècle) ", *Afriques* [on line], 01. URL : http://afriques.revues.org/470

Zergaw Asfera, 1973, "Some Aspects of Historical Development in Amhara/Wällo (ca. 1700–1815)", B.A. thesis, Haile Selassie I University.

Weld Blundell, Herbert, 1922, *The Royal Chronicle of Abyssinia, 1769-1840*, Cambridge, Cambridge University Press.

Fig. 1 - **Genealogy of the Mammedoch of Wello**
from *Shaykh* Nur Husayn to *Imam* Amedé Kolasé

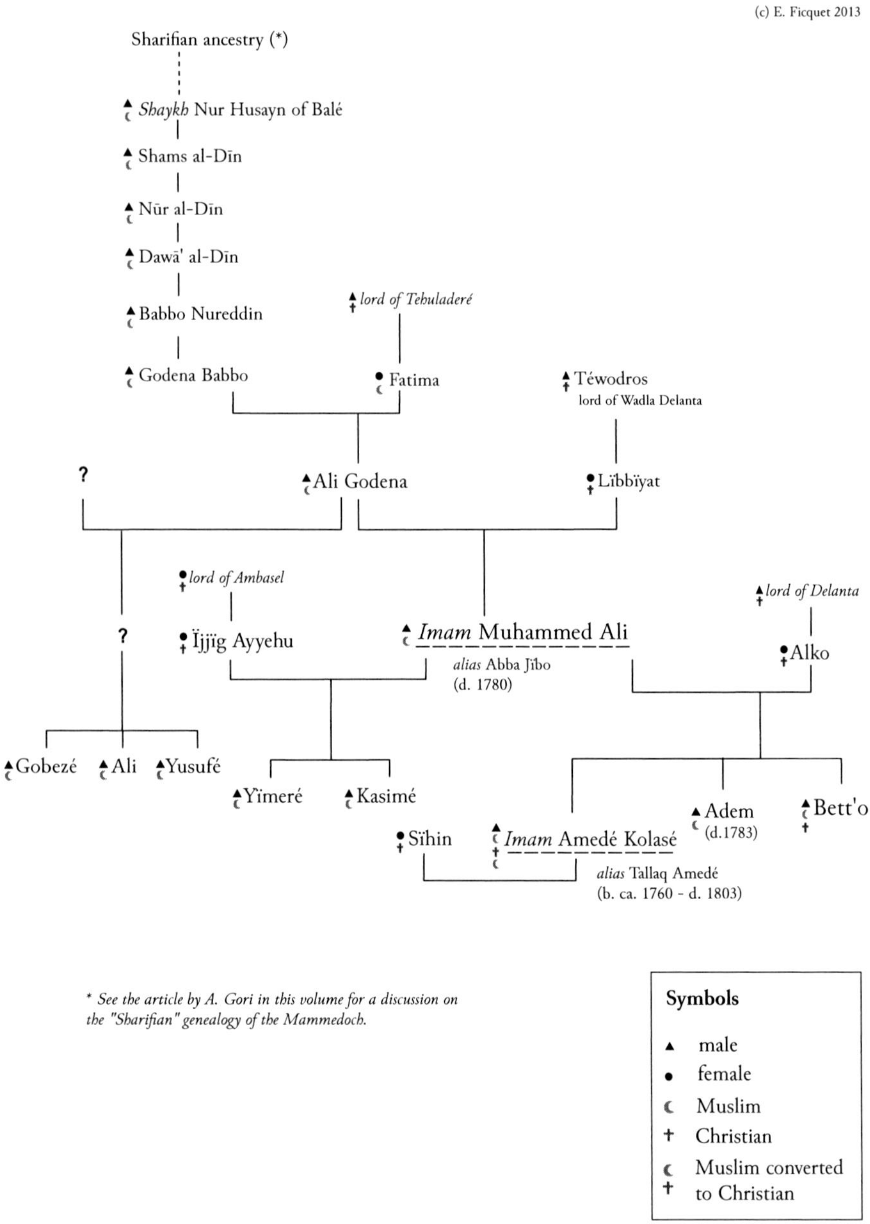

* *See the article by A. Gori in this volume for a discussion on the "Sharifian" genealogy of the Mammedoch.*

Fig.2 **Genealogy of the Mammedoch of Wello**

From *Imam* Amedé Kolasé to the two last *Imam-s* who were baptized in 1878

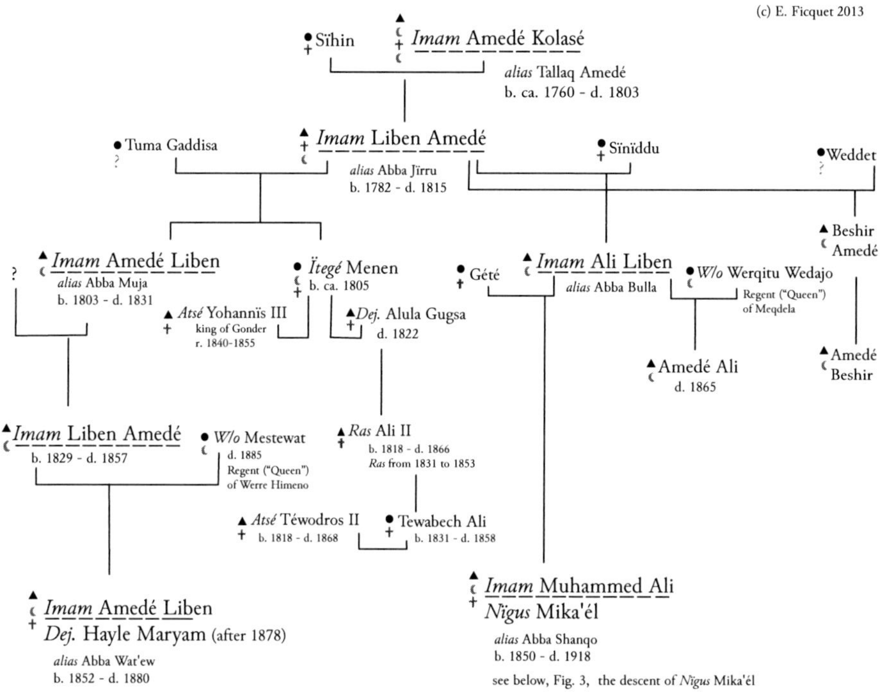

Fig. 3 **The descent of *Nïgus* Mikaél (Muhammed Ali)**

With focus on the most prominent figures

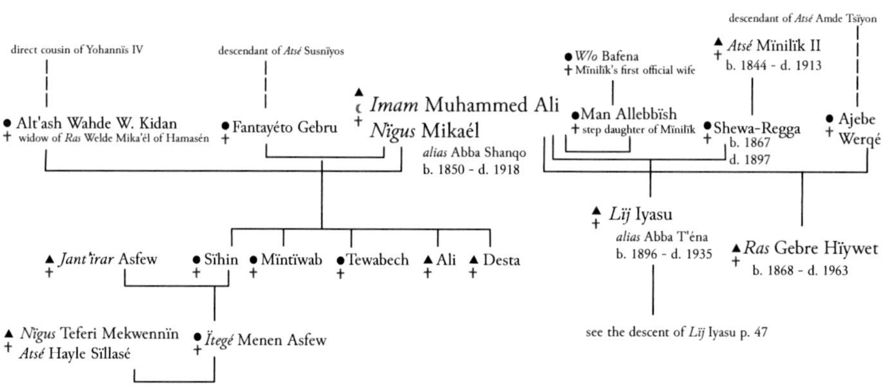

Some Observations on a Sharifian Genealogy of *Lij* Iyasu (Vatican Arabic ms 1796, folio 22v)

Alessandro Gori *

Prolegomena

There is an enormous lacuna in our present knowledge of Islam in Ethiopia: the lack of information about the human groups, families and clans that claim an Arab ancestry. As it is well known from other parts of the Islamic world, these groups have played and still play a crucial role in many aspects of the Islamic societies. This is particularly true for the *sayyid* and *šarīf* lineages, directly related to the Prophet Muḥammad. However, also other lineages originating from the two first caliphs (Abū Bakr and ʿUmar: the *Bakrī* or *Ṣiddīqī* and *ʿUmarī* or *Fārūqī* ancestry), from clans of the Banū Hāšim and Qurayš and from companions of the Prophet (*Anṣārī* or *Ṣaḥābī* ancestry) tend to build up clearly identifiable social and cultural groups, with their own peculiar way to interact with the surrounding human environment, their own family history and a specific connection to the past of the Islamic communities where they live in.

This exceptionally important social and historical function of the groups of Arab descent has been relatively well studied in Somalia where not only the territorial location and diffusion of the numerous *ashraaf*, Bakrī, ʿUmarī and other generally Arab lineages are well known but also the different genealogical traditions have been collected and more or less carefully analyzed.[1]

As a matter of fact, the first and fundamental way to gain insight into the complicated but vital universe of the different human groups that claim an Arab origin in the area is to collect their genealogies, especially those preserved in manuscripts.

Genealogical documents function in a double direction: vertically, they locate the group in a historical space-time dimension, keeping memory of the origins and the successive displacements through countries and regions. Horizontally, they describe a sort of social geography, building relationships with groups of more or less close

* Department of Linguistics University of Florence. The following paper is based on a research carried out in the summer of 2009 at the Hiob Ludolf Zentrum für Äthiopistik of the University of Hamburg thanks to the generous support of the Alexander von Humboldt Foundation.

1 See for example Lewis (1994).

relatives, delimiting territories of allies and foes, creating friendships and enmities. Of course, the frame which a genealogy sets up is not fixed once and forever. A same genealogical document may be read differently according to changing social or historical circumstances, paving the way for alliances instead of conflicts; moreover, the possibility of rewriting or reshaping a genealogical tradition is always at hand and can be used whenever necessary to correct the chain of names and adjust it to some new exigency.

In the Islamic tradition, a specialized category of learned men was and is in charge of preserving and transmitting the genealogical knowledge. The *nassāb* (pl. *nassāba*) are the recognized keepers of the science of *nasab* (pl. *ansāb*).[2] Their work, their books, their huge collections of intricate genealogical trees, whose branches extend through centuries and countries, are the only reference to rightly classify the lineages. The judgment of a *nassāb*, who has gained fame in his field and is considered reliable in disentangling the bulk of the genealogical material, is the most important touchstone in the evaluation of a *nasab* chain. An Arab ancestry which has been approved by a renowed *nassāb* is thus a decisive element for the history and the social position of a human group living in a Muslim region.

One has to admit that scholars of Islam in Ethiopia have only a very vague idea of all this extremely complex and at the same time crucial manifestation of the Islamic culture and society.

The genealogical documents of most of the Ethiopian Muslim communities and families are practically unknown. Comparison among different *ansāb* is an untouched field and even the simple but exact knowledge of the geographical distribution of the groups boasting an Arab ancestry is still a desideratum. The name of no famous Ethiopian *nassāb* is known until now.

The urgent need to acquire information in this field is felt not only by the scholars but also by conscious Ethiopian Muslims: in this very year, a Muslim young man *sayyid* Abū al-Qāsim Ḥusayn al-ʻAlawī, who started a personal research on the genealogy of his family, managed to put on line a first collection of Ethiopian *ansab*[3]: it is a first step in the right direction and I hope that it will be followed by many others.

In this general frame I should like to locate also the genealogy of *Lïj* Iyasu that I am going to present and publish here. It is self evident that the nature of the personage not only allows but even imposes other interpretative approaches to the document. However, as the present speaker is basically an Islamicist, it is from the above sketched perspective that I prefer to conduct my analysis.

2 On *nasab* in general see Franz Rosenthal, "Nasab", in *Encyclopaedia of Islam*[2], vol. 7, p. 967.

3 The collection with an interesting introduction in Arabic is called *al-Saʻy wa-al-ʻaṭaš li-taʻrif ašraf al-Ḥabaša*. In the introduction the author laments the carelessness of the Muslims of Ethiopia in the field of genealogy. He explains this lack of interest also as a consequence of the respect due to noble families: no one has dared so far to ask them to show the documents proving their ancestry.

The document

The genealogical document I am going to deal with can be found in folio 22v of the Arabic manuscript number 1796 of the Vatican Library (fig. 1). The manuscript was acquired in Harar by Enrico Cerulli who published many of the texts which it contains. It was then donated by the Italian Ethiopianist to the Vatican Library. In 1965 Giorgio Levi Della Vida catalogued and described it (Levi Della Vida 1965: 158).

It is a simple half page written by a quite coarse and unrefined hand but in clear and readable *ductus*. Nothing is known about the scribe and also the origin of the text remains obscure. The writing presents a certain incertitude in the spelling of some names and from the point of view of grammar, a glaring error is present. The names in the *nasab* are numbered so that the reader is facilitated in distinguishing them getting at the same time an impression of accuracy.

Here I retype the *nasab* reproducing exactly the text as it is in the manuscript.[4]

هذا المرقوم نسب الملك الملوك[sic!]
امبراطور الحبش سيد الياسوا ابن ١نجس ميكائيل ابن ٢امام علي ابن ٣امام ليبن ابن ٤امام محمد ابن ٥امام احمد ابن ٦امام محمد ابن ٧علي ابن ٨گودَانا ابن ٩بابو ابن ١٠داؤ الدين ابن ١١نور الدين ابن ١٢شمس الدين ابن ١٣نور حسين ابن ١٤دِمَلگَان ١٥ابن عبد الحميد ابن ١٦عيسى ابن ١٧سخي الله ابن ١٨امام نور ابن ١٩يعقوب ابن ٢٠جوهر ابن ياقوت ابن ٢٢محمود ابن ٢٣تاج الدين ابن ٢٤تَمام ابن ٢٥محمد ابن ٢٦ابراهيم ابن ٢٧خليل ابن ٢٨نور ابن ٢٩احمد ابن ٣٠اسماعيل ابن ٣١يحيى ابن ٣٢تقي الله ابن ٣٣عمر ابن ٣٤موسى الكاظم ابن ٣٥عبد الله ابن ٣٦محمد ٣٧باقير ابن ٣٨زيد [sic!] العابدين ابن حسن وحسين ابن علي ابن ابي طالب[5] ابنا فاطمة بنت رسول الله صلى عليه وسلم ابن عبد الله

Here follows the translation and transcription of the genealogy:

This numbered text is the genealogy of the king of the kings.

Imperator of Ethiopia sayyid Iyāsū son of nigus (1) Mikāʾīl son of imām (2) ʿAlī son of imām (3) Liban son of imām (4) Muḥammad son of imām (5) Aḥmad son of imām (6) Muḥammad son of (7) ʿAlī son of (8) Kawdānā son of (9) Bābū son of (10) Dawū' al-Dīn son of (11) Nūr al-Dīn son of (12) Šams al-Dīn son of (13) Nūr Ḥusayn son of (14) Dimalkān son of (15) ʿAbd al-Ḥamīd son of (16) ʿĪsā son of (17) Saḫī Allāh son of (18) imām Nūr son of (19) Yaʿqūb son of (20) Jawhar son of (21) Yāqūt[6] *son of (22) Maḥmūd son of (23) Taj al-Dīn son of (24) Tamām son of (25) Muḥammad son of (26) Ibrāhīm son of (27) Ḫalīl son of (28) Nūr son of (29) Aḥmad son of (30) Ismāʿīl son of (31) Yaḥyā son of (32) Taqī Allāh son of (33) ʿUmar son of (34) Mūsā al-Kāẓim son of (35) ʿAbdallāh son of (36) Muḥammad (37) Bāqīr son of (38) Zayd al-ʿĀbidīn son of Ḥasan and Ḥusayn - son of ʿAlī b. Abī Ṭālib - two sons of Fāṭima daughter of the Messenger of God (May God bless him and grant him salvation) son of ʿAbdallāh.*

4 For technical reasons, I am not able to put the order number over the name of each bead of the chain of the genealogy as it is in the manuscript. I thus put it before the name and after the always repeated "Ibn"

5 The name is written between the lines in the reverse way.

6 The name Yāqūt was written over the line after Yaʿqūb was canceled; Yaʿqūb is however still clearly readable.

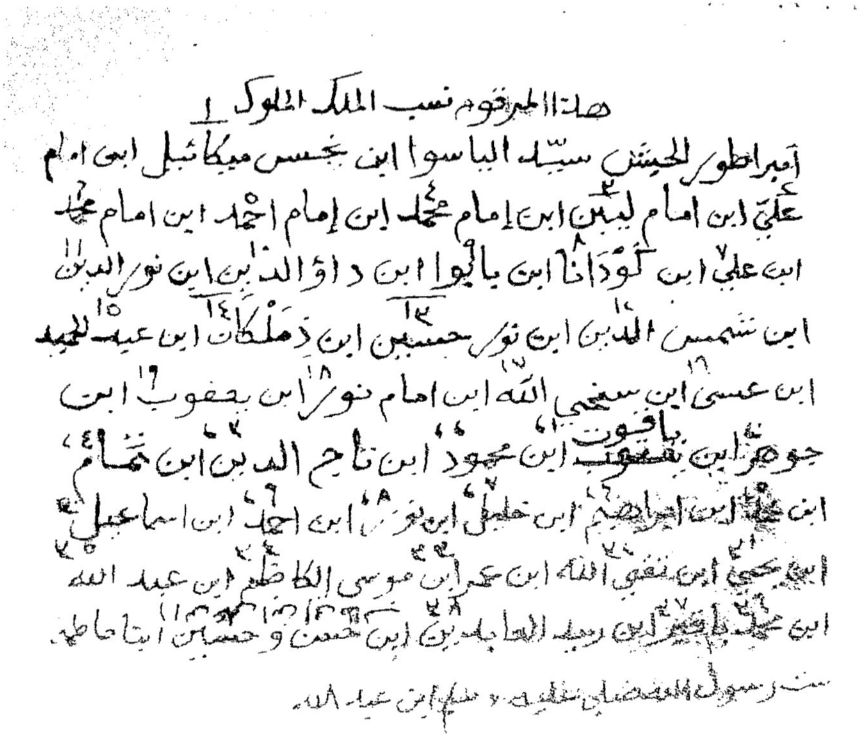

Fig 1.: Vatican Arabic ms 1796, folio 22v

Some first observations

This is not the first time that a genealogy of *Lïj* Iyasu comes into discussion. More exactly: the genealogy of the Mammedoch dynasty to which the Ethiopian ruler belonged had already attracted the attention of the scholars and the ancestry of *Nïgus* Mika'él, father of Iyasu, was fairly well known. Moreover, the idea that *Lïj* Iyasu had spread among his Muslim subjects a genealogy which made him a descendant of the Prophet Muḥammad is widely attested in several sources of different origin and bias.[7]

Summarizing the available data on this point, one finds:

- a genealogy of *Lïj* Iyasu published by Budge (1928: 546-547) which retraces his ancestry to the Prophet Muḥammad. It is not clear where Budge read and transcribed his source.
- Domenico Brielli (1945) edited by Carlo Conti Rossini reconstructing the history of Wello dealt at length with the *Mammedoch* and enumerated all the member of the ruling family.
- The regretted Hussein Ahmed (2001: 203) published a genealogy of the *Mammedoch* family down to *Lïj* Iyasu that he drew from oral sources and from the scholarly literature.
- Finally Eloi Ficquet (2007) collected together all the previous information in a encyclopedic article.

The more or less significant differences between the known genealogical lists and the present Arabic document will be mentioned in the following. This is definitely the first time that an Arabic *nasab* of *Lïj* Iyasu is published.

To analyze with ease the content of the genealogy, I will divide it in three sections: starting from Iyasu up to (8) Kawdānā son of (9) Bābū; then, from (10) Dawū' al-Dīn to Dimalkān son of (15) ʿAbd al-Ḥamīd; and finally, from (33) ʿUmar son of (34) Mūsā al-Kāẓim to Muḥammad the Prophet.

The first section of the nasab

The first section of the *nasab* is the commonly known genealogy of the *Mammedoch* family which ends with the founder of the dynasty Godaanaa son of Babboo. In this part of the *nasab* one may find only one major peculiarity: *imām* (3) Liben is said to be the son of *imām* (4) Muḥammad son of *imām* (5) Aḥmad (i.e. *imām* Amedé Kolasé or K^{w}elasi or *tïllïq*). The insertion of the name of an *imām* (4) Muḥammad son of *imām* (5) Aḥmad contradicts most of the known genealogies of the *Mammedoch* where Liben is son of Amedé Kolasé and an *imām* Muḥammad is not mentioned. It is not apparently explainable from where this name actually came: it is nevertheless attested also in the genealogy of Iyasu published by Budge where "Imam Lihan" [sic !] is son of "Imam Muḥammad II".

7 See for example Hayle Sillasé I (1965 a.m.: 31) and Asfa-Wossen Asserate (2007: 31, 376)

The second section of the nasab

(10) Dawū᾽ al-Dīn is clearly a misspelling of the scribe for the name Dawā᾽ al-Dīn (ar. "the medicine of the religion") which is also mentioned in the list of Budge.

The names up to (13) Nūr Ḥusayn: (11) Nūr al-Dīn son of (12) Šams al-Dīn are present also in the genealogy of the *Mammedoch* published by Hussein Ahmed.

Nūr Ḥusayn is the most revered Muslim saint of Ethiopia. His full genealogy is well known and was published together with his two hagiographies several times in the country. It is thus possible to make a comparison.[8]

The string (12) Šams al-Dīn son of (13) Nūr Ḥusayn son of (14) Dimalkān is problematic as Nūr Ḥusayn is not given a son named Šams al-Dīn in his *nasab al-šarīf*; as for Dimalkān, it is an evident misspelling for Malkā᾽ī, the nickname of Ibrāhīm, father of *šayḫ* Ḥusayn.

The ancestry given in this genealogy for Nūr Ḥusayn son of (14) Dimalkān up to (34) Mūsā al-Kāẓim is really puzzling and quite astonishing.

The *nasab al-šarīf* of *šayḫ* Ḥusayn does not claim a *šarīfian* origin for the holy man of Bale but retraces his forefathers up to ʿAqīl b. Abī Ṭālib, older brother of ʿAlī b. Abī Ṭālib and cousin of the Prophet. The *ʿAqīlid* ancestry is a widespread *nasab* in Northeast Africa.

As for the present genealogy, one has moreover to note that the whole series of name from (14) Dimalkān up to (34) Mūsā al-Kāẓim cannot be found elsewhere. It really an *unicum*, at least so far.

The third section of the nasab

The third part of the genealogy is easy to check as it has its pivotal point in (34) Mūsā al-Kāẓim (d. around 800) the seventh *imām* of the Twelver Shia whose *nasab* up to ʿAlī b. Abī Ṭālib and Fāṭima daughter of the Prophet Muḥammad is of course very well known and established once forever.

Once more one cannot help feeling much surprised by some evident mistakes in the succession of the names in the chain. The string (33) ʿUmar son of (34) Mūsā al-Kāẓim son of (35) ʿAbdallāh son of (36) Muḥammad (37) Bāqīr son of (38) Zayd al-ʿĀbidīn son of Ḥasan and Ḥusayn - son of ʿAli b. Abī Ṭālib - two sons of Fāṭima daughter of the Messenger of God (May God bless him and grant him salvation) son of ʿAbdallāh is a collection of errors and shortcomings.

8 The *nasab* of *šayḫ* Ḥusayn was printed for the first time in the *Kitāb rabīʿ al-qulūb fī ḏikr manāqib wa-faḍā᾽il sayyidina al-šayḫ Nūr Ḥusayn Raḍya Allāh ʿanhu wa-yalīh kitāb nuzhat al-asrār wa-ṭahārat al-aqḏār fī manāqibih wa-faḍā᾽ilih ayḍan*, Addis Ababa: al-Maktaba al-Ḥusayniyya - Cairo: Maṭbaʿat al-šarq, 1927 (1345 a.h.), pp. 63-71. See also Andrzejewski (1975: 139-140).

First of all, Mūsā is son of the sixth *imām* Ğaʿfar al-Ṣādiq (d. 765) and grandson of the fifth *imām* Muḥammad *al-Bāqir* (d. around 735): the name ʿAbdallāh as the one of his father was perhaps originated by the *kunya* of Ğaʿfar – Abū ʿAbdallāh; the separation of the name of Muḥammad from the nickname *Bāqir* as if they were two distinct persons is really inexplicable. Almost every average Muslim – Shiite and Sunni as well - knows the nicknames of the twelve imams and could not sever Muḥammad from *al-Bāqir*.

Secondly, the name of the son of Mūsā al-Kāẓim (33) ʿUmar is not attested in any of the collections of genealogical traditions of the descendants of ʿAli b. Abī Ṭālib: it is thus an *apax*. This is perhaps the most sensitive point in the whole genealogical chain, as ʿUmar represent the link between the Alid – prophetic section of the *nasab* and the Ethiopian descendents: an evident inconsistency in the name of this link person means a failure in the whole structure of the genealogy.

Some tentative conclusions

To sum up: I have briefly scrutinized this Arabic *nasab* of *lij* Iyasu in the light of some current but accredited sources of the Arabic Islamic genealogical science and in comparison with one of the best known Ethiopian Islamic genealogies (*šayḫ* Ḥusayn). The clear result is that this genealogical document suffers of an intrinsic weakness: not only it has many scattered inaccuracies and shortcomings but also it is clamorously inconsistent in retracing the ancestry of its most famous names. The result is that the *nasab* is at great variance with other similar documents and presents many *apax* that set it completely apart from the conglomerate of trees and branches of other sharifian families.

This is to say that this genealogy does not reach the standard of reliability according to the criteria fixed by the science of Islamic *nasab*. One can infer from the reading of the succession of the names that the writer of this *nasab* was not sufficiently acquainted with the principles of the science of traditional Islamic genealogy.

It is not known whether the document circulated or not among Muslims. Also the circumstances of its writing are obscure. The question of who was this clumsy *nassāb* and why he took the decision of writing such an unsatisfying genealogical document must for the moment remain unanswered.

It is however quite evident that a claim of a sharifian ancestry could not be seriously supported among at least learned Muslims by such a document which on the contrary could have given rise to many serious doubts in its readers.

Bibliography

Andrzejewski, Bogumił W., 1975, "A Genealogical Note Relevant to the Dating of Sheikh Hussein of Bale", *Bulletin of the School of Oriental and African Studies*, 38, pp. 139-140.

Asfa-Wossen Asserate, 2007, *Ein Prinz aus dem Hause David und warum er in Deutschland blieb*, Frankfurt am Main, Fischer Verlag.

Budge, E.A. Wallis, 1928, *A History of Ethiopia, Nubia & Abyssinia (according to the hieroglyphic inscriptions of Egypt and Nubia, and the Ethiopian chronicles)*, vol. 2, London, Methuen.

Brielli, Domenico, 1945, "Ricordi storici dei Uollo (con note di Carlo Conti Rossini)", in Conti Rossini, Carlo, ed., *Studi Etiopici*, Roma, Istituto per l'Oriente, pp. 78-110.

Ficquet, Eloi, 2007, "Mammädoc dynasty", in S. Uhlig, ed., *Encyclopædia Æthiopica*, Wiesbaden, Otto Harrassowitz, vol. 3, pp. 715-717.

Hayle Sïllasé I, 1965 a.m., *Hïweténna ye-Ityopya Ïrmïjja*, Vol. I, Addis Ababa. Bïrhanïnna Selam.

Hussein Ahmed, 2001, *Islam in Nineteenth-Century Wallo, Ethiopia. Revival, Reform and Reaction*. Leiden, Brill.

Levi Della Vida, 1965, *Secondo elenco dei manoscritti arabi islamici della Biblioteca Vaticana*, Città del Vaticano, Biblioteca Apostolica Vaticana (Studi e Testi, 242).

Lewis, Ioan M., 1994, "Myth and History in Somali Genealogies", in I. M. Lewis, *Blood and Bone. The Call of Kinship in Somali Society*, Lawrenceville, The Red Sea Press, pp. 95-111.

Lïj Iyasu's Marriages as a Reflection of his Domestic Policy

Zuzanna Augustyniak

Introduction

In 1916, when the Shewan nobles decided to take over power in Ethiopia, they accused *Lïj* Iyasu of betrayal of Christianity by marrying several wives in accordance with Muslim customs. However, a reassessment of *Lïj* Iyasu's reign seems to imply rather that his marriages served as a tool for the accomplishment of an internal policy aimed at gaining support of the Muslim inhabitants of eastern and southern Ethiopia. He also used this strategy to achieve his genuine idea of uniting the peoples of Ethiopia. The aim of this article is to show that despite his young age and limited experience *Lïj* Iyasu was not simply a ruler with an endless sexual appetite, as he is often presented, but a conscious policymaker with a complete and complex vision of his empire.

When in the 1960s Donald Levine collected material for his book *Wax and Gold* (1972) in Addis Abeba, he asked in one of his questionnaires after the most and the least popular historical personalities. According to the results of the survey, the most negative historical personality was *Lïj* Iyasu. University and college students justified their negative evaluation by writing that the ruler was an "*incompetent ruler*", "*encouraging Islam*" and was "*chasing after women*" (Levine 1972). Nowadays, the reason for such a perception of Iyasu seems obvious, because it emerged as a part of Hayle Sïllasé's policy of undermining Iyasu's historical role. Also the discussion on different aspects of policy led by Iyasu has been opened and the workshop in Desé in November 2009 stands as the best example for this.

A number of new sources related to Iyasu's rule resurfaced in recent years. Together with other well-known sources they provide information on different aspects of the heir to the throne's life and his times. They leave no doubt, that Iyasu's policies were not arbitrary, but systematically responding to both the domestic and external situation of the country. Iyasu's view on how to rule the Ethiopian Empire can – as an enlightening example – be analysed through the marriage-unions, in which he was involved. According to Bahru Zewde's article in *Encyclopaedia Aethiopica*, Iyasu had twelve wives with whom he had many children.[1]

1 Bahru Zewde, 2007: 255; Gebre Ïgziyabïhér Elyas (1994: 358) mentions only ten wives of Iyasu.

Marriages in Ethiopia

There is a long history of political marriages in Ethiopia, which were very important for the political system and networks in the Ethiopian Empire in the 19th century. For example, *Ïtégé* T'aytu, answering the critics of her decisions, explained that arranged marriages are like mixing water with milk, where "*the last whitens the first*" (Bairu Tafla 1972). Those who were supposed to get married often did not have any choice about who would become their spouse and when. Sources for the history of Ethiopia show that a man "*asked for a wife from the court*" while women were told to get married (Heran Sereke-Brhan 2005).

The main goal of political marriage was strengthening or expanding the sphere of influence by making new unions. Thus, this kind of marriage could neutralize potential threats. For example, when in 1868 *Wag Shum* Gobezé of Lasta made himself emperor Tekle Giyorgis, he used arranged marriages as one of the tools to control the chaos in the country abandoned by its previous emperor, Téwodros II. Already before being emperor, Tekle Giyorgis arranged several marriages, which were supposed to give him support.

The other reason for arranged marriages was the fact, that thanks to marrying a certain person one could become regularly guest at a court, which, in turn, often created the opportunity to realize one's political aspirations (Heran Sereke-Brhan 2003: 266-274). If one was fortunate, one could even become regent or even emperor. This method was used for example by *Ïtégé* T'aytu, who, knowing that she cannot give children to Mïnilïk, decided to put one of her relatives on throne.

Political marriages also served the purpose of resolving conflicts and strengthening alliances within the aristocracy and leaders belonging to different faiths, for example Muslims or Béte Isra'él, and ethnic groups such as Oromo (Pankhurst 1997: 206-220). 19th century Gonder was ruled by the Yejju family. In those times, there were many marriages between Muslims and Christians. Obviously, that kind of marriages could function only under the condition that one of the partners changed his faith. Almost always it was the person who followed Islam, who thus entered into the Christian highlands' power networks (Heran Sereke-Brhan 2005).

Lïj Iyasu's marriages

Lïj Iyasu's first wife was Princess Romane Werq, granddaughter of emperor Yoḥannïs IV, who at the day of her wedding was only seven years old.[2] The marriage was arranged by King of Kings Mïnilïk, who wanted to strengthen *Lïj* Iyasu's position as the official heir to the throne. This move was supposed to weaken the well-known opposition of the Tigrayan rulers (Bartnicki & Mantel-Niećko 1987: 333). It was also

---

2 Gebre Ïgziyabïhér Elyas writes that Romane Werq was twelve when she married *Lïj* Iyasu. The wedding took place shortly after *Ras* Tesemma's death. According to Chris Prouty (1986: 320) the princess was six years old. The same sources confirm that her name was Astér Mengesha. See: Molvaer (1994:358).

supposed to stop *Ïtégé* T'aytu from forcing in Zewditu – married to T'aytu's nephew – as a candidate to become the heir to the throne (Marcus 1975: 238). Paradoxically, however, this marriage also supported the plans of the ambitious *Ïtégé*, because Romane Werq was also T'aytu's relative (Bahru Zewde 1996: 117). Thanks to this marriage, the *Ïtégé* could still continue to develop her network of family connections and at the same time exert her influence on political decisions made in the Ethiopian Empire.

According to Mersï'é Hazen Wolde Qirqos, the marriage ceremony and a huge wedding feast took place in Mïnilïk's palace on 16 May 1909 (Mersé Hazen 2004: 50).[3] *Fitawrari* Habte Giyorgis was acting on behalf of *Ras* Mengesha, who was Romane Werq's father and who could not be present at the wedding (Gebre-Igziabiher Elyas 1994: 358). We do not know whether the princess's mother, *Weyzero* Kefay (the daughter of *Ras* Walé Bït'ul, the brother of *Ïtégé* T'aytu) was present. After the wedding the bride was given a new name - Astér Mengesha (Mersé Hazen 2004: 50). Before that she used to be called Tsïgé Roman Mengesha. When she was married to *Lïj* Iyasu, she was supposed to be six years old (she was born in June 1903). The groom was seven years older than her (Mersé Hazen 2004: 50). Probably Romane Werq was the only one of many Iyasu's wives whom he married according to Christian Ethiopian rite (Gebre-Igziabiher Elyas 1994: 358). After the wedding, it was decided that Astér Mengesha should be raised up in her aunt's, *Weyzero* Gashasha (wife of *Qeñazmach* Kefelew), home. She was built a special pavilion and was treated with the highest honors (Mersé Hazen 2004: 50).

Due to the young age of the newlyweds, the marriage was never consumed. Therefore there were no problems with getting a divorce. Little more than year after they got married, at the end of June 1910, *Lïj* Iyasu divorced Astér (Marcus 1975: 246). Later Astér Mengesha got married with *Ras* Gétachew Abaté, but they divorced soon after their first son, named Abate, was born.[4] It is rarely pointed out that at a later period also Teferi Mekonnïn wanted to marry Astér. He was planning to divorce Menen and take Astér as his wife. Yet his counselors, mainly the *Ïch'egé* and *Ras* Kasa Haylu, advised him not to engage in this relationship. They said that Teferi could not send his consort away after she supported him during his conflict with *Lïj* Iyasu, opposing her against her own family (Gebre-Igziabiher Elyas 1994: 358).

Lïj Iyasu's next relationship was informal according to Ethiopian Orthodox Church rules. That is why Mïnilïk's counselors tried to arrange another marriage for the young prince; this time with the representative of one of powerful Christian families. Their choice was fourteen years old *Weyzero* Seble Wengél Haylu, the daughter of the Gojjamé ruler, *Ras* Haylu. The purpose of this marriage was the reduction of *Ïtégé* T'aytu's influence, as Seble Wengél was not related to the family of Mïnilïk's wife.

3 According to Heran Sereke-Brhan (2005) the wedding took place in 1908.

4 From this relationship Astér Mengesha had also a daughter.

Soon enough *Lïj* Iyasu left his wife and his baby girl (called Alem Tsehay) for, as Gebre Ïgziyabïhér Elyas wrote, “Muslim girls”.[5] Nevertheless, before that Iyasu was in a relationship with *Weyzero* Tisemme Andargé, another representative of Christian aristocracy (Gebre-Igziabiher Elyas 1994: 358).

In the literature that deals with the era of *Lïj* Iyasu’s rule, especially in Ethiopian sources, it is often written that Mïnilïk’s grandson converted to Islam. Iyasu himself denied it telling that he was still a Christian, though he liked to spend time with his Muslim friends and then he wore their traditional clothes (Prouty 1986: 342). Nevertheless those Christian nobles who were not in favor of Iyasu stressed the fact of his marriages with daughters of Muslim noblemen and criticized him for neglecting those with daughters of Christian rulers from Wellega, Gojjam and Yejju. After *Lïj* Iyasu’s downfall the Christian Ethiopians were told that Iyasu was sponsoring the construction of mosques, but only few acknowledged that he was also sponsoring the building of numerous churches (for example Qech’ené Medhané Alem) and that he regularly donated money to the covenant of Debre Libanos (Bahru Zewde 1996: 124). The propagandistic needs of that period did not take into consideration that marriages with daughters of Muslim lords may have been just a part of *Lïj* Iyasu’s domestic politics, whose main goals were to integrate the peoples of Ethiopia and enlarge the Empire’s territory. In that sense, *Lïj* Iyasu was just continuing his grandfather’s politics. Mïnilïk extended the country to the south and Iyasu was trying to extend it to the east. Emperor Mïnilïk’s grandson was not, as it was usually asserted, a ruler with an endless sexual appetite, but a conscious policymaker with a complete and complex vision of the Empire. And to put this vision into practice, he just simply used the same tools as *Ïtégé* T’aytu did.

At the turn of 1912, *Lïj* Iyasu traveled to “Adal province” to pacify the region where people “*lived like bandits (shifta) and caused a lot of trouble*”, as Christian highland writers put it (Gebre-Igziabiher Elyas 1994: 331); this refers to a journey to the sultanate of Awsa, Adal being the Amharic term for “ᶜAfar” in general and in particular being also the name of the former Muslim state, of which Awsa was a successor, both are often confused in Christian sources. Soon he arrived to a city called Sidina. The people living there were so terrified by his fearless army that they succumbed at once. “Abeto *Iyasu, seeing their fear, took pity on them and without fighting them he subdued them in love*” (*ibid.*: 332). In these times, the source narrates, the chiefs in Adal and Yïfat fought with each other for power. *Lïj* Iyasu reconciled both neighbors. This refers to the period when the sultan of Awsa was *Amoyta* Yayyo Mahammad, who had emerged out of a fierce ten-years civil war only a few years before and had consolidated his control of Awsa[6]. Gebre-Igziabiher Elyas further narrates that in order to strengthen the bond between himself and the two chiefs, *Lïj* Iyasu took as his concubine and then married in a civil ceremony the daughter of an ᶜAfar notable.

5 Gebre-Igziabiher Elyas 1994: 358; Prouty 1986: 333 and Heran Sereke-Brhan 2005.

6 See Morin (forthcoming).

In some narrations this event is confused with the important, but much later marriage of 1916 with Fatuma Abubakar Muhammad, a daughter of the "Adal notable" (in this case "Adal" simply meaning ^{c}Afar) *Neggadras* Abubakar[7], and granddaughter of *Neggadras* Muhammad Abubakar from the Obakarto lineage of the ^{c}Afar rulers of Zayla^{c}.[8] From that relationship Iyasu had a son who was named after his grandfather Mïnilïk (on this marriage s. Smidt 2007: 927).

Gebre Ïgziyabïhér Elyas also writes that *Lïj* Iyasu then married two other women from "Adal". One of them was probably from Harer (the former capital of the defunct Muslim state of Adal), the other one was a Somali (Gebre-Igziabiher Elyas 1994: 332, 358). The former is probably a reference to the marriage with the daughter of the influential trader of Harer ^{c}Abdullahi ^{c}Ali Tsadiq, a former diplomatic envoy of Emperor Mïnilïk (Pankhurst – Gérard 1996; Bairu Tafla 2003:38).

After the pacification of the two regions Awsa and Yejju, on 2 June of the same year 1912, *Lïj* Iyasu traveled to Jimmaa.[9] The ruler of the province, *Abbaa* Jiffaar, received him with honors. The feasting took eight days. Next, when he finished inspection in the region, Iyasu arranged with Jiffaar that he would marry Jiffaar's daughter through a *sirat* ceremony. It is very interesting to discuss why *Lïj* Iyasu decided to take this step. Perhaps the Ethiopian prince wanted this marriage to become the most important alliance among his inner-Ethiopian alliances. Probably the Jimmaa ruler was supposed to become Iyasu's main supporter. For this to happen, the daughter had to become a Christian and subsequently, the baptism ceremony took place in Addis Abeba.

Dembi Dolloo in Wallagaa was the next stop on Iyasu's journey. During his stay there, the young prince got engaged with *Weyzero* Askele, one of *Dajjazmach* Jootee (the ruler of Dembi Dolloo) daughters (Mersé Hazen 2004: 121). The already consumed marriage with Jiffaar's daughter did not constitute a problem for this new marriage. The marriage in Dembi Dolloo was profitable for both sides. The girl's father was so pleased with the marriage, that he offered Iyasu 100 *gasha* of coffee land. In return, the prince granted the sons of his new father-in-law with military titles (Gebre-Igziabiher Elyas 1994: 335).

From Dembi Dolloo *Lïj* Iyasu traveled to the lands of *Dajjazmach* Kumsa, also in Wallagaa. During the stay at his house, the young prince met the host's daughter – Dasshe.[10] He wanted to marry her, but it was impossible. According to Ethiopian

---

7 Tibebe Eshete (1998: 170) claims that Abobaker was the ruler of ^{c}Afar, which is a confusion, as the ^{c}Afar were not unified under one ruler, but belonged to different sultanates and clans' territories; in fact, he was an ^{c}Afar notable (see for this confusion also the next footnote).

8 In some sources the girl's father is called Abubakri *Basha* from Awsa, cp. Bartnicki & Mantel-Niećko 1987: 340. This illustrates the unreliability of secondary sources regarding Iyasu's relations with Muslims, as they often strongly depend on Christian highland sources, which show a very poor knowledge of the semi-independant Muslim polities of the east and north-east and even of the most important Muslim notables of the Mïnilïk and *Lïj* Iyasu periods; Awsa had no ruler of this name.

9 Tibebe Eshete (1998: 170) claims that it was on 2 June 1914.

10 The girl used two names. Dasshe was her Oromo name. Her Amharic name was Sïhin. Cf. Molvaer 1994: 336.

common law, there are two types of kinship – by blood and the social one. This means that if the parents of a groom are by any means related with the family of the bride, a marriage was not allowed. Since *Dajjazmach* Kumsa was a god-child of emperor Mïnilïk, Ethiopian customary law did not allow for such a marriage, as groom and bride were regarded as "sister and brother".[11]

In 1915 the *Abéto* married a daughter of *Emir* Abdullahi, a Somali (Mersá Hazen 2004: 152, 163). Mersï'é Hazen Welde Qirqos writes that *Lïj* Iyasu was also married to *Weyzero* T'ïru Werq Aligaz from Yejju.[12] Gebre Ïgziyabïhér Elyas also mentions this woman, claiming that she was a Muslim, probably an Oromo, from a family of *shaykh*-s. This chronicler refers also to two other wives of *Lïj* Iyasu, without mentioning their names. One was a descendent of a well-known clan from Adal (again certainly with the general meaning of "ᶜAfar"), the other was a descendent of Swalih family from Timuga (Gebre-Igziabiher Elyas 1994: 359). The reference to Adal certainly means his prominent marriage to Fatuma of 1916, already treated above, which was his most important link with the ᶜAfar.

In summer of 1916 *Lïj* Iyasu planned to marry Muhammad Abdille Hassan's daughter, in an ambitious project to ally himself to the de-facto-independant ruler of the rebel Somali territory within the British colonial sphere of Somalia. In August, the *Abéto* (as *Lïj* Iyasu was also called) sent his trusted men to Taleh, where his future father-in-law lived. According to one narration, which still needs to be checked with other sources, they were told to offer engagement presents and bring the future bride to Addis Abeba. The coup d'état in September 1916 and the loss of crown by the *Abéto*, however, put an end to those plans (Tibebe Eshete 1998: 173).

In addition to his wives of important families, notables and rulers, married according to different local customs, *Lïj* Iyasu had many mistresses; also his relationships with these were not unimportant for the political history of Ethiopia. Gebre Ïgziyabïhér Elyas writes that *Ligaba* Beyyene joined the conspiracy against *Lïj* Iyasu because the latter had "*a sexual relationship with his wife, Weyzero Yïgemmitu Abbay*" (Gebre-Igziabiher Elyas 1994: 355).

One of Iyasu's mistresses was Atsede-Maryam Tekle-Maryam, the daughter of *Meggabi* Tekle-Maryam from Bulga. She had a son with Iyasu named Melake-Tsehay Iyasu, who on 2 September 1937 was crowned Emperor of Ethiopia "*by the patriots in Bulga, in northern Shewa.*"[13]

11 Mersï'é Hazen (Mersé Hazen Wolde Qirqos 2004: 122) notes that the Wallagaa ruler was called Gebre Ïgziabïhér.

12 In another chapter of his book Mersï'é Hazen writes that T'ïru Werq was only Iyasu's lover and the young prince was not proud of this relationship, cf. Mersé Hazen Wolde Qirqos 2004: 160 and 170

13 More about this subject: Gebre-Igziabiher Elyas (1994: 571-575).

Evaluation

Not so long ago most historians, both Ethiopian and western, perceived the rule of *Lïj* Iyasu solely as an interlude between the two great rulers of Mïnilïk II and Hayle Sïllasé I. *Lïj* Iyasu was considered as an emperor without a clear vision of his rule, who liked to indulge in his passions. This opinion was popularized by the Shewan noblemen's and *Ras* Teferi Mekonnïn supporters' propaganda. Now, however, it is often said that the young prince had his own vision of Ethiopia in the 20th century.

Emperor Mïnilïk's incorporation of vast lands, which once had been separate kingdoms with different religions, to a certain degree disturbed the inner balance of the Ethiopian Empire. The aim of *Lïj* Iyasu's domestic policy was to integrate the peoples of Ethiopia. In the same time, the aim of his foreign policy was to expand the Ethiopian borders up to the sea (Mersé Hazen 2004: 121; Molvaer 1994: 335). Both aims could be achieved by precise political moves and arranged marriages with political overtones. The *Abéto* decided to focus on the latter. What some Ethiopian noblemen saw as an erotic escapade all over the country was in fact a precisely planned political operation. Thanks to his marriages *Lïj* Iyasu linked himself with many noble and rich Ethiopian families. His fathers-in-law were politically and economically powerful men like *Ras* Haylu of Gojjam, the Muslim trader ^{c}Abdullahi ^{c}Ali Tsadiq from Harer, or the Obakarto family from Zayla^{c}.

There is no doubt that most, if not all, marriages were political. *Lïj* Iyasu wished for women he married to give him descendants that could rule over their grandfathers' provinces. Thus, the young prince's policy was similar to that of his step-grandmother, *Ïtégé* T'aytu. He had learnt from her mistakes though. He was aware that allowing his extended relatives to rule over the lands would not guarantee the subordination of the local chiefs. That is why he decided to give the power over regions to his own children from the marriages with daughters of local rulers. In this manner both sides would be satisfied and the country would become integrated.

It is very difficult to decide how the Ethiopian Empire would have looked like, if *Lïj* Iyasu had been able to realize his plan till the end. *Lïj* Iyasu had a vision of an empire where Muslims and Christians were equal, or at least he wanted to have the support from the lands where Muslims lived. This goal was easier to achieve due to the fact that his own father was originally a Muslim lord. Marriages contracted by Iyasu were tools by which the young prince could gain wide support in the Ethiopian Empire. Unfortunately, they did not yield the expected result – forces that were against Iyasu stopped the idea from developing. On 27 September 1916, Ethiopian noblemen in Shewa staged a coup d'état with the approval from *Abune* Matéwos and overthrew *Lïj* Iyasu frustrating all his plans.

Bibliography

Bahru Zewde, 1996, *A History of Modern Ethiopia*, London: James Currey.

Bahru Zewde, 2007, "Iyasu", *Encyclopaedia Aethiopica*, vol. 3, Wiesbaden: Harrassowitz, p. 255.

Bairu Tafla, 1972, "Marriage as a Political Device: an Appraisal of a Socio-political Aspect of the Menelik Period 1889 – 1916", *Journal of Ethiopian Studies*, 1, pp. 13 – 22.

Bairu Tafla, 2003, "ᶜAbdullāhi ᶜAlī Ṣādiq", *Encyclopaedia Aethiopica*, vol. 1, Wiesbaden: Harrassowitz, p. 38.

Bartnicki, Andrzej & Mantel-Niećko, Joanna, 1987, *Historia Etiopii*, Wrocław: Ossolineum.

Heran Sereke-Brhan, 2003, "Drying Bad Blood: Notes on Elite Marriages, Politics and Ethnicity in 19th and 20th century Imperial Ethiopia", *Proceedings of the Fifteenth International Conference of Ethiopian Studies*, pp. 266 – 274.

Heran Sereke-Brhan, 2005, "Like adding water to milk: Marriage and Politics in nineteenth-century Ethiopia", *International Journal of African Historical Studies*, 38 (1), pp. 49-77.

Levine, Donald, 1972, *Wax and Gold. Tradition and Innovation in Ethiopian Culture*, Chicago: University of Chicago Press.

Marcus, Harold G., 1975, *The Life and Times of Menelik II, Ethiopia 1844-1913*, Oxford: Clarendon.

Mersé Hazen Wolde Qirqos, 2004, *Of What I Saw and Heard. The Last Years of Emperor Menelik II and the Brief Rule of Iyassu*, Addis Abeba: CFEE.

Molvaer, Reidulf K., 1994, *Prowess, Piety and Politics. The Chronicle of Abéto Iyjasu and Empress Zawditu of Ethiopia (1909-1930) by: Aleqa Gabra-Igziabiher Elyas*, Köln: Köppe.

Morin, Didier, forthcoming, "Yayyo Maḥämmad", *Encyclopaedia Aethiopica*, vol. 5, Wiesbaden: Harrassowitz.

Pankhurst, Richard & Gérard, Denis, 1996, Ethiopia Photographed, *Historic Photographs of the Country and Its People, Taken Between 1867 and 1935*, London.

Pankhurst, Richard, 1997, "Dynastic Inter-marriage in Medieval and Post-medieval Ethiopia", *Proceedings of the Thirteenth International Conference of Ethiopian Studies*, vol. 1, pp. 206-220.

Prouty, Chris, 1986, *Empress Taytu and Menelik II: Ethiopia 1883 -1910*, Trenton: The Red Sea Press.

Smidt, Wolbert, 2007, "Mənilək Iyasu", *Encyclopaedia Aethiopica*, vol. 3, Wiesbaden: Harrassowitz, p. 927

Tibebe Eshete, 1998, "A Reassessment of Lïj Iyassu's Political Career", in: Page M. et. al., eds., *Personality and Political Culture in Modern Africa. Studies Presented to Professor Harold G. Marcus*, Boston: African Studies Center, Boston University.

Fig 1: **The marriages and the descent of Lïj Iyasu**

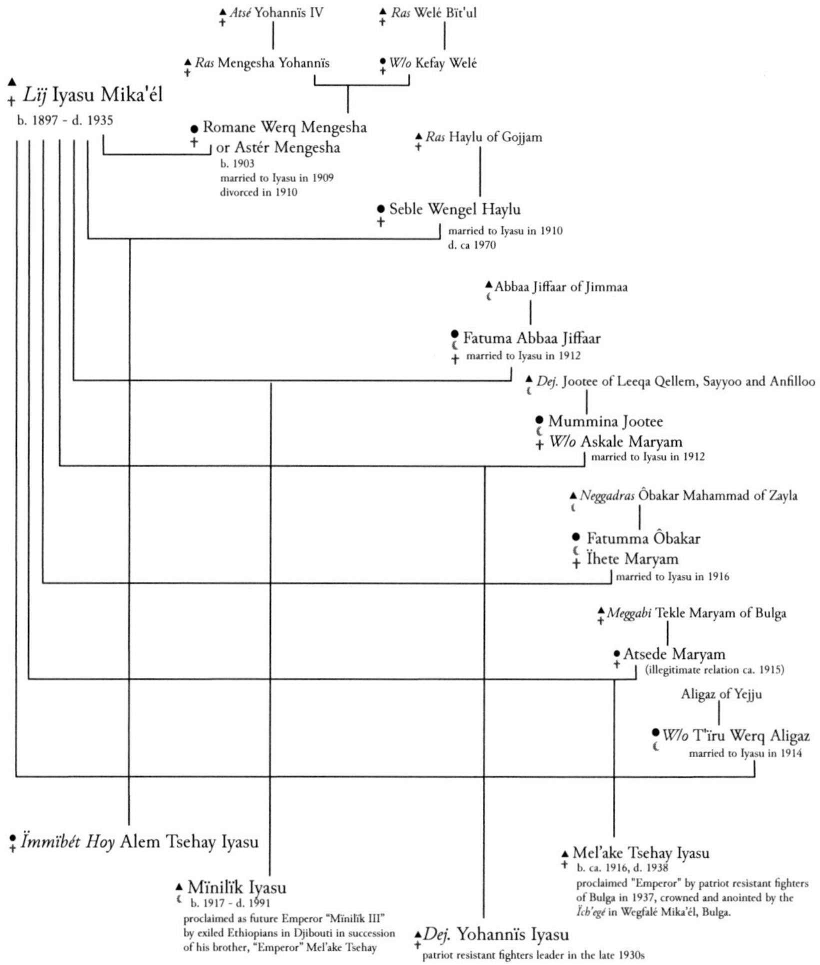

Part II - The Heir: Between Ethnic and Religious Pluralism, Reform and Continuity

Portraits of an Ethiopian prince, *Lïj* Iyasu*

Estelle Sohier

Much of the reign of *Lïj* Iyasu remains obscure because his memory was elaborated during the rule of his successor and political adversary Teferi Mekwennïn, king of kings under the name of *Atsé* Hayle Sïllasé from 1930 to 1974. During this period, the memory of Iyasu was sullied by official historiography, or, to the contrary, exalted by his partisans in private. Accused of having put Ethiopia in jeopardy with ill thought international and local political decisions, the heir of Mïnilïk II was portrayed by his successors as an apostate, of lax morals and of an impetuous and violent character. Concomitant to this, the publication of documents on his reign was tacitly prohibited by the monarchy. However, various materials published since the 1990s allow to shed a different light on the period, and to nuance the accusations with which the posterity of the prince has been burdened. Amongst these documents are found a certain number of photographs. The art of photography was blooming under Iyasu's period, and the prince had inherited a pictorial policy developed by his grandfather and predecessor, king of kings *Atsé* Mïnilïk II.

The portraits discussed in this article were collected for an exhibition dedicated to *Lïj* Iyasu at the National Museum of Ethiopia on the occasion of the centenary of his nomination. [1] They come from private collections in Ethiopia, from public archives in Italy and Switzerland, and from old and more recent publications. What knowledge do these images provide upon princely education in Ethiopia, upon the mechanisms of political transition as well as upon the complex and controversial personality of Iyasu?

---

* This article is the edited version of "Portraits of an Ethiopian Prince" *in* Sohier (2012).

1 "Lights and Shadows: insights in the photographic heritage of *Lij Iyasu* (1898-1935)", exhibition organised by Estelle Sohier at the National Museum of Ethiopia (November 2009-January 2010) with the support of the French Centre for Ethiopian Studies of Addis Abeba, CEMA*f* (Paris 1 University - CNRS), "*Orientale*" University of Naples and GEMDEV (Paris 8 University). The photographs are also permanently exhibited at the Museum of Dessie. We would like to particularly thank Ambassador Zewde Retta, *Ato* Tadele Y. Tessema, *Ato* Saladdin Mohammed, *Ato* Ahmed Zekaria, Dr Wolbert Smidt and Mr Denis Gérard who gave us the opportunity to discover and publish these documents.

Childhood photographs: the creation of an heir (1897-1909)

Iyasu was photographed from the tender age of 4, sometimes on horseback, or reading, alone as well as surrounded by servants, or even other children, bearing weapons, flowers, books or talismans, and all this on the orders of his grandfather, *Atsé* Mïnilïk II.

What purposes did the king of kings have in mind for these images?

The descendants of the king are difficult to discern, as he had no children from his first wife Bafena, or from T'aytu, wed in 1883. The king of Shewa had other wives and concubines, but none of his male descendants survived.

The oldest son, Wesen Seged, from an earlier marriage, was brought up in the king's entourage, who had thought of making him his successor. He had a genetic disorder that had impeded his growth, nevertheless, some of his portraits were staged, in order to hide his small height and enhance his princely status. Mïnilïk II had however to renounce making Wesen Seged his heir, because of his handicap, and the prince passed away at the age of 23, in March 1906 (Marcus 1975: 231).

After the accession of Mïnilïk to the throne of Ethiopia in 1889, his succession became the object of manifold political manoeuvres at the court (Bairu Tafla 1972). Mïnilïk II hoped to acquire a grandson, by marrying his daughters Zewditu and Shewaregga, to the most influent chiefs of the country. *Lïj* Iyasu was the third and last child of Shewaregga, an illegitimate daughter of the king that he recognised in his waning years. After a first union with the son of one of Mïnilïk's paramount chiefs to whom she bore a son, Shewaregga was married in 1891 to *Ras* Mika'él. Formerly a Muslim ruler, with the name of Muhammed Ali and title of *Imam*, he had converted to Christianity upon becoming governor of the province of Wello in 1878. Two children were born from this union: Zennebe Werq and then Iyasu, who was born in 1897, six months before Shewaregga passed away (Gebre-Igziabiher Elyas 1994: n. 1, p. 558).

Zennebe Werq was brought up at the king's court before being wed at the age of 10 to the son of the influential *Nïgus* Tekle Haymanot of Gojjam. It seems that she died in 1903, perhaps during childbirth (Prouty 1986: 224). Her younger brother, Iyasu, was another solution to the royal succession dilemma.

"Hidden from the Gaze of Men"

Iyasu was born on 27 *T'ïr* 1890 A.M., that is to say 3 February 1897, in Desé, a town founded by his father. Iyasu then grew up in Ankober with the guardian of the state prison, *Wehni Azzazh* Welde Tsadiq (Bairu Tafla 1968: 123, 125), to whom he had been entrusted soon after his birth. This transfer to Ankober placed the heir midway between the courts of his father, to the north, and of his grandfather, to the south. It brought Iyasu geographically, but also culturally and symbolically, closer to his grandfather, as Ankober was the king's birthplace and the ancient capital of Shewa.

Two series of snapshots dating from this period have been identified. The first was probably staged by Alfred Ilg, the Swiss adviser of Mïnilïk II, the second by Doctor De Castro. The latter recounted in great detail in his travel book how the king had sent him with his Kodak to photograph his grandson in the surroundings of Ankober (De Castro 1915, vol. 2: 215-256). The king had written a letter of instruction about the staging of the images and the clothes and regalia of the prince. Iyasu, for example, was to ostensibly bear a bouquet of artificial flowers specially obtained for the occasion. The flowers were a symbolic element of church paintings. In the photographs of the king's grandson the flowers possibly were to signify the double inheritance of Iyasu, consisting in both royal power and the Ethiopian territory.

Fig.1 –Photoreportage about the education of the Prince, here reading the Psalms. Dr. L. De Castro, Ankober, 1903. Published in De Castro (1915, vol. 2, fig. 193)

Iyasu, in the photographer's frame, is posed sitting, astride a mule, as well as studying in front of a *Dawit*, the Book of Psalms (Fig. 1). The image reflects the daily life of the prince, whose "tutor is on his back from morning to night to teach him to read and write" (De Castro 1915: vol.2, 225). The presence of church clergy in some of the shots illustrates the Christian dimension of his education, especially because of Iyasu's background as the son of a Muslim convert. The costumes he wears signify his rank as prince. They also make him a "miniature copy" of his grandfather, Mïnilïk II, of whom he bears the visual signs of recognition.

This photo shooting took place in February 1903, a few days before the commemoration of the battle of ʿAdwa celebrated with great pomp in Addis Abeba. The photographs were to show the continuity of his rule to all those gathered in the capital – allies, enemies and potential foes. The photographs demonstrated the correlation between the heir's education and the needs of the crown, solving the paradox between the need to protect the prince by keeping him hidden, and the need to celebrate his origins.

First official portraits in Addis Ababa

Iyasu was transferred to the court of Mïnilïk II in Addis Abeba two years later, at the age of 7 (Bahru Zewde 2007: 253). He continued his education at court in order to be initiated into the protocol and to develop his social relations. More photographic shoots were organized for Iyasu and other dignitaries' sons at the *gïbbi* [palace]. The visible lack of willingness with which he took part in these sessions reminds us of testimonials bearing witness to the child's aversion for official ceremonies (Ydlibi 2006: 152-153). These sessions contained an educational element: they were to teach the prince the politic symbolism of manner, clothes and other paraphernalia, but also the use of the image; they enabled him to acquire a mastery of his body and appearance that would be necessary for his future role. His early encounters with photographers also taught him the symbolic impact of this technology imported from abroad. The outside world had by then acquired a considerable importance within Ethiopian politics.

The education of the prince was all the more taken seriously as Iyasu had been chosen by Mïnilïk II long before being officially appointed, in 1909. That seems to be proven by certain sources (Berhanou Abebe 2001: 311), amongst which several childhood photographs. Mïnilïk II, for example, sent to the German Kaiser, Wilhelm II, a portrait of the Ethiopian heir dated 4 July 1907 (Fig. 2). This photograph served as a proof that the succession was being prepared. Its objective was probably to allay the fear of a vacancy of power after the death of Mïnilïk II, a fear prevalent amongst the official representatives of the foreign powers in Addis Abeba.

We still have no portraits of Shewaregga, or any photographs of Iyasu as a child with his father, *Ras* Mikaʾél. Such documents had no place in the political sphere. The official nomination of Iyasu was done progressively, while the king's health was degrading. Mïnilïk II suffered from several strokes, starting from 1906. In December 1909, the prince was officially proclaimed heir to the throne, and *Ras* Tesemma Nadew designated as his tutor.

Church paintings: God, the *Abun* and the dignitaries, guarantors of the royal succession (1909-1913)

Mïnilïk II had chosen Iyasu as heir from the very start of the 1900s, however, this choice was not unanimously supported at the court. *Ïtegé* T'aytu was the first to try to thwart the royal plans (Bairu Tafla 1972: 16). Her supporters opposed the partisans of Iyasu as soon as the first signs of the king's physical decline became apparent. At the beginning of the 20th century, as in earlier periods, the royal succession gave room for a "winner takes all" scramble for the crown. The heir chosen by the sovereign was only one candidate amongst others, and any perceived weakness - for example the great youth of the heir - could give birth to a power struggle, where the highest bidder won (Toubkis 2004: 231).

After his official designation to the throne, Iyasu's photographs became commonplace and were reproduced on the mural paintings of a number the royal churches.

The Church and the transmission of power

The royal church of Sïllasé [Trinity] is situated to the north of the *gïbbi* in Addis Abeba. Three portraits of Iyasu can still be seen there today.He appears with Mïnilïk II and the leader of the Ethiopian Church, *Abune* Matéwos. On the northern wall, the trio is surmounted by Saint Marc and a lion, an allusion to Mïnilïk's royal motto, "he has conquered, the Lion of Judah". This association symbolizes the historical alliance with the Church, as the Apostle Marc is considered to be the founder of the Coptic Church, as he evangelized Egypt. A double transmission is thus represented: a vertical transmission between Saint Marc, the leader of the Church and the king of Ethiopia, and a horizontal transmission, from Matéwos and Mïnilïk II to Iyasu. In a painting on a pillar of the eastern wall (Fig. 3), Iyasu holds with his right hand a sword in its scabbard, symbolising a latent force, already seen in some of his childhood pictures. The *Abun* shows the holy book and the cross, both symbols of his function, while Mïnilïk II holds a stick symbolizing his power and age. The composition evokes the authority of the prince, surrounded and supported by the two principal figureheads of the country. In the third and last portrait, the heir is included in a series depicting T'aytu and Mïnilïk II. Wearing a *gofer* (lion's skin) and an *anfero* (lion's mane), he is not yet a sovereign but a triumphant warrior.

The paintings of Sïllasé show a power in the making under the auspices of the Church. Starting from the end of the 19th century, the *Abun* played an increasingly political role inside the Ethiopian monarchy. Matéwos was a key figure in the transmission of power as he had sworn to excommunicate anyone who would attempt to thwart the officially sanctioned choice of Iyasu. The paintings of the palace's church underline this determination and request it to be respected. They enshrine the pact made between the royal power and the Church, between the faithful of this place of worship, that is to say the dignitaries of the Church itself and the court. Sïllasé Church was at that time one of the stages of Ethiopian political life, and harboured for example the discussions around the succession. The paintings of the church reminded everyone of the commitment undertaken before the king's disappearance.

Wheeled throne and crown suspended in the air: the paintings of Addis Alem

The biggest pictorial representation of Mïnilïk II's transmission of power can be found in Saint Mary's in Addis Alem. Founded in 1900 by Mïnilïk II, this town was planned to become the new capital of Ethiopia. The king finally renounced the idea of moving his court here, but the town became famous when a *Nïbure Ïd* (religious governor) was designated, making Addis Alem the new sacred city of Ethiopia, in the heart of the territories conquered by Mïnilïk II.

The church, dedicated to Mary, was built on a rectangular plan, in reference to the church of Tsïyon in Aksum, and relatively spacious, which explains the width of the scene. On the western wall (Fig. 4) Mïnilïk II and Iyasu are placed underneath a representation of the Virgin and Infant and the Passion of Christ. To the left of the heir to the throne, and side by side, are found *Fitawrari* Habte Giyorgis, and Gebre Sïllasé, the king's chronicler and recently appointed *Nïbure Ïd* of the church, and finally, the *Afe Nïgus* Ïst'ifanos. The three dignitaries represent respectively, the armed forces, the Church, and the justice, the key institutions guaranteeing the transmission of power. The painter and his child also appear in the background. Mary's sign of benediction points towards Iyasu, who is the only one who directly looks at the viewer. The visitor is hence invited to contemplate, recognize and support the prince, and in this way joins the scene: The viewer, same as the other personalities shown in the image, looks at Iyasu and in this sense becomes an integral part of the depicted situation of adoration.

All painted portraits of the high officials are modelled on photographs. Mïnilïk II's portrait, for example, was modelled on a snapshot taken by the Italian Bertolani. The painting is hence a twice-staged event, with some elements copied and others added. The throne has been equipped with wheels, perhaps to evoke Mïnilïk II's paralysis, called "illness of the feet" in his chronicle (Guèbrè Sellasié 1931: 535). The king of kings continues to reign, but no longer rules. Iyasu alone stands with a lion at his feet: the motto "he has conquered, the Lion of Judah" has already almost been adopted by him.

Multiple sources bear witness to the importance of the events organized in Addis Alem at the beginning of the 1910s. The consecration of the church in 1911, followed by the commemoration of its foundation were accompanied by very large ceremonies, as six hundred members of the clergy were assigned to the service of the church (Mersé Hazen 2004: 89). Iyasu and other members of the court took part. The church was hence conceived as a stage for the representation of power and its continuity, both both through painting and through the means of ceremony. These two means of demonstration of power complete and mirror each other. The paintings testify the represented leaders had visited the church. Through their presence, the members of the royal court could witness the unity of the state. To take part in a ceremony in this church was to worship both the saints and the state, but also to pay allegiance to a hierarchy in its current structure. Saint Mary's had no doubt been planned by Mïnilïk II to be the location of his heir's coronation. Iyasu used this place of worship as a visible demonstration of his legitimacy, but he was never to be crowned there.

Iyasu, or the quest for the perfect representation

Starting from the age of only 13, Iyasu emancipated himself. He categorically refused the new regent that the court's dignitaries tried to impose on him after the sudden death of his tutor, *Ras* Tesemma, in April 1911. In December 1913, Mïnilïk II died in secret after having been hidden the public for several years, paralysed and mentally incapacitated. The death of the king of kings was not announced, as, along the lines of royal succession, his heir should have been crowned only in the moment he could affirm his power with total legitimacy. However, even if the prince had already progressively seized power, he postponed his coronation for obscure and probably manifold reasons, and in agreement with the different regional chiefs quickly summoned to Addis Abeba in January 1914. The coronation of Iyasu was delayed, but the foundations of his power were reinforced by the decision to crown his father Mika'él, who was eventually proclaimed *Nïgus* of Wello and Tïgray in May 1914.

This transitional period weakened the Ethiopian government. All the more the kingdom had to face domestic political upheavals in the north of the country. The uncertainty was deepened by the international context, as the outbreak of the World War I in August 1914 sent shockwaves into the Horn of Africa.

To face these challenges, the young Iyasu (17 years old in 1914) took audacious political measures. Starting from 1912, he criss-crossed the country, forging pacts with the different regional chiefs. Being experienced in the manipulation of pictorial symbols since his childhood, he started now to commission his portraits himself, and radically changed the political use of images.

A master of photography

Several professional photographers opened studios in the capital with the support of Mïnilïk II, offering the monarchy better quality images than those of the amateurs who had been employed until then. Iyasu used their services and became particularly close to the two pioneers, the Armenians Bedros Boyadjian and Levon Yazedjian, to whom we owe several of his portraits.

A painter and a photographer, Yazedjian may have also served Iyasu as the chief of his secret police.[2] Iyasu was photographed, in private or in public, in Addis Abeba or in the provinces, alone or surrounded, and in his different roles: supreme judge of the court; royal spectator at the Addis Abeba race track; supreme armed forces commander; with his troops, his collaborators, or his associates...

The son of two kings

After the disappearance of Mïnilïk II, new "family" portraits were made by Boyadjian. Although the prince was probably never represented with his father during his childhood, he now figured several times in his presence at the court of Desé, accompanied by Boyadjian (Smidt 2001: 372-373).

On Fig. 5, the heir to the throne poses kneeling at the feet of Mika᾽él whose right hand lies on the bowed head of his son.[3] This gesture appears as a confirmation of succession. Iyasu figures in a subservient position, but fixes the lens: this is all about his own power, emanating from his father's position.

One can understand this posture from the texts used as reference by the Ethiopian monarchy, and particularly the Bible. It could mirror certain passages where the heir is designated by the right hand of the father (*Genesis* 48: 19), right hand mentioned many times in the Psalms: it represents the support of the father but also of God; it is linked to the idea of strength and victory (*Psalms* 139: 10). Mïnilïk II is evoked metonymically in the picture's composition, by way of his crown, brought to Desé on the occasion of the coronation of Mika᾽él. The crown is both a reminder of the deceased sovereign but also of the supreme power that Iyasu has inherited.

This picture illustrates the newly established closeness between Iyasu and his father, and the political role with which the latter was bestowed upon his coronation in May 1914. The two men also hereby convey several messages to their contemporaries and for posterity, by reinterpreting the political inheritance built by Mïnilïk II for his heir. By putting publicly the emphasis on his paternal descent, Iyasu becomes not only a grandson of a king of kings but also the son of a king. The promotion of Mika᾽él enabled Iyasu to reinforce his political position inside the kingdom, by associating himself with an unwavering and powerful ally who could even out the power of the chieftains of the court of Shewa. Several sources tell us that Iyasu could have been reticent to become his father's sovereign, as Mika᾽él would have had to swear allegiance to his own son upon his coronation (see Ydlibi 2006: 259). The photographs of Iyasu and Mika᾽él show that the filial and power relationships between the two men were problematic, and the object of negotiations both on a political and a symbolic level.

2 Several members of the Armenian community of Addis Abeba bear witness to this. See Berhanou Abebe, 2003: 24.

3 On this coronation and the story of the crown see Smidt, 2001 and Smidt, 2007-2008.

But, by creating such images, Iyasu nevertheless emphasised what Mïnilïk II had tried to occult: he was symbolically linking himself with the figure of his father, an ex-Muslim chief converted to Christianity by political necessity and the governor of a predominantly Muslim region of the kingdom

Photography, a pact between enemies?

Iyasu posed, of course, with his allies, but also with characters with whom he held more complex relationships, particularly Teferi Mekwennïn. The relationship between the two young chiefs started to unravel in 1916 and broke down completely in September of the same year, when Teferi was named heir to the throne in the place of Iyasu, impeached. The two cousins had grown up side by side for some time in the *gïbbi* of Mïnilïk II. Upon the nomination of Iyasu, Teferi payed an oath of allegiance to the heir, together with the other dignitaries. The two men posed together several times in the photographic studios of Addis Abeba and in the town of Harer. They sometimes have similar poses and clothes, the pre-eminence of Iyasu signified by a few details: on one snapshot, the coloured fringe of his *shamma*, the regal bearing of his head and the forward thrust of his weapon, whereas Teferi holds his sword discreetly at his side

These photographs were undertaken inside a larger more complex and ambiguous relationship, sometimes full of tension. Iyasu told one of his advisers, Tekle Hawaryat, that he was terrified by Teferi (Bahru Zewde 2002: 167), notwithstanding his pre-eminence. On the other hand, Teferi's private secretary asserted in his correspondence, that Iyasu was his worst enemy.[4] These few lines suffice to evoke the nature of a complicated and complex political relationship, made up of family links, maybe a little friendship, and certainly solemn oaths, but nevertheless marked by feelings of rivalry fanned by others. The group portraits of Iyasu and Teferi seem to be the expression of a pact underwriting a consensus that was unstable but fundamental for the peace of the realm. The photographs were perhaps created to highlight to all the understanding between both men and belie the rumours of discord.

The prince's body, a mirror for multiple identities

The *Lïj* also fostered links with political and cultural groups that had been recently incorporated into the kingdom by his grandfather. During his long expeditions throughout the country, he allied himself to the dignitaries of the peripheral regions by conducting an active matrimonial policy and by surrounding himself with Muslim followers (Mersé Hazen 2004: 159). This official political acknowledgement of the country's religious and cultural pluralism was reflected in the prince's image policy.

4 Letter from Samuel to Jarosseau from Addis Abeba the 20 April 1914. Capuchin Missionary records, Harar. (1911-1914). Miss reel. 12, archives of the IES, Addis-Abeba.

Iyasu adopted the same practises with these dignitaries that he had used with his Christian allies: he posed by their side, but disregarded the dress conventions of the Ethiopian court. In Harer, where he stayed regularly starting from 1915, he for instance posed in elegant Muslim garb, his head swathed in a turban, in the company of one of the town's dignitaries, Abdullahi Ali Tsadiq (Fig. 8). The prince had kindled a friendship with this man whom he often met and whose daughter he had wed.[5] These links took on heavy political implications, as it seems the Harer notable was the source of the prince's interest in Somalia, and the preference given to the Turks and Germans against the other colonial powers (Gebre-Igziabher Elyas 1994: 561). He may also have been the intermediary between Iyasu and the Somali chief Muhammad Abdallah Hasan (Bairu Tafla, 2003: 38). A trader in contact with all of the principal commercial centres of the region, Abdullahi Ali Tsadiq had already served as secret intermediary between the Somali chief and Mïnilïk II, who had sent him on an official mission to the Ottoman court in 1904. The understanding between Iyasu and this Muslim dignitary was therefore in a certain manner a continuation of his grandfather's policies.

The photographs of Iyasu in Muslim dress can be compared with other images just as audacious and unexpected for a Christian prince. A photograph published by Wilfred Thesiger (1987), of unknown provenance, unveils the prince with bare feet and chest, wearing a simple wrap around his hips in the fashion of the ʿAfar, whose knife he bears (Fig. 9). Yet another novelty: Iyasu was the first Ethiopian sovereign to wear an European suit (Fig. 7). These iconoclastic portraits offended the sensibilities of the Ethiopian Christian dignitaries who, if they hadn't seen the pictures themselves, had heard of them by word of mouth (Mersé Hazen 2004: 159).

All the same and despite his apparent closeness with some of his Muslims subjects, Iyasu nevertheless remained a practising Christian. Iyasu's audacious pictorial policy was therefore not – or not only – due to his inclination for provocation and to his insouciant youthfulness, as he was conversant with the creation and manipulation of symbols and images.

Donald Crummey underlined the weaknesses of the Solomonian ideology in Ethiopia, noting that at the beginning of the 20th century the majority of the population of the country didn't master the Semitic language in which it was propagated (Crummey 1988: 38). The same can be said of the iconographic representations of the state which spoke, until then, only to the Christian audience. By inventing new pictorial forms, Iyasu was in a certain manner correcting this ideological lapse. Iyasu adopted the same policies towards the groups incorporated into the realm by his grandfather as he did towards the ruling class of the high plateaux. However, it seems that the photographs of the prince in Muslim or ʿAfar attire for example were

5 Testimonial of R. K. Molvaer after an investigation conducted in the 1980s (Gebre-Igziabher Elyas 1994: 560).

very limited in their distribution and were essentially destined to the political interlocutors of the prince. In adopting their guise, Iyasu was officially expressing the acknowledgement by the Ethiopian state of other cultures, a necessary step for the foundation of a real political, military and economic partnership.

On the other hand, by this means Iyasu also sought to consolidate his stature as future king of kings, in order to be recognised by the Christian chiefs, but also by other groups officially belonging to the Ethiopian polity. In accomplishing this, he was not putting an end to the ideological system on which his power was built, but, on the contrary, was seeking to adapt it to the reality of the land that had been handed down to him by Mïnilïk II. The pictures were both reflections and actors of his policy. They were all the more important that the impact of symbols is exponential in a context of uncertainty and instability.

By using Muslim symbols, the prince however upset the political and institutional balance set up at the end of Mïnilïk II's reign to ensure a peaceful succession with the help of the Church. His policies also stoked anxiety among the neighbouring states, England, France and Italy, that watched over the prince's alliances in these times of world war with increasing vigilance.

Denunciation by the image... and disappearance

By manipulating his appearance and the political symbols of royalty, Iyasu might have played with fire, as it seems he was squeezed out by the means of just such a photograph. The *coup d'état* instigated against him in September 1916 was due to a combination of factors. The pressure brought about by the diplomats of the three Allied countries were a decisive factor in the impeachment process: the English, French and Italian legations were afraid of the pro Turkish and German proclivities of the prince. Their agitation was successful as it found a favourable echo amongst the dignitaries of the court, that the *Lïj* had alienated (Mersé Hazen 2004: 125). He had brought the uneasiness of the Shewan nobility to a head by delegating a part of the royal power towards the court of his father in Wello (see Smidt, 2007), and had surrounded himself and promoted dignitaries from other regions and social classes, had committed petty gestures against chiefs from his grandfather's court, but also, had initiated fiscal investigations which sought to bring to book the grandees of the court (Mersé Hazen 2004: 162).

The day of the feast of the finding of the True Cross, the 27th of September 1916, the *abuna* Matéwos accepted to release the dignitaries from their oath of allegiance to the heir of Mïnilïk II by excommunicating him for apostasy, the prelude to his impeachment. Iyasu was stripped of his rights to the crown.

The daughter of Mïnilïk II, Zewditu, was crowned in his stead Queen of Kings on 11 February 1917, as Teferi Mekwennïn was promoted to *Ras* and *Ïnderasé* at her side. From this date onward the portraits of Iyasu are few and are all the more significant.

A photograph for a coup?

As a number of historians before him, Berhanu Abebe described how a doctored photograph which showed the prince wearing a turban had been used as incriminating evidence in September 1916, among others in order to encourage the *Abun* to excommunicate him (Berhanu Abebe 2003: 19-41). Produced in great numbers, this forged photograph was perhaps commissioned by the British, the famous secret agent T.E. Lawrence himself having perhaps played a role in the plot.[6] Uncertainties linger around this mysterious picture, as no copy of it has ever been found. Perhaps this story is the product of a blurred memory, an imaginary recreation of Iyasu's reign, a fantasy produced by the silence imposed during the reign of his successors, and beyond? What one can say it that the story of this forgery is relevant in the context of a World War characterised by an increased use of propaganda by all belligerents, propaganda facilitated by the technical improvements of fixed and moving images and new means of reproduction.

German representatives for example kindled friendships with Ethiopian chiefs and celebrated - inside their legation - all the victories of the Axis, sometimes exhibiting a full sized photograph of the Kaiser (Mersé Hazen 2004: 157). One can imagine that the portrait of Iyasu in European dress at the side of a European (German?) diplomatic delegate (Fig. 7) was undertaken in the same context. The prince no doubt believed in the victory of the Germans and Turks. In the opposing camp, different means were used by the Allies to compete with German propaganda.

Disappearance and concealed photographs

At the moment of the coup d'état, in September 1916, Iyasu was in the region of Harer. After an unsuccessful attempt at armed resistance, he escaped, and was finally captured many years later in a church in Tigray in January 1921 (Bahru Zewde 2007: 255). The grandson of Mïnilïk II lived his last fourteen years in prison out of sight of the Ethiopian public.

He was first imprisoned in Fiché, in the domains of *Ras* Kasa, a follower of Teferi. After a failed breakout in May 1932, the prince was transferred to Gara Mulleta, where he experienced a harsher regime and enhanced surveillance. He is confined here until the middle of the year 1935, when he was probably assassinated following an order by Hayle Sïllasé, while Italian troops invaded the country. But even if Iyasu physically disappeared from the public sphere when his captivity started, he was still theoretically

6 Greenfield (1965: 138) quoted by Berhanu Abebe (2001: 323).

present in the Ethiopian political scene, his successors being torn between their guilt at having the grandson of Mïnilïk II endure such a predicament, and the fear of his return to power. For the prince was still popular and enjoyed potential support in the country.

One photographer alone seems to have been able to shatter this isolation leaving a thin visual trace of *Lïj* Iyasu. The story of these documents is rather exceptional even if we are still left with gaps.

Two photographs show the prince crossing a river surrounded by an escort (doc. 39). The caption indicates that this river would be the Blue Nile, in the Gojjam region, after the re-capture of Iyasu in 1932. Strapped to a float and held by the men surrounding him, Iyasu still finds the time to smile to the photographer. His body is heavy and his face has aged. Sixteen years separate this picture from the last known portraits.

The third and last picture was taken before or just after his escape from the prison of Fiché. With the play of the light which structures the picture, the prince and his photographer may have wanted to evoke a decision taken, or the prince's future outside the prison cell. The length of Iyasu's hair is really quite unusual for an Ethiopian aristocrat. It physically expresses his marginalization from aristocratic society and/or a desire to resist the establishment.

Two of the three photographs were published in the last few years[7], rendered public and handed over to us by *Ato* Tadele Yïdneqachew Tesemma, today the trustee of these pictures and their story[8]. These clandestine images had been given to the father of *ato* Tadele, *ato* Yïdneqachew Tesemma, by *Ato* Mekesha Welde Mesqel (1902-2001) who had been in the service of the father of Yïdneqachew, the famous Tesemma Ïsheté, since the reign of Iyasu. Formerly the minister of Post and Telegraphs, and an adviser of the *Lïj*, to whom he was particularly close, Tesemma was a self-taught man of many talents, being notably one of the first photographers of Ethiopian nationality. Tesemma was to have a complex and ambivalent relationship with the successor of Iyasu, Hayle Sïllasé, for the rest of his life.

He secretly kept these documents pertaining to the reign of Iyasu during all of his life, assisted by his secretary, Mekesha Welde Mesqel. The latter only transmitted the photographs of Iyasu from his prison just shortly after the death of Yïdneqachew in 1987. Why were these pictures concealed with such precaution while their content does not show, it would seem, any elements which could pose a threat to the apparatus of State? The photographs of the prince, however, provide clues; they are a clear revelation and are *proof* of his existence on the margins of society. Different testimonials show that Iyasu was still present in people's minds, both at court and in

7 Yïdneqacchew Tesemma (1992-1993: 19-20); Gérard & Pankhurst 1996; Bahru Zewde (2007: 255).

8 All of the information pertaining to the photographs and their story were transmitted to us by *Ato* Tadele Yïdneqachew Tesemma in November 2009. I would like to thank him here warmly.

the capital and certain regions. These photographs of the prince alive could have rekindled his memory with his partisans, but could also have enabled them to *imagine* a different political way, the prince being still alive, what is more, sane of body and mind. These documents could also have shocked the Ethiopians, reverent of the memory of the king of kings Mïnilïk II and his grandson, as the conditions of Iyasu's imprisonment apparent in the pictures were unsuitable for a person of his rank. The pictures had a great potential of negative symbolism for the Ethiopian royalty at large, by showing one of their members in isolation and disgrace.

Today, these fragile and fugitive documents remind us that there are many aspects of the last years of Iyasu's life on which all the light has not been shed. His death wasn't announced publicly, the circumstances surrounding his disappearance and his burial place in November 1935, were suppressed. This concealment is comparable, in some ways, to the secrecy in which the last photographs were held. Its aim was no doubt to snuff out the memory of the prince, preventing partisanship in favour of him and his memory – both on the terrain and in imagination –, and to prevent any reuse of his physical remains by his descendants, of which several could have claimed the throne and taken the lead of contestation movements.

Irony of history, one can draw a parallel between Iyasu's tragic end and the destiny of his successor and enemy, Hayle Sïllasé, he himself having been assassinated and buried in secret in an unlikely location at the heart of Mïnilïk II's palace. However, while the body of Hayle Sïllasé was found and subsequently reburied in the year 2000 with dignity after the downfall of the Derg, the location of Iyasu's tomb still remains unknown. New research into this subject would enable to reincorporate the body of Iyasu into Ethiopian society and to rehabilitate his role in the complex history of the monarchy in the 20th century.

* * *

The end of the reign of Mïnilïk II and the reign of Iyasu were marked by great political, geographical and cultural shifts in Ethiopia. We can compare the Ethiopian court of this period to a laboratory, where the use of photography and the manipulation of visual symbols in different media played a role in the making of the heir. The use of photography by Iyasu is to be seen as a continuation of the education that he had received, marked by a political culture of an imagery rich with meaning, a great distrust towards the colonial powers, and finally an ability to put to use new technical means imported from abroad in a novel manner. His reign shall not be interpreted as a messy interlude of the history of the contemporary Ethiopian monarchy, but it illustrates the adaptation efforts of the monarchy to the unprecedented changes experienced by the kingdom.

The images commissioned by Iyasu after his accession to power were both reflections as well as agents of his attempts to manage the complex political and cultural field that his grandfather had passed down to him after his conquests. The son of a former Muslim chief who had received a proper royal and Christian education, Iyasu was of course, himself, a product of this policy. His images show and illustrate his specific and somewhat fumbling approach in managing the complexities of his own identity and that of his country.

Bibliography

Bahru Zewde, 2002, *Pioneers of Change in Ethiopia. The Reformist Intellectuals of the Early Twentieth Century*, Addis-Abeba, London, Ohio: James Currey, Eastern African Studies.

Bahru Zewde, 2007, "Iyasu", *Encyclopaedia Aethiopica*, Wiesbaden: Harrassowitz, vol. 3, pp. 253-256.

Bairu Tafla, 1968, "Two Ethiopian Biographies", *Journal of Ethiopian Studies*, 6 (1), pp. 123-130

Bairu Tafla, 1972, "Marriage as a Political Device: an Appraisal of a Socio-political Aspect of the Menelik Period, 1889 – 1916", *Journal of Ethiopian Studies*, 1, pp. 13 - 22

Bairu Tafla, 2003, "Abdullahi Ali Ṣadiq", *Encyclopaedia Aethiopica*, vol. 1, p. 38

Berhanou Abebe, 1998, *Histoire de l'Éthiopie d'Axoum à la révolution*, Paris, Maisonneuve et Larose, CFEE.

Berhanou Abebe, 2001, "Le Coup d'État du 26 septembre 1916 ou le dénouement d'une décennie de crise", *Annales d'Éthiopie*, 17, pp. 309-359.

Berhanou Abebe, 2003, "Montages et trucages photographiques dans l'Éthiopie moderne", *Annales d'Éthiopie*, 19, pp. 19-41.

Crummey, Donald, 1988, "Imperial Legitimacy and the Creation of Neo-Solomonic Ideology in 19th Century Ethiopia", *Cahiers d'études africaines*, 109, pp. 13-43.

De Castro, Lincoln, 1915, *Nella Terra dei Negus*, (R.S. Geografica Italiana), Milan: Fratelli Treves editori, 2 vols.

Gebre-Igziabiher Elyas, 1994, *Prowess, Piety and Politics, The Chronicle of Abeto Iyasu and Empress Zewditu of Ethiopia (1909-1930)*, Reidulf K. Molvaer (ed.), Köln: Rüdiger Köppe Verlag.

Gérard, Denis & Pankhurst, Richard, 1996, *Ethiopia Photographed. Historic Photographs of the Country and its People taken between 1867 and 1935*, London, New York: Kegan Paul International.

Guèbré Sellassié, 1930-1932, *Chronique du règne de Ménélik II, roi des rois d'Ethiopie*, Paris: Maisonneuve frères, vol. 1, 1930, vol. 2, 1932.

Le Roux, Hugues, 1901, *Ménélik et nous*, Paris: Librairie Nilsson.

Le Roux, Hugues, 1914, *Chez la reine de Saba*, Paris: E. Leroux.

Marcus, Harold G., 1975, *Life and Times of Menelik II, Ethiopia 1844-1913*, Oxford: Clarendon Press.

Mersé Hazen Wolde Qirqos, 2004, *Of What I Saw and Heard. The Last Years of Emperor Menelik II & the Brief Rule of Iyassu*, trans. by Hailu Habtu, Addis Ababa: CFEE & Zamra Publishers.

Palma Silvana, 2005, *L'Africa nella collezione fotografica dell'IsIAO. Il fondo Eritrea-Etiopia*, Rome: IsIAO.

Pankhurst, Richard, 1992, "The Political Image: the Impact of the Camera in an Ancient Independent African State", in E. Edwards, ed., *Anthropology and Photography 1860-1920*, New Haven, Conn., London: Yale University Press, pp. 234-241.

Perret Michel, 1995, "Photographie et histoire. Le portrait du roi de Ménélik à Haylä Sellassié", dans Triulzi Alessandro, ed., *Fotografia e storia dell'Africa*, Napoli: Istituto Universitario Orientale, 1995, pp. 71-85.

Smidt, Wolbert G.C., 2001, "The Coronation of Negus Mikael in Desse in May 1914: A Photograph from the Nachlass Jensen and its Historical Background", *Annales d'Éthiopie*, 17, pp. 361-373.

Smidt, Wolbert G.C., 2007, "The Coronation of Negus Mikael, King of Wollo and Tigray, in May 1914: New findings", *Annales d'Éthiopie*, 23, pp. 413-434.

Sohier, Estelle, 2011, *Portraits controversés d'un prince éthiopien. Iyasu (1897-1935)*, Montpellier: L'Archange Minotaure.

Sohier, Estelle, 2012, *Le Roi des rois et la photographie. Politiques de l'image et pouvoir royal en Éthiopie sous le règne de Ménélik II*, Paris: Publications de la Sorbonne

Thesiger, Wilfred, 1987, *The Life of my Choice*, New-York, London: W.W. Norton & Co.

Toubkis, Dimitri, 2004, "Je deviendrai roi sur tout le pays d'Éthiopie ». Royauté et écriture de l'histoire dans l'Ethiopie chrétienne (XVIe-XVIIIe siècles)", PhD dissertation, Paris I University.

Ydlibi, May, 2006, *With Ethiopian Rulers. A Biography of Hasib Ydlibi*, Bahru Zewde (ed.), Addis-Abeba: AAU Press.

Yïdneqachew Tesemma, 1992-93, *Semïnna Werqu Tesemma Ïsheté*, published by Tadele Yïdneqachew, Addis-Abeba.

Fig.2 – The first diplomatic portrait.
By Bédros Boyadjian, Addis-Abeba, July 1907.

Fig.3 – Wall church painting: Mïnilïk II, *Abune* Matéwos and *Lïj* Iyasu
Addis-Abeba, Old Sellasé Church, eastern wall, c. 1909.
Painting by Kasa Arägahäñ. Photographed by Claire Bosc-Tiessé, 2009.

Fig. 4 – Wall church painting: From right to left: Mïnilïk II, Iyasu, *Fitawrari* Habte Giyorgis, *Nïbure Ïd* Gebre Sïllasé, *Afe Nïgus* Ïst'ifanos, underneath a representation of the Virgin and Infant. Addis Alem, Saint Mary's church, western wall, c. 1909.
Photographed by Sohier, 2009.

Fig. 5 – The son of two kings: *Lïj* Iyasu, *Nïgus* Mikaél and Mïnilïk's crown.
Desé, 1914
Photographer : Bédros Boyadjian
Published in: Henri de Monfreid, *Le masque d'or*, Paris, 1936.

Fig. 6 – Iyasu with a warrior dress from Shewa at the age of 18.
Addis-Abeba (?), 1915, author unknown.
From Guèbrè Sellasié (1930, pl. LXI).

Fig. 7 – Iyasu in a European suit with an European (unidentified) diplomat
Date, place and author unknown.
© Ambassador Zewde Retta
It may be the only picture where Iyasu wears a European costume, and the first time that an Ethiopian ruler is dressed in a « modern » fashion.

Fig. 8 – Iyasu dressed as a Muslim with Abdullahi Ali Sadeq's family
Harar, c. 1916, author unknown.
Courtesy of Mr Salah ed-Dinn Mohamed. Reproduction: Denis Gérard.

Fig. 9 – Iyasu in Afar's dress
Date, place and author unknown
From Thesiger (1987).

The lion, the lion cub, the oxen and the pigs: Interpreting a 1900's Ethiopian political popular painting

Valeria Semenova

The Ethiopian collection of the Museum of Anthropology and Ethnography of the Russian Academy of Sciences (MAE RAS) in St. Petersburg includes several traditional paintings gathered at the beginning of the 20th century. One of the paintings of this collection (№ 4055-14) has struck our attention as it reflects the indigenous representation of the general structure of Ethiopia at the end Mïnilïk's reign, before *Lïj* Iyasu's succession.

The museum got this painting in 1930 from State Hermitage as a part of Professor Boris Turaev's collection. In turn Boris Turaev obtained it from the Russian doctor A. I. Kohanovski who worked in Addis Abeba from 1905 to 1913 and collected during his stay several fine pieces of Ethiopian traditional art produced in the early years of the 20th century now kept at the MAE RAS in St. Petersburg. A considerable part of his collection gives an idea of secular themes characterized by the representation of historical personalities and portraits.

This "*political popular picture*", as B. A. Turaev (1915: 195) called it, follows a "*patriotic theme*" according to Richard Pankhurst's taxonomy (1966:33). It is a brightly-coloured painting executed on paper. Its size is 55.5 cm by 38 cm. It was framed in Russia. An elaborate structure characterizes the composition. The upper half of the picture is occupied by a large circle, filled in red (the sun?), surrounded by the strips of a rainbow, the inner strip being dark blue followed by strips of the colors of the Ethiopian flag (green, yellow, red). There are two lions within the circle, a big one and, below, a smaller one, or a lion cub. The big one is obviously the Lion of Judah, passant, holding in the right paw a long stick ended on both sides with crosses and bearing an indeterminate shape that could be a flag (not the Ethiopian one as colors are blue-green-blue) or a blade. Its head is covered with a crown, and the symbol is completed by the Geez motto of the monarchy: **ሞዓ አንበሳ ዘእምነገደ ይሁዳ** – "The Lion of the tribe of Judah has prevailed". The caption on the left refers this lion to Emperor Mïnilïk: **ምኒልክ ዳግማዊ ሥዩመ እግዚያብሔር ወንጉሠ ነገሥት ዘኢትዮጵያ** – "Mïnilïk the Second, God's vicar and King of kings of Ethiopia"

The pose of the lion cub is not heraldic. It is crowned with flowers and identified as: **ኢያሱ ምኒልክ ዳግማዊ** – "Iyasu [son of] Mïnilïk the Second".

Such captions describing the names and ranks of figures are characteristic features of the popular Ethiopian painting of this period. Most of the texts are in Amharic, the dominant spoken language. Some sentences are written in Geez, referring to quotations from the Bible, and giving a more formal tone to the whole work.

To the right of the Lion of Judah a dove in a halo of light is depicted. It bears a bunch of flower to Mïnilïk and is also turned towards Iyasu. A phrase commented on this image seems to be a key for understanding the entire picture: **ምሳሌ ርግብ ወዘመንፈስ ቅዱስ የምስራች አበባ ይዛ እንደመጣች ነው** – "Allegory of the dove (representing) the Holy Spirit, when she comes bearing the flower of good news". This caption is followed up by a text in Geez: **ወትቤ ርግብ ዓመተ ምሕረት ዳግማዊት ነትገ ዓመተ ፍዳ ቀዳማዊ** – "and says the dove: the second era of mercy abolished the first era of punishment". This sentence refers to the Old and the New Testament, the "punishment" being the banishment of Adam and Eve from the Garden of Eden.

Inside this circle a greeting in Amharic is also included: **እንቍጣጣሽ ዓመት ካመት ዘመን ከዘመን ያሸጋግርዎ እላለሁ አሽከርዎ** – "*Ïnqwït'at'ash* [traditional garland of grass and flowers], my best wishes for the New Year, let Him pass you over years and centuries. Your servant".

Below the circle in the centre of the painting Ethiopia is represented as a woman carrying on her head a *mesob*, a traditional Ethiopian wicker table here filled with flowers. The dress of the woman looks also like a traditional *qemis* with a cloak (*kaba*) usually worn by nobles. The figure is enveloped in a yellow light. On either side of her, from top to down, there are flocks of lions, oxen and pigs. The captions equate the lions with the nobles and dignitaries (**መሣፍንት ወመኳንንት**), the oxen with the people (**ሕዝብ**) and wild pigs as pagan peoples (**አሕዛብ አረማውያን**).

Then to the left of the woman a description in Geez explains that **ዛቲ፡ ይእቲ፡ ሐገርን ኢትዮጵያ ወእሙ ለምኒልክ ትሲሲ ለኵሉ ምግበ ፍሥሐ ወትፀውር ማዕደ ፍሥሐ** "It is our country Ethiopia and a mother for Mïnilïk: for all she carries the food of joy on a table of joy". To the right again an approximate translation of this phrase in Amharic is given: **የምኒልክ ሃገር ኢትዮጵያ መሶብ ተሸክማ ለሁሉ እንዳበላችው** "Ethiopia, the country of Mïnilïk, bearing a basket to feed all the people".

Under the woman there is one more sentence about "Ethiopia stretching forth her hands to God", referring to the well-known biblical statement of Psalm 67:32 **ኢትዮጵያ ታበጽሕ እደዊሃ ሃበ እግዚአብሔር**

The background of the entire picture is strongly faded dark-green. Out of the image extremely right is found the signature of the painter: **ይህ ሥራ ዘአለቃ ሐዲስ የገነት ሰዓሊ** "It's a work of *Aleqa* Haddis the painter of paradise".

Painting № 4055-14
Museum of Ethnography and Anthropology of the Russian Academy of Sciences
Collection Boris Turaev
Author: *Aleqa* Haddis; date: ca. 1910 place and author unknown

This painting is pleasant for its fanciful and brightly-coloured design. It has also a certain cultural-historical interest. Firstly it shows a popular expression on how the succession of *Atsé* Mïnilïk by *Lïj* Iyasu was understood. The painter placed the lion cub symbolizing *Lïj* Iyasu directly under Mïnilïk. This dual and transitional representation of power can be observed on other paintings by A. I. Kohanovski and kept at the MAE RAS.

The painting № 2594-22 represents Mïnilïk and T'aytu in the centre. Under them, *Lïj* Iyasu is depicted with the designation of "the son of Mïnilïk". To the left and right are placed nobles and officials of Mïnilïk's state administration.

A similar kind of representation is found on another painting № 2594-18. As in the previous picture, *Lïj* Iyasu is "the son of Menelik the Second" (*weldu le-dagmawi Mïnilïk*). The composition is interesting: under the representation of the Trinity Mïnilïk and Iyasu are together placed to the left, whereas Empress T'aytu is placed with Zewditu, the daughter of Mïnilïk, to the right.

In a triptych of the same collection, № 2594-30, *Lïj* Iyasu is represented as the central character. Traditionally, the central panel is meant for the image of Virgin with Christ. It shows that the authority of *Lïj* Iyasu was already recognised before the beginning of 1913, when A. I. Kohanovsky returned to Russia.

This picture is a kind of greetings card for the New Year that could have been addressed to Emperor Mïnilïk himself. Though the production for foreign visitors by painters based in Addis Abeba was already well developed during this period, it is reasonable to suppose that this picture was an order of local people or at least produced for local purposes.

Our painting seems to be one of the first attempts to express the idea of Ethiopia as a single country inhabited by different peoples under a single authority. The image of the woman equated with "our country Ethiopia" looks like a forerunner of the well-known image of Mother Ethiopia which would become a common theme some years latter in popular iconography. Two paintings of the years 1930s-1940s published by R. Pankhurst (Pankhurst 1966: 46, 65) represent the image of Ethiopia stretching forth her hands to God, side by side with Emperor Hayle Sïllasé. After liberation some paintings of Mother Ethiopia were also produced for the decoration of the *t'äj bét*-s.

The emblem of the Lion of Judah and its associated motto drew on ancient royal traditions. These symbols were refined and systematically employed as symbols of Solomonic dynasty under the reign Mïnilïk II first on seals, then through extended use on coins, official letters, newspapers, monuments, public buildings and so forth (Rubenson 1965; Pankhurst 2007).

Finally we can note that another characteristic of this picture is the vertical representation of social classes, through an allegory with domesticated and wild animals. Discussions on the structure of the feudal monarchy were vivid in the educated circles, particularly among clergymen. Such intellectual debates were intensified in the context

Addis Abeba, the most progressive city of Ethiopia since its recent establishment as the capital city. Critical thought on social classes is found in Ethiopian literature, for example in the work of Abba Bahrïy on the Oromo history that was written in the late 16th century, that was rediscovered and discussed in the end of the 19th century by Atsmé Giyorgis (Bairu Tafla 1987).

To conclude, this painting is a fine and singular example of visualization of social and political structure of the Ethiopian feudal monarchy of that period. It is an innovative composition mixing traditions with new models that can be interpreted as a prototype of further creations in popular painting. Unfortunately we haven't succeeded to find any information about the author, *Aleqa* Haddis, a talented and even bold painter who was probably established in Ethiopian the capital city in the beginning of the 20th century.

Bibliography

Bairu Tafla, 1987, *Aṣma Giyorgis and His Work: History of the Gāllā and the Kingdom of Šawā*, Stuttgart, Franz Steiner.

Pankhurst, Richard, 1966, "Some Notes for a History of Ethiopian Secular Art", *Ethiopia Observer*, 10 (1): 5-80.

Pankhurst, Richard, 2007, "Lions in Ethiopian culture", *Encyclopaedia Aethiopica*, 3: 572-575.

Rubenson, Sven, 1965, "The Lion of the Tribe of Judah: Christian Symbol and/or Imperial Title", *Journal of Ethiopian Studies*, 3(2): 75-85.

Turaev, Boris, 1915, "Abissinskaya politicheskaya lubochnaya kartina moego sobraniya", *Hristianskiy Vostok*, 3 (2): 195-196.

Lïj Iyasu: A Reformist Prince?

Ahmed Hassen Omer

If the term reform is making something better by removing faults and errors, a reformer can be described as someone, who could make improvements at country level by removing faults and abuses especially in moral, social, economic political senses. Basically, a reformist is a person who advocates possible means to bring about social, economic and political reform.

The objective of this article is to test whether or not some of the endeavours of *Lïj* Iyasu could qualify him as a reformist prince or not.[1] To undertake this task one has to deal with contemporary sources and assess the socio-political and economic environment of *Lïj* Iyasu's career during his short but turbulent reign (1910-1916).

A Historical Antecedent

One of the very critical and meticulous writers of the early 20th century Ethiopia was *Neggadras* Gebre Hïywet Baykedañ, who argues that the reign of Emperor Mïnilïk II (1889-1913) was relatively peaceful. It seems this relatively peaceful time and opportunity allowed him to reside in his alternative palaces at Ïnt'ott'o, Addis Alem and Addis Abeba. Gebre Hïywet was in safe situation when he, based on objective reality, compared and contrasted the Mïnilïk era and that of his predecessor in pinpointing that as opposed to his predecessors such as Emperor Téwodros II (1855-1868) and Emperor Yoḥannïs IV (1872-1889), Mïnilïk never spent much of his time in tents. The intention of Gebre Hïywet was not to undermine the value Meqdela seat of Téwodros or those palaces of Yoḥannïs at ʿAdwa and Meqelé. Instead, his intention was to underscore that the two predecessors of Mïnilïk successfully engaged themselves in chaotic wars either with local rebels as in the case of Téwodros or a series of foreign aggressors which eventually made the 17 years of Yoḥannïs IV's imperial rule more dark and very bloody (Gebre Hïywet 1912: 341).

1 The first draft of this paper was read at the International Conference on *Life and Times of Lïj Iyasu: New Insights*, Wallo University, Dessie November 8-10, 2009. I am grateful to Dr, Eloi Ficquet, Director of the French Centre for Ethiopian Studies (CFEE) for invitation. Dr. Thomas Osmond, my French colleague, has also extended his close encouragement in France or here in Ethiopia. I extend my thankfulness to him.

What is of historical importance is that as opposed to the times of Téwodros II and Yoḥannïs IV, the reign of Mïnilïk witnessed relative peace and stability, an era in which the people of Ethiopia did not engage in long series of rebellion against their royal master. Mention should be made of the fact that Ethiopia under Mïnilïk II got both internal strength and wider territorial extent (Gebre Hïywet 1912: 340). This was a historical task unmatched by the leaders before him. Ethiopia enjoyed both its diplomatic and sovereign rights. There was, however, a reasonable and convincing doubt as to whether or not the power and energy which Ethiopia had experienced under Mïnilïk could be sustained in the following decades. The critical assessor of the Mïnilïk era concludes that the strength of the Ethiopian state under Mïnilïk was the order of the day not that much because of the effective and well organized administration. Instead, it was due to the personal strength and wisdom of Mïnilïk's leadership. It was a sad story that the personal strength and wisdom of the indefatigable Mïnilïk gradually deteriorated ever since the very day Mïnilïk faced the first stroke in 1906. This was indeed the beginning of the end for the noble idea of modernization which Mïnilïk had put on the agenda.[2]

The question to be raised is why Mïnilïk's ambition was not followed by his officials? Gebre Hïywet is of opinion that the majority of Mïnilïk's officials were careless to the extent that they did not bother if the emperor's agenda would go down the drain or if it would be successful. It seems that things had to wait the accession to power of his grandson, *Lïj* Iyasu, who implemented a series of reforms above all against the evils of feudal system and many other impediments that were blocking an old African nation not to embark on the path of modernization and social development (Gebre Hïywet 1912: 346).

The Reformist Intent of *Lïj* Iyasu

The reign of *Lïj* Iyasu (1910-1916) was short but eventful. Although short, his reign was characterized, for a careful observer, by chains of incidents such as elements of social progress, factual disinformation, political treachery, and leadership's inconsistencies to handle the affairs of the country with maturity. Nevertheless, the achievements of his short reign should not haphazardly be dumped into the bulwark of incompetence and his multifaceted tasks as only mere escapades of a spoilt young man. This can be safely argued based on the major issues he raised some of which were not dreamt neither by his predecessor and nor by his successor as well. Among such major issues was that of reform. And, the main objective of this paper is to pick this task of him and attempts to put the reformist career of *Lïj* Iyasu Mïnilïk in its proper historical setting.

2 Gebre Hïywet 1912: 346. See also Ydlibi 2006: 133-155.

What tasks accomplished and qualified *Lïj* Iyasu as a reformer and which sources are of vital importance to help us understand this problematic from the grass root level should be brought together. The best available primary source, in this regard, is Gebre Hïywet's account which evidently underscores that Mïnilïk II was attacked by a serious stroke and left his hopes and tasks of reforming and modernizing Ethiopia. The ingenious Gebre Hïywet comments his enthusiastic hope on *Lïj* Iyasu, thus:

> "*All these* [reforms] *may have been thought by Mïnilïk to be accomplished. Alas! Almost nothing is seen on the ground. Indeed, let us hope this noble task would be accomplished towards final by His Excellency, Prince Iyasu, heir to the throne which he deserves so far. Big responsibility is also upon his shoulder being an Ethiopian king. Ignorance, in the past, is a queen on this earth. Today, it is under strong challenge by its enemy. Its enemy is the European mind. Those ready to open their room for it would be advanced and enriched their capacity.*" (1912: 354)

There is another inquisitive point raised in Gebre Hïywet's work with respect to how Ethiopia under *Lïj* Iyasu should have embarked on the path of development. He, in this regard, proposed an "extra-European" task and lesson to be considered by the young prince. Gebre Hïywet's hope further hints that *Lïj* Iyasu, the heir presumptive of Mïnilïk II should assign someone or a group to study how the Japanese government tackled its problems and if possible follow the itinerary of the Japanese experience.

Any student of Ethiopian history, who sets out to discuss the reformist stand of *Lïj* Iyasu should carefully compare and contrast the stands of contemporary independent sources and will see that much of Mïnilïk's efforts were still on the agenda at the very moment of his death in 1913. The intention of this article is neither to discredit the noble efforts made by the enthusiastic Mïnilïk nor to demote or promote the role played by *Lïj* Iyasu as his immediate successor. Instead, it is to learn why Mïnilïk failed to achieve his policy of modernization and equally in which way *Lïj* Iyasu took over Mïnilïk's unfinished agenda. The logical justification is well forwarded by Gebre Hïywet Baykedañ (1912: 345-346). He bluntly argued that Mïnilïk was sandwiched between the Ethiopian public of his time, who did not give due attention to education, and a few Europeans, upon whom Mïnilïk put his confidence but only to be betrayed for this or that reasons.

Count Pietro Antonelli the Italian architect of the infamous Wuch'alé Treaty of 1889 can be mentioned in this regard. It seems due to this reason that it took Mïnilïk some time to think and search for European advisors. In fact, his wisdom to wait and see the white men's trek to Ethiopia in the latter part of his long reign helped him to carefully distinguish the best white men on his side. Hasib Ydlibi, Alfred Ilg, Casimir Mondon-Vidailhet, Léon Chefneux, Pierre Arnoux and others may be seen along this line.

However, during the last decade of Mïnlïk's reign, Ethiopians who were educated abroad were not less than Europeans to advise him on matters regarding both foreign and domestic issues. Not that much was registered as long a lasting achievement. The fulfilment of Mïnilïk's agenda had to wait not only the arrival of *Lïj* Iyasu as his grandfather's successor but also the short reign to succeed the longer one. In actual fact, it should be underlined that some of the reforms *Lïj* Iyasu undertook could have needed a longer time span than the brief six years of his reign. But some major achievements were accomplished within that brief period.

It is interesting to see that, *Lïj* Iyasu was not only seeking foreigners as advisors but also gave them the possibility to be directly employed in his bureaucracy. Some of the foreigners coming to Ethiopia were individual entrepreneurs in search of, according to Bahru Zewde, both "fame and fortune" (Ydlibi 2006: x). Hassib Yidlibi, who won the special appreciations from Mïnilïk, won even greater support in the times of *Lïj* Iyasu, as he was employed as governor of Dïrré Dawa and *Neggadras* of Harer. It seems he and many other foreigners had their pieces of advice behind *Lïj* Iyasus' reform deal. In some cases strong criticism were roaring against his delay to embark on the track of social reform. For the purpose of this paper, it is useful to bring to light the debate exchanged between Iyasu and Ydlibi during one Sunday dinner at the latter's house. *Lïj* Iyasu's inertia is more evident when we see the questions posed by Ydlibi:

> *"What are you doing Lïj Iyasu? Where are you drifting? What has become of our revered Mïnilïk's reforms, barely commenced and then abandoned? Do you realize that by the terms of your treaty with France,*[3] *you were given ten years during which to introduce reforms? Do you realize that those ten years will soon be ended? What are you going to do about it?"* (Ydlibi 2006: 207).

Lïj Iyasu had tried to justify that Europe was busy in its Great War and that it could not display ample time to the Ethiopian issues. The intelligent Yidlibi did not take time to respond that this was really the case but frankly explained to the young prince that he should not think as if the war in Europe could sustain for long time. By way of advising the young Prince, Ydlibi precisely remarked that he should not waste his time here and there but should pay more attention to Europeans to make them think positively about him. In the course of the dinner get-together, everything was raised and for much part of that session *Lïj* Iyasu was a good listener by plunging himself in such a dimly thought. In the last minutes, however, he raised some key issues he wanted to explain or make clear to Ydlibi:

> *"Abba* [Father] *Ydlibi, it is easy to scold, and to find fault, but that does not advance matters a bit. Instead, why don't you help me? Why not teach us the things we should do? Would you agree to do that? Would you agree to be the governor of a town, for instance, and, by putting it in order, set the example for the other towns to copy?"* (Ydlibi 2006: 207).

3 This was a Treaty of Commerce and friendship signed with France in July 1907. For further reference see, among others, F.O. 401/11: Thesiger to Sir Edward Grey, Addis Ababa, April 28, 1911; see also the English version of the Treaty F.O.403/420.

Pleased by the demand of the young prince Ydlibi's reply was so positive underscoring that he would certainly extend his services in much the same vein as to that of *Lïj* Iyasu's grandfather, Emperor Mïnilïk II. Moreover, Hasib Ydlibi promised to the young Prince that he should count upon him for whatever he could wish. He asked to Iyasu if he could precisely expose his immediate need. Yidlibi was quickly demanded if he would accept to become governor of Dïrré Dawa with an additional office to be bestowed upon him as *Neggadras* of Harer. *Lïj* Iyasu further informed Ydlibi that he would have free hand to make his own rule and introduce the best reforms for the benefit of the two cities. He underlined to Ydlibi that his governorship of Dïrré Dawa should become a model for all Ethiopia. This was above all acceptable to the chiefs and the public at large. *Lïj* Iyasu's intention was to introduce through the efforts of Hasib Yidlibi a system of government similar to the one which Britain had employed in Cyprus, where Ydlibi used to work earlier. It was well considered; however, from the very outset this model from Cyprus should not have been "photocopied" since some modification was essential to meet the Ethiopian realities still intact with medieval garbs.

Why did *Lïj* Iyasu choose Dïrré Dawa for the implementation of his reform endeavor? This town represented a lucrative source of revenues with its customs office that was one of the most important in the country. The intention was that a new type of administration with substantial tax incomes could further help to undertake extra reforms in other parts of Ethiopia.[4] The chosen town of Dïrré Dawa itself was, however, facing serious difficulties that were obstacles against any reform program. In particular, theft, robbery, corruption and backwardness were very rampant in those days. Part of *Lïj* Iyasu's reform was targeted against the system which was by then known as *quraña* (the situation of imprisonment under which both the accused and the plaintiff were chained together until final solution would arrive); and, the *lebashay*[5] (traditional way of detecting theft). The young prince's intention was to make such series of changes that social evils would be overcome once and for all, both at the national level and at the micro level of Dïrré Dawa. In doing so, it is clearly established that he had a strong foreign advisors backing him. Nevertheless, *Lïj* Iyasu himself had received some modern education from which he could at least have obtained the basic understanding of the need for modernization in Ethiopia. Even if *Lïj* Iyasu's "New Deal" had a clear sense and intention to modernize his administration, using both local and foreign capacities, the Ethiopian public response was both marked by joy and confusion.

While some considered his policy quite impressive, other sections of the Ethiopian public perceived his reformist zeal with deep suspicion. Those who appreciated his endeavor perceived it by relating his efforts directly to his contact with skilled foreign personnel; and, due to encouragement he used to win from the local contemporary

4 F.O.371/228: Walker to Sir Edward Grey, February 5, 1915.

5 See Gebre-Igziabiher Elias 1936 e.c.: 25-36.

intellectuals. In this regard, the foreigner Hasib Ydlibi became his skilled town governor and played the role of motor in his reform plan (Ydlibi 2006: 207-209). Moreover, *Lïj* Iyasu disclosed to Ydlibi, on their visit to Djibouti, that he wanted to visit Europe if European countries were not at war with each other:

> "*Abba Ydlibi, if Europe were at peace, I would have continued the journey now. When they have finished fighting, I will go to Europe, and you must promise to accompany me!*" (Ydlibi 2006: 24).

This by itself is a clear testimony regarding the young prince's intention to visit and benefit from the experiences he could get from the developed world.

In terms of hope and encouragement which he extended and the confidence he developed towards *Lïj* Iyasu, the Ethiopian foreign educated intellectual, Gebre Hiwet Baykedagn's view convincingly surpasses his contemporaries. Gebre Hiwet did not underestimate the due efforts made by the untiring Emperor Mïnilïk II, who tried his best in seeking ways through which Ethiopia should properly embark on the path of development. Unfortunately, death detached him from some of the noble tasks he intended.

It was hoped that *Lïj* Iyasu, as well indicated by Gebre Hïywet (1912: 354), could follow in the footstep of his grandfather. Indeed, what can be said in this regard is that *Lïj* Iyasu had followed in his grand father's footsteps in as far as continuity was concerned. Nevertheless, there was a big change and difference between Mïnilïk's reforms and Iyasu's "New Deal" (Marcus 1996: 18-19, 22-30). What was conceived as reform or modernization was on the agenda of both the grandfather and the grand son. It should, however, made be clear that they were not on the same track in as far as their methods were concerned. Gebre Hïywet Baykedañ, ingenuously shown that Emperor Mïnilïk had not that much introduced new policies in as far as reforms and modernization go. This view was contrary to the pro-Shewan claim that was ostensibly rubberstamped by Afeworq Gebre Iyyesus (1901 E.C.). For Gebre Hïywet, Mïnilïk instead praised and sealed for the Ethiopian people to retain the tradition of their forefathers. This was nothing more than the *status quo ante* together with little advances along the road of Imperial tradition. Emperor Mïnilïk was nothing else than an Empire builder. He did not, after all, try to challenge his people accept new things. Sending abroad a few sons of nobility and aristocracy, introducing one school, one hospital, one hotel and the railway had been something that could be counted on fingertips in front of the bulwark of the Ethiopian backwardness in those days. Seen in the context of the time, however, it was no doubt a step forward (Gebre Hïywet 1912: 334).

Lïj Iyasu, during his short reign, represented a challenge to the imperial tradition. He clearly departed from that imperial thoroughfare and remained as a singular nation builder in the historical saga of the 20th century Ethiopian leadership. The period of diarchy (1916-1930) that succeeded the short reign of Iyasu was only to realize the political deceitfulness of then *Dejjazmach* Teferi Mekonnïn, who eroded the power of Queen Zewditu Mïnilïk to finally clear the road of his aspiration for power. Seen from different historical perspectives, however, the longevity of Hayle Sellasé's reign, under which the reformist tasks of *Lïj* Iyasu were firmly erased by the imperial rubber. One shall also argue that the communist regime was there only to waste time by covering the last two decades of the 20th century Ethiopia.[6]

Coming back to *Lïj* Iyasu, it was his departure along the different route of social considerations, by betraying the old imperial highway, which could later reduce him being victim of the conspiracy of the Shawan nobility. It, therefore, goes without saying that the religious indicts which the Shewan establishment and his foreign enemies brought against him in reality shrouded their political concern. It was such political calculation of the anti-*Lïj* Iyasu camp which until our own times almost permanently obscured the historical facts behind the young prince than clarifying it.[7]

Lïj Iyasu's Reforms: The Achievements

In the preceding section of this article, attempts have been made, based on sources, to revaluate the main intentions of his reformist endeavors. The task of this last section of the article is, however, to briefly consider the attempted reform undertaken by *Lïj* Iyasu with respect to economic and social security. The leading historians specialized on this period have confidently considered his attempts as progressive. Among such historians, who scored the high point of scholarly achievement on the history of early 20th century Ethiopia, Bahru Zewde's expressive remarks, in his *A History of Modern Ethiopia*, stand out quite clearly:

> "*In addition to the guaranteeing of property and more equitable system of Asrat collection...he put to the quragna system, whereby the plaintiff was chained to the defendant and the creditor to the debtor until justice was delivered. He also tried to mitigate the abuses of the lebashay, a whimsical traditional mode of detection of criminals, in which a young boy would be given a powerful drug and let loose in the neighbourhood; the unfortunate owner of the house where the boy finally collapsed would be declared the culprit.*" (Bahru Zewde 2001: 121-122)

Lïj Iyasu's reform, besides what one could observe in the above quotation was the introduction of the institution of municipal police force commonly known as the *Trimbulle*, a corrupted Amharic term to referring to Tripoli, as those *Trimbulle*, almost all of them, had been returnees from Tripoli where there was the campaign of Italian annexation of Libya a task they started in the year 1911.

6 Informant: the late *Lïj* Mika'él Imru interviewed at his home in Addis Ababa in April, 1993. I am grateful to the late Dr. Berhanou Abebe for a week end arrangement for the interview; cf. Bahru Zewde (2001: 121).

7 Gebre-Igziabiher Elias 1936 E.C.: 25-49; Bahru Zewde 2001: 124.

One point to be raised is why the reforms undertaken by *Lïj* Iyasu, faced such a sharp opposition from two internal corners, i.e. the Shewan nobility and the Ethiopian Orthodox Church. The former hated him for he was a challenge to their political supremacy. The latter did the same, albeit for different reasons. It questioned his Muslim ancestry which lent steadfastness to such stand against the young prince. *Lïj* Iyasu's donations to different Orthodox Monasteries were not that much appreciated. The founding of the church he executed in Addis Abeba was ignored from being a Christian commitment he supposed to have accomplished. The church finally served the propaganda role for his opponents above all by amplifying his association with the daughters of Muslim Ethiopian chiefs, the intimate connections he extended to the Muslim inhabited areas such as Harer, Dïrré Dawa and Jijjiga, in the latter case the construction of a mosque by the young prince was quite highlighted. Although the local anti-Iyasu elements fabricated propaganda particularly in relation to his conversion to Islam, external sources have increasingly shown their impartiality with maximum veracity that the young prince had no intention to do anything dangerous against the church in favor of Islam (Bahru Zewde 2001: 124).

Finally, this paper has no intention neither to discredit all efforts made by Emperor Mïnilïk II in his reform endeavor nor did it condemn the political calculations by the Shawan nobility or the Orthodox Church which led *Ïcheggé* Wolde Giyorgis to eventually join the anti-Iyasu propaganda camp. The objective stand of the *Abun* should not be misunderstood as he only reluctantly stood in favor of those believing in *Lïj* Iyasu's conversion. By the same token no intention is prepared behind this paper to credit or endorse every task undertaken by *Lïj* Iyasu. The basic contribution of this short paper is to underscore that *Lïj* Iyasu's policy can be regarded as a tangible reaction to former injustices committed by his predecessors. If Iyasu's reforms are to be appreciated, it is because that he attempted them after carefully considering the question of national integration, that of religious equity and social and economic injustice. It seems he attempted to prepare the fertile ground and the mind free of doubts before he decided to embark on his reformist plan. This attempt was aborted as the tragedy of his short reign shows. It seems due to this reason that his tasks had attracted the intellectuals of the time. It was not only Gebre Hïywet Baykedañ, who by then stood in favor of his reform agenda. Many others did the same for that matter. *Bïjïrond* Tekle Hawaryat Tekle Maryam had been one of the intellectuals who contemplated that there might have been a better opportunity to carry out reform under *Lïj* Iyasu than under his grandfather, Emperor Mïnilïk II. In fact, Tekle Hawaryat did not stay to the last minute after he carefully realized some of the weak points of *Lïj* Iyasu. The particular weak point he had seen, with wisdom, in the personality of the young prince was nothing but what Bahru Zewde (2002: 59) aptly puts as lack of "seriousness of purpose and steadfastness of application".

Bibliography

Afeworq Gebre Iyyasus, 1901 E.C., *Degmawi Mïnilïk*, Roma.

Ahmed Hassen Omer, 2007, "Islam, commerce et politique dans l'Ifat (Éthiopie centrale) au XIXe siècle : L'emergence d'une ville Carrefour, Aleyuu Amba" (Thèse de doctorat d'histoire, Université Paris I, Panthéon, Sorbonne.

Bahru Zewde, 2001, *A History of Modern Ethiopia: 1855-1991*, Second Edition, Oxford/Athens/Addis Ababa: James Currey, Ohio University Press, Addis Ababa University Press.

Bahru Zewde, 2002, *Pioneers of Change in Ethiopia: The Reformist Intellectuals of the Early Twentieth Century,* Oxford, James Currey.

Gebre Hïywet Baykedañ, 1912 E.C., *As'é Mïnilïk-ïnna It'yop'ya* [Emperor Mïnilïk and Ethiopia], Asmara, Bïrhan Yïhun.

Gebre-Igziabiher Elias, 1936 E.C., *Ye Tarik Mastawesha*, Addis Ababa.

Marcus, Harold G., 1996, *Haile Sellasé I: The Formative Years, 1892-1936*, Lawrenceville, Red Sea Press.

Rouaud, Alain, 1991, *Afe-Werq: un intellectuel éthiopien témoin de son temps, 1868-1947,* Paris: éditions du CNRS.

Ydlibi, May, 2006, *With Ethiopian Rulers. A Biography of Hasib Ydlibi*, Bahru Zewde (ed.), Addis-Abeba: AAU Press.

The Reign of *Lïj* Iyasu – as Avedis Terzian Saw it

Richard Pankhurst

Avedis Terzian son of Emperor Mïnilïk's Armenian aide, the entrepreneur Sarkis Terzian,[1] was a largely self-educated historian (Zervos 1936: 496). Though keenly interested in Ethiopian history he wrote little about it, but confided many of his thoughts and memories to the present author, who tape-recorded them at Terzian's house in Addis Abeba in 1979.

The Armenian's recording, which is impressionistic rather strictly factual, was based largely on his own observations, and conversations with Ethiopian nobles of the older generation – with many of whom he was on visiting terms. He also relied on the recollections of his father Sarkis Terzian, and of the wider Armenian community, which was in closer contact with the Ethiopian population, it should be emphasized, than any other group of foreigners.

In the course of one of our tape-recording conversations Avedis Terzian recounted the story of *Lïj* Iyasu. This account, which embodied statements of varying credibility, is interesting in that it indicates how the rise and fall of Ethiopia's uncrowned Emperor appeared to the Armenian.

Historical Context

Looking at *Lïj* Iyasu's accession to power in its historical context Terzian recalls that his friends in the Palace had emphasized the significance of two important events which had preceded it.

The first was the death in 1906 of *Ras* Mekonnïn, whom many had conceived as Mïnilïk's chosen successor. This death had been followed by looting in Addis Abeba, which had caused Mïnilïk to recognize the need to obviate a similar reaction in the event of his own demise. This contributed, Terzian claimed, to the Emperor's decision to appoint a successor.

The above contention, though entirely plausible, would seem uncorroborated. The present commentator has failed to trace evidence of looting in 1906, though it undoubtedly followed the death of *Lïj* Iyasu's tutor *Ras* Tesemma in 1911.[2]

1 On the life of Sarkis Terzian see Pankhurst 1981.

2 Montandon 1913 : 379-80; Mérab 1921-1929: vol.2, 246.

The second event bearing on Mïnilïk's successor also dated back to 1906. It was the signing by the British, French, and Italian Governments of that year's Tripartite Treaty, which partitioned the country between them into three spheres of interest. This prompted Mïnilïk - allegedly *"on that very day"* - to seek an alternative access to Europe – by opening up diplomatic relations with a fourth Power: Germany. This was significant for *Lïj* Iyasu because it reduced his dependence on the three neighbouring Colonial Powers, Britain, France and Italy, and increased the number of European States with which he could maneuver.

Family Background, and Accession to the Throne

Turning to *Lïj* Iyasu's family background Terzian recalls that this Prince was, as everyone knows, the son of *Nïgus* Mika'él of Wello by Mïnilïk's daughter Princess Shewa-Regga Mïnilïk.[3] Elaborating, on this descent he tells us that Iyasu, at that time, did not see his father, and that his mother had died while he was only a baby. The result was that the infant had been immediately dispatched to Addis Abeba – and accordingly "grew up in the Palace".

It was while he was thus still only a child at the Palace – in 1909 - that his grandfather, Mïnilïk, came to a decision about the succession, after which Terzian relates:

> "[Mïnilïk] *gathered all the dignitaries at Jan Méda,* [a large open field near the Addis Abeba Palace], *and issued a Proclamation in which he described his life and his efforts to unite Ethiopia – and he explained to them* [the nobles] *that he was not immortal, and could die at any day*".

It was for this reason, Terzian continues, that the aged - and ailing - Emperor appointed *Lïj* Iyasu as his heir, after which the courtiers *"signed a very formal document"* doing so – and Abune Matéwos, the Egyptian head of the Church, supervised the nobles in taking an oath of loyalty. The last sentence included the curse that anyone overturning this oath should *"beget a black dog"*.

Terzian goes on to state that after 1906 Mïnilïk's powers declined – and T'aytu *"became very active"* in building up dynastic and other support for herself.

Ras Tesemma

Iyasu was at that time under the tutorship of one of Mïnilïk's most trusted courtiers, *Ras* Tesemma Nadew. The latter had been chosen, Terzian tells us, because his father had been Mïnilïk's own tutor. Tesemma, he says, was "an old man... a very simple-minded man, a very good Ethiopian - but knew nothing about diplomacy". By the time he died, in 1911, Iyasu, Terzian explains, had *"become very unruly",* He was encouraged

3 Terzian, by a slip of the tongue actually referred to this princess as Teñañe Werq.

in this, Terzian claims, by Tesemma's wife, or widow. It was a "secret", the Armenian adds, that she was a "very young", and "very good-looking" woman – who "*began to court* Lïj *Iyasu*". The latter, according to Terzian, was fourteen or fifteen years old when he began his "love affair" with his tutor's wife [or widow].

Possible corroboration of this statement about Tesemma's widow found in the observation of the Georgian pharmacist Dr Mérab that she was one of several "princesses" in whose houses Iyasu occasionally resided.[4]

After Tesemma's death Iyasu, the Armenian continues, "*felt himself more emancipated*" and "*began to associate with younger people*".[5]

Tesemma's death, it is generally agreed, was a major turning-point in Iyasu's life. The Prince was quoted by the Swiss scholar George Montandon as pointedly declaring: "*My father Menilek gave me a Regent, but God took him away*" (Montandon 1913: 381).

Iyasu's Ambition, Character, and Relations with the Chiefs

It was not long, Terzian continues, before Iyasu wanted "*to continue his grand-father's consolidation of the unity of Ethiopia and the centralization of Imperial power*" – which had been "*the great dream*" first of Téwodros and later of Mïnilïk.

Terzian, while recognizing the grandeur of Iyasu's ambition – rejects the then widely circulated contention that the Prince ever became a Muslim. He nevertheless takes the view that the young man's character was seriously flawed. Mïnilïk's heir, he claims, "*was spoiled and began to maltreat the great chiefs, to insult them, and do things that were not proper*". Elaborating on this statement, Terzian observed:

"*The great military leader* Fitawrari *Habte Giyorgis was rheumatic, and had difficulty riding or walking – but he* [Iyasu] *made him walk with him. He* [Iyasu] *was a giant... athletic.., and behaved very badly to him*". He also, according to Terzian, "*behaved badly*" with a number of Mïnilïk's other courtiers, whom he called his father's "sheep", because they were fat. That Iyasu insulted them in those words is corroborated by other writers, among them Iyasu's chronicler Gebre Egzi'abïher Elyas.[6]

Worse still, according to Terzian was that, Iyasu "*began to sleep with the chiefs' wives*".[7] Generalizing on Ethiopian tradition Terzian declares that it was considered

4 Mérab (1921-1929: vol.2, 256). For a brief overall history of Iyasu see Anon (in fact Sergew Hable Sellassie), "Iyasu Mikael, Lïj", in *The Encyclopaedia Africana Dictionary of African Biography*, (New York, 1977), pp. 91-92; and, more recently, Bahru Zewde 1991. For photographs of Iyasu as a child reading the Psalms of David, see De Castro 1915, vol.2: plates 39, 112 and 129.

5 After the death of Tesemma , "*Lïj Iyasu took the whole business of governing in his own hands, and became greatly feared... He refused to take the advice of officials and nobles. His council and conduct were with youths and women, and he visited Ethiopia's provinces to the right and the left.*" (Gebre-Igziabiher 1994: 321).

6 The chronicle notes that Iyasu criticized them, saying that they had grown old and fat (Gebre-Igziabiher 1994: 327, 350).

7 On Iyasu's relationship to women see Mérab 1921-1929: vol. 2, 249.

permissible for a monarch to have as many concubines as he liked, but he was not expected to play about with other men's wives. Iyasu's relationship with the wives of his chiefs was thus, in Terzian's view, a major factor leading to the Prince's growing unpopularity among the ruling elite.

Assertions of Iyasu's relations with the wives of the nobility are in the nature of things difficult to document – or refute. The only nobleman mentioned in the literature as having been alienated from Iyasu on account of sexual jealousy would seem to be *Ligaba* Beyyene Wendémegeñahu who, according to Gebre Egzi'abïher Elyas (1994: 355), suspected Iyasu of having "*had a sexual relationship with his wife*".

This suspicion, if it existed, would however have been by no means unimportant, for *Ligaba* Beyyene played a major role in Iyasu's subsequent overthrow. The chronicle reports that early in the subsequent Shewan noblemen's agitation against the Prince the *Ligaba* pulled out his sword, and uttered a war cry against Iyasu and his Muslim supporters - and later read out the speech deposing him (Gebre Igziabher 1994: 360-64). Beyyene subsequently also played a major role in the fighting which led to Iyasu's fall from power (Gebre Igziabiher 1994: 365, 370-76).

World War I - Iyasu's religious beliefs

Terzian then turned to Iyasu's position in relation to World War I (between Britain, France, Italy and Russia on one side, and the German, Austrian and Turkish empires on the other). He claims that at the outbreak of hostilities in 1914 the German Legation in Addis Abeba "*became very active*", and "*began to cultivate* Lïj *Iyasu*". He adds that an alliance with the Turks was not abhorrent to Iyasu in that his father, *Nïgus* Mika'él, had been born a Muslim, and had only been converted to Christianity by force. The "*majority of the people of Wello*, he adds, *had remained Muslims*".

Discussing Iyasu's religious beliefs, Terzian declares himself "*uncertain*" as to the extent of the young man's Christianity, but dismisses the idea, canvassed by the Shewan nobles at the time, that Iyasu had become a Muslim. He sees the Prince rather as a "*very ambitious*" young man, who "*felt very strong*" and "*thought he was all-powerful*" in relation to the Great Powers. Elaborating on the young man's attitude to the latter he states that the British Minister, Wilfred Thesiger, had sought to befriend Iyasu, but that the later had deliberately shunned him: whenever the Minister searched for him in Addis Abeba the Prince would escape to Ankober – This evasive policy is not mentioned in Thesiger's diplomatic reports!

The Germans, according to Terzian, had meanwhile promised Iyasu "*all the coast* [i.e. the neighbouring European Colonies or Protectorates] *if he joined Germany in the war*"- and for this reason became "quite influential at Iyasu's court. Prominent among them was Lorenz Jensen, who, according to Terzian, spoke Amharic "perfectly", and used it to make direct contact with the Ethiopian chiefs.

Seeking to define Iyasu's somewhat ambiguous attitude to the war Terzian asserts that there was "*a tendency in the Palace to become pro-German without realizing the implications of joining the war*". This statement should be read in conjunction with the observation attributed to Iyasu by the pro-British Syrian merchant Hasib Ydlibi that the Prince wished to be "*perfectly neutral*", but "*admired the efficiency of the Germans*" (Ydlibi 2006: 252).

Iyasu, Terzian explains, nevertheless developed amicable relations with Ethiopia's Muslim population - for example by visiting the Mosque in Harer, and fathering a child by an ʿAfar noblewoman.

Adding a personal touch to his account the Armenian claims that Iyasu was a "*very good friend*" of his father, Sarkis Terzian, whose house the Prince frequently visited. The young man, he claims, also spent many hours in the public baths at Fïlwïha, which Sarkis Terzian had erected - and on one occasion "*stuck a pen-knife into my father's leg to test whether my father was brave*".

As for Iyasu's attitude to Christians and Muslims, Terzian recalls that the Prince had on one occasion told his father that he considered himself "*Emperor of all Ethiopians, regardless of religion*" – and encouraged Islam with the hope of conquering the outlying territories. This reported utterance is once again supported by Ydlibi (2006: 250), who quotes Iyasu as saying to him:

> "*I have not changed my faith. I would never think of doing so. It is perhaps true that when I am in the country of Muslim subjects I might favour them, but I do the same to the Oromos when I am in their country. They are all my subjects and I believe they are each entitled to every mark of favour in equal shares, be they Christian, Muslim or even heathen*".

Terzian, turning to his own reminiscences, also told of relations between Iyasu and the latter's cousin Teferi Mekonnen (the future Emperor Hayle Sellasé). He states that Iyasu, when "*just a child... used to come to our house, and leave Teferi outside... He disliked Teferi, and used to call him* ch'ach'ut *which means a "chicken"*[a chick or small chicken]. *This was "because Teferi was very thin*" - with a wrist only half the width of that of Terzian, while Iyasu was "*twice the size*" of him.

Elaborating on Teferi's subordinate status at that time Terzian quotes the slave-girl who brought him up as saying:

> "*We all felt very sorry when* Lïj *Iyasu used to come, and enter the parlour with your father, and leave Teferi outside, holding the gun. We knew him* [Teferi] *as the son of* Ras *Mekonnen* [i.e. the former governor of Harer] *and felt ashamed that he should wait on the balcony while* Lïj *Iyasu went inside*".

On another occasion Iyasu and Teferi, Terzian reports, rode together to the Hotel de France to play billiards, a game then popular among the young Ethiopian nobility. Iyasu, addressing Teferi, who by then held the title of *Dejjazmach*, said to him, "*Pick up your cue, and let's play for Champagne – if you lose, you pay for Champagne for all the soldiers outside*". So they played. Teferi, though normally the better player, lost the game. Iyasu thereupon insulted him, telling him to "*use some of the money which your father left in London*" – the implication being that that the *Ras* had appropriated State property when travelling to Britain to attend King Edward VI's coronation way back in 1902.

Reverting to Iyasu's political and religious agenda Terzian explains that it aroused the opposition of Britain, at the very time when the chiefs were increasingly resenting Iyasu's arrogant attitude to them – and his seductive approaches to their wives.

The Coup d'Etat of 1916

Terzian presents an interesting account of the coup d'état which resulted in Iyasu's overthrow. Arguing that the Prince had by then become "*a danger to the Allies*"; he recalls that, during his absence in Harar, the Shewan nobles met together to depose him, on the excuse that he had become a Muslim. Summing up the situation Terzian declares:

> "Lïj *Iyasu became a danger to the Allies, and to the Chiefs, so they met together here* [in Addis Abeba] *while Iyasu was away in Harer, for his political reasons; and the Abun was called to join them. The Chiefs said, "Our ruler has become a Muslim; he has abandoned the Faith, and is behaving in an improper manner. You must dethrone him*".

The *Abun*, however, refused to absolve them of their oath of allegiance to Iyasu. The Chiefs, Terzian continues, then approached the British Minister Wilfred Thesiger, who, he claims, went to discuss the matter with the *Abun*, The British Minister's interpreter, Terzian claims, was an Armenian, who subsequently described the ensuing conversation, in which Thesiger reportedly declared to cleric (who was of course an Egyptian – and as such well aware of British military might), "*You know our guns; we can remove him – but you must sign* [the dethronement proclamation]".

Terzian claims that Thesiger offered the prelate one hundred thousand Maria Theresa dollars, and that the prelate thereby absolved the Chiefs of their Oath of Allegiance.

There is, one should emphasize, no record of any such a bribe in British Foreign Office archives. One has therefore to assume that the payment was the fruit of the Armenian's imagination – or that the British Minister somehow disposed of unrecorded funds.

Reverting to the opposition to Iyasu, Terzian goes on to state that one of the Prince's loyal supporters then telephoned his master, urging him to return to Addis Abeba, as he was "*being deposed*". His master merely laughed, and asked contemptuously whether his followers in Addis Abeba were merely women.

The plotters meanwhile "*all agreed to use Mïnilïk's daughter Princess Zewditu, and to make her Empress*". They sent a delegation on horseback to bring her to the capital, "*but Zewditu was frightened – she said: How can I replace my nephew?*". They were, Terzian claims, "*all afraid of* Lïj *Iyasu. He was so fierce, athletic and powerful*". Moreover "*Zewditu was a woman – and people asked how could she rule Ethiopia ?*"

To make the Princess's appointment more palatable to the Shewan nobility it was decided, Terzian recalls, that she should divorce her husband *Ras* Gugsa Wellé, because it was felt impossible to have a Gonderé *Dejjazmach* as husband of the Queen.

The next question, according to Terzian, was who should share power with her. There were two possible candidates. One was *Ras* Kasa, who had the better claim to the throne, and was supported by the British, but, "*being very religious*" was unwilling to assume the position, The other candidate was *Dejjazmach* Teferi Mekonnïn, who had the backing of the French. On *Ras* Kasa's rejection of the position, Teferi gained the support also of the British. Terzian who once again claims to have received his information from Thesiger's Armenian interpreter, asserts that the British Minister said to Teferi, "*You will be the Crown Prince of Ethiopia; you will be the Regent to help the Empress". Teferi, Terzian declares, was at first "frightened*"; "afraid" to go against the Prince who had "dominated him, and who was the "direct heir of the great Emperor [Mïnilïk]".

Teferi, Terzian states, however duly agreed, after which the plotters drank their health in Champagne.

The "Doctored Photographs"

Terzian gives credence to the report that "doctored photographs" of *Lïj* Iyasu were used to discredit the Prince. He states that the latter's opponents "*sent messages into the interior, describing* Lïj *Iyasu's bad behaviour*" – to which they "*attached a photograph, a photograph of* Lïj *Iyasu with a turban and a loin cloth*".

> "*A photo montage was prepared with the help of the British Legation which paid, I think, five thousand Maria Theresa dollars to an Armenian photographer, Mr Levon Yazedjian,*[8] *who made three thousand copies of the photo montage which was sent into the interior*".[9]

Mention of such photographs was also made by Hasib Ydilbi's daughter May Ydlibi, who reports that:

> "*The plotters took a photograph of* Lïj *Iyasu to an artist begging him to design a turban on the head, after which the print was re-photographed reproducing the prince*

8 On this photographer see Pankhurst 1981: 381-82

9 On the use of photo-montage in Ethiopia in this period see Pankhurst 1992; Smidt 2001; Berhanou Abebe 2003.

as wearing a turban. The faked photograph was printed in hundreds and distributed freely among the public as absolute proof of the charge proffered against him".[10]

It is curious that the photograph, supposedly produced at the behest of the British Legation, is not mentioned in the Foreign Office archives – and that, despite its alleged wide diffusion, no copy has thus far been traced.[11]

The Battle of Segelé

Coming to the battle of Segelé, which sealed Iyasu's fate, Terzian claims that the French were at first "very worried" about its outcome. They were "*not sure*" that Teferi and his allies would "*succeed in the battle, because Mika'él was very brave and courageous, and had a very good army*". He had moreover been "*heavily*" supplied with fire-arms by his son, who had "sent a lot of weapons from Addis Abeba".

Terzian goes on to recalls what he terms "*a very strange anecdote*" which, one may assume, circulated among the Armenian community. This held that French, fearing that their side might lose the battle, and be obliged to retreat:

"*prepared a railway coach with Teferi to hide in... and they decided that he should wear women's clothes. They found an Armenian lady who was of his size, and the plan was to shave his beard, and put him in the Armenian lady's clothes, take him to the [Dïrré Dawa] railway station, and to take him to Jibuti*".

The battle turned, however, in Teferi's favour, as a result of which the need for his disguise, whether true or imagined, was obviated. Mika'él was duly captured, and taken to Addis Abeba, after which he was imprisoned at Holeta. Iyasu for his part made his way to Desé, and later to Meqdela, but could not continue the struggle. "*He fled*", Terzian recalls, "*into the Danakil Desert in 1916*" and "*roamed freely about the desert*" until 1923 when he surrendered to *Ras* Sïyyum at Meqelé, after which he was taken to Addis Abeba as a prisoner. Teferi, Terzian claims, demanded that the deposed monarch should be handed over to him, but Zewditu, who was the latter's aunt, refused, declaring: "*We cannot hand give him into the hands of his opponent – you being his opponent*".

Iyasu was accordingly entrusted to *Ras* Kasa, who kept him as a prisoner at Fiché in the mountains of northern Shewa, where Terzian's story of the Prince comes to an end.

---

10 Ydlibi (2006: 258). For an alterative theory involving a photograph taken by the Italian consul in Dïrré Dawa see Berhanou Abebe (1998: 152). Yet another theory is found in Zishka (1936), which suggests the involvement of the British adventurer Colonel T.E. Lawrence, widely known as Lawrence of Arabia. This latter supposition was based on a confusion between T.E. Lawrence and another British official, Arthur Salisbury Lawrance (*sic),* who was involved in Somali affairs – on this confusion see Sharf and Pankhurst (2004: 242-44).

11 For apparently genuine photographs of Iyasu in Muslim clothes see Thesiger 1987.

Conclusions

Terzian's testimony on the reign of *Lïj* Iyasu would seem to present a useful account of an important period in Ethiopian history. The recording indicates in the first place that the interviewee rejected the then widely canvassed view that Mïnilïk's heir had embraced Islam. The text also provides interesting endorsement to the widespread – but still unproven - belief that those deposing the Prince made extensive use of a fake photograph produced by one of Terzian's compatriots.

Terzian's recording is interesting also in that it reports a succession of events, and situations, not elsewhere recorded. These, if corroborated, would seem to add significantly to the historical picture. They include the Armenian's statement that *Ras* Mäkonnen's death in 1906 was followed in Addis Abeba by extensive looting which helped to persuade Mïnilïk to finalize his own succession; and the statement that Iyasu's tutor *Ras* Tesemma was selected because the latter's father had been Mïnilïk's own tutor. Also generally unknown is the young man's affair with his tutor's widow; the derogatory nickname he gave to his young kinsman Teferi Mekonnen; the manner in which Iyasu evaded the British envoy Thesiger by riding off to Ankober; the way in which Thesiger reportedly bribed the *Abun* to allow the Ethiopian nobles to abandon their oath of allegiance; and the never-implemented plan devised to save Teferi in the event of the latter losing the battle at Segelé.

Terzian was clearly such an objective – and fair-minded – student of Ethiopian history that most of his account, if uncorroborated, may be taken in trust.

Bibliography

Bahru Zewde, 1991, *A History of Modern Ethiopia, 1855-1991*, Oxford: James Currey.

Berhanou Abebe, 1998, *Histoire de l'Ethiopie d'Axoum à la révolution*, Paris.

Berhanou Abebe, 2003, "Montages et truquages photographiques dans L'Ethiopie moderne (1915-1955)", *Annales d'Éthiopie*, 19, pp. 19-41.

De Castro, Lincoln, 1915, *Nella Terra dei Negus*, (R.S. Geografica Italiana), Milan: Fratelli Treves editori, 2 vols.

Gebre-Igziabiher Elyas, 1994, *Prowess, Piety and Politics, The Chronicle of Abeto Iyasu and Empress Zewditu of Ethiopia (1909-1930)*, Reidulf K. Molvaer, ed., Köln: Rüdiger Köppe Verlag.

Mérab, Paul, 1921-1929, *Impressions d'Ethiopie. L'Abyssinie sous Ménélik II*, Paris, 3 vols.

Montandon, Georges, 1913, *Au pays Ghimirra. Récit de mon voyage à travers le massif éthiopien (1909-1911)*, Neuchâtel.

Pankhurst, Richard, 1992, "The polical image: The impact of the camera in an ancient African state", in E. Edwards, ed., *Anthropology & Photography 1860-1920*, Yale University Press, pp. 234-41.

Pankhurst, Richard, 1981 "The history of Ethiopian-Armenian Relations (III): The late nineteenth an early twentieth century", *Revue des Etudes Arméniennes*, 15, pp. 355-400.

Sharf, F.A. and Pankhurst, R., 2004, *Letters from Abyssinia 1916 and 1917 by Majot Hugh Drummond Pearson*, Hollywood, California, Tsehai Publishers.

Smidt, Wolbert, 2001, "The coronation of negus Mikael in Dessie in May 1914: a photograph from the Nachlass Jansen and its historical background", *Annales d'Ethiopie*, 17, pp. 361-74

Thesiger, Wilfred, 1987, *The Life of my Choice*, New-York, London: W.W. Norton & Co.

Zischka, Anton, 1936, *Abissinia, Ultimo Problema Irresoluto dell'Africa*, Firenze, Sansoni.

Ydlibi, May, 2006, *With Ethiopian Rulers. A Biography of Hasib Ydlibi*, Addis Abeba University.

Zervos, Adrien, 1936, *L'empire d'Ethiopie. Le miroir de l'Ethiopie moderne 1906-1936,* Alexandrie.

Part III
Lij Iyasu's Foreign Relations

The foreign politics of *Lïj* Iyasu in 1915/16 according to newly discovered government papers

Wolbert G.C. Smidt

This paper discusses the administrative correspondence of the Ethiopian foreign minister Beyyene Yïmer, which covers the period from his nomination in December 1914 until early 1916. These documents are an extremely important source showing the government of a traditional polity on its way to modernisation. They allow most valuable insights into the functioning of the government of lïj Iyasu, whose reign is still largely unstudied and obscure, due to the lack of primary sources

Introduction

Recently the full administrative correspondence of *Qeñazmach* Beyyene Yïmer of 1915 until early 1916, then Foreign Minister of *Lïj* Iyasu's government, has been made accessible by his family.[1] This comprises very short letters (e.g. concerning the issuing of permits for foreigners travelling to the Ethiopian borders), but also detail correspondence regarding the minister's dealings with foreign powers. They are addressed to foreigners (mainly the ministers of the legations present at Addis Abeba), members of the government, *Lïj* Iyasu and his father *Nïgus* Mika'él.

The letters discuss questions concerning weapons import and other affairs related to World War I, conflicts with Europeans, who broke Ethiopian laws, the introduction of passports in Ethiopia and other measures of modernization, the establishment of an Ethiopian consulate in the Colonia Eritrea etc. These interesting documents, written in Amharic, permit a deep insight into the functioning of the government of Ethiopia,

---

1 The exact circumstances how these documents were preserved are not known to me. When the coup d'état against *Lïj* Iyasu took place on 16 Meskerem 1909 Ethiopian Calendar (27 September 1916), *i.e.* shortly after the Ethiopian New Year, *Qeñazmach* Beyyene was among those, who joined the putchists (see his name listed in the chronicle of Gebre-Igziabiher Elyas, 1994). His exact motives are not documented. Allegedly, Beyyene wanted to preserve his Ministry's documentation from destruction and was hiding these documents at home. I am extremely grateful for the fruitful discussions with Tadele Y. Tesemma and with Yasin Mohammed Yasin, who both greatly helped me in the understanding of the Amharic texts with their respective translations, and I very warmly thank Hailemelekot Agizew, who was the first to show me these documents. I also thank the family deeply for making these documents accessible.

only eight years after its formal establishment by Emperor Mïnilïk II.[2] They also shed a new light on the foreign politics of Ethiopia during World War I and help us understanding better the largely mis-perceived government of *Lïj* Iyasu. The documents are an extremely important source showing the government of a traditional polity on its way to modernisation. The following paragraphs discuss some of the aspects of modern Ethiopian history, to which these documents contribute new insights.

A number of legends, which had been spread by Iyasu's enemies, do not find confirmation at least by these documents. The documents do not suggest any preparation of war-alliance with Germany and Turkey against the other powers (but confirm good relations with their representatives); there is no sign for a conversion of *Lïj* Iyasu to Islam;[3] also the alleged disorder of government, so dramatically underlined especially by the French and British ministers, does not find any ground in this primary source. This shows that we have to treat the widely believed allegations at least with some degree of skepticism. While other sources show close strategic relations of Iyasu with Germany and Turkey in the context of World War I (see the contribution by Haggai Erlich), and also his strategical and personal closeness to Islam, these papers show that those tendencies were only one element of his politics and personality, while the Ethiopian Ministry of Foreign Affairs continued to function on the basis of the well-established bureaucracy which did not get involved into these – rather personal? – leanings.

Technical remarks

The handwritten manuscript, which has more than one hundred pages, bears no title. It contains the handwritten copies of 312 documents, mostly letters, which are separated from each other by the naming of an addressee in the beginning and the naming of the sender and (in most of the cases) a date at the end. Most documents are letters which had been written by the Foreign Minister *Qeñazmach* Beyyene to other members of the government, to *Lïj* Iyasu and his father, *Nïgus* Mika'él, and to foreign diplomats. There are, however, also copies of other letters, e.g. letters from foreign diplomats to *Lïj* Iyasu or his father, and very few notes on telephone messages and oral communications. This shows that it is the official proceedings of the Foreign Minister himself, containing the quasi-totality of his official correspondence. Such proceedings are not known from previous ministers. Probably the beginning of the exact

2 *Atsé* Mïnilïk II established a government following the European model in 1907, nominating ministers of justice, interior, foreign affairs etc.

3 For a discussion of the background of Iyasu's alleged conversion to Islam, used in the coup d'état of 1916 against him, see Finke (2007) - with new information based on Turkish sources -, Rubinkowska (2005:1081), Smidt (2007-2008), Id. (2007a).

documentation of government letters predates this manuscript, but it seems probable that this administrative measure had been introduced only with the introduction of ministries by Emperor Mïnilïk in 1907 or slightly later.[4]

The paging is quite disturbed, so that documents dated to quite different periods directly follow each other. In some cases a document, which starts at the end of one page, is not continued on the next page, and - vice versa - the beginning of some documents is missing on some pages. These incomplete documents do not pose a major problem, however, as in most cases the missing part can be found somewhere in the manuscript. Document number 102 (containing the beginning of the text), for example, is completed by document number 282 (containing the end of the text). The period covered by the documents ranges from the 4 Tahsas 1907 Ethiopian Calendar (document number 46, date of the nomination of *Qeñazmach* Beyyene Yïmer as Minister of Foreign Affairs) until 11 Yekkatit 1908 Ethiopian Calendar (document number 221), i.e. about 14 Ethiopian months (if we count P'agumen as a month). In European terms this means the period between 13 December 1914 and 18 February 1916.[5] A few documents randomly bear dates outside this time range, but this is evidently due to mistakes in the writing.

The reconstruction of the original order of the documents will take some time. After a first trial to reconstruct it, it seems to me that a part of the original pages are lost (e.g. most documents dated to Yekkatit 1907 are missing), but that the greatest part of the Minister's letters are preserved. It is still unclear, if the manuscript is a secondary (later) copy of the Minister's collection of letters or if it had been produced during his time as Minister, in his Ministry.

Iyasu and government affairs

Qeñazmach Beyyene was nominated Minister of Foreign Affairs by *Lï'ul lïj alga werash* Iyasu *weldu le dagmawi* Mïnilïk *Nïguse negest ze'Ityop'ya* ('Highly [or His Highness] Prince Iyasu, heir-to-the-throne, son of Mïnilïk II, king of kings of Ethiopia') on 4 Tahsas 1907 (i.e., 13 December 1914). The documentation starts with Iyasu's official announcement to the foreign legations of Beyyene's nomination, in which it is stated that all the contacts between the foreign and Ethiopian governments should pass through him (document no. 46, originally being the first document in the collection). The second document in the collection (no. 47) is Beyyene's own announcement of his

4 The memories of the Christian Syrian merchant Ydlibi contain some interesting details on his role in the modernisation of the government's administration; it might well be that the introduction of proceedings, i.e. the exact documentation of records following the example of merchants, is based on an advise given by him (Ydlibi, 2006).

5 This means that the documentation stops more than seven months before the coup d'état against *Lïj* Iyasu. We do not know what happened to the ministry's proceedings covering the period between 18 February 1916 and 27 September 1916. They might have been destroyed during the coup d'état.

appointment to the same legations. The addressees are (in this order) Brice, the French minister plenipotentiary, von Syburg, the German minister plenipotentiary, conte Colli di Felizzano, the Italian minister plenipotentiary, Vinogradoff, the chargé d'affaires of the Russian legation (of the "Moskob" government), and Doughty Wylie ("David"), British chargé d'affaires.

The full title of *Lïj* Iyasu – as mentioned above – repeatedly appears in these documents. This is also interesting, as historiography until now has not mentioned this title. It contributes an interesting slight modification to the title normally used in historiography, *Lïj* ('Infant', 'Prince') or *Abéto* ('Prince').[6] Often it is assumed that the term " *lï'ul* " was only added to princely Ethiopian titles starting from the reign of Hayle Sïllasé; the documents presented here, however, show the abundant usage of it in the official titulature of Iyasu.[7] While keeping the unambitious title of *Lïj* (thus confirming his own minority and the superiority of his father, *Nïgus* Mika'él), the addition of *lï'ul* ('high') clearly underlines his primary position, elevating him above all the other princes. There are a number of variants of the usage of the term *lï'ul* when Iyasu is addressed by Beyyene and other notables of his government. It often appears, most of the time as *Lï'ul Lïj* (e.g., no. 37, 175), sometimes only *Lï'ul* (no. 61, 108), and also as *Lï'ul Gétayé* ('my high master', no. 20).

We can now also conclude that the historical rumour that Iyasu did call himself *Nïguse negest ze Ityop'ya* ('king of kings of Ethiopia') does not have any basis. The origin of the rumour is clear: it is based on the misreading of his full title and name, which includes the formula 'son of Mïnilïk II, king of kings of Ethiopia'. The rumour, however, is not without any reason. When Iyasu refers to Mïnilïk, he does not simply construct a genealogy, but indirectly also claims succession. Also the fact that the full title and name ends with *Nïguse negest ze'Ityop'ya* bears this connotation; that he does not claim to already bear the title at present, however, is underlined by the term *Alga Werash*, 'heir-to-the-throne'. It is important in this context, that Emperor Mïnilïk does appear himself in the documents, too (e.g., no. 153 speaking of *Janhoy*, 'Majesty', referring to him, not to Iyasu). One document speaks of the Emperor's birthday celebration on 12 *Nehasé* 1907, as if the Mïnilïk was still alive (no. 89). In fact, the documents support the impression that even in 1915 Iyasu maintained the official version that he reigned in the name of his (sick) grandfather. Even if references to Mïnilïk are extremely rare, his death is virtually inexistent in these documents.[8] When

6 As in the chronicle of Gebre-Igziabiher Elyas, 1994.

7 The title *Lï'ul Lïj* had already been used by him at least starting from 1913, see another document published by me (Smidt, 2007b).

8 Even if both foreigners and Ethiopian nobles heard of Mïnilïk's death already in December 1913 (Marcus, 1995: 261), this was not officially announced; the first official announcement of Mïnilïk's death was done only in 1916, on the occasion of the coup d'état. One has very much attacked Iyasu for the secrecy he built around his grandfather's death; the exact reasons for this still need thorough historical study. It is clear, however, that it should not be linked with his youthful arrogance and irresponsibility, as the putchists claimed in 1916 (in

one of Mïnilïk's "famous horses" died, it was announced as an important event (evidently considered as a sad affair, no. 305).

Many of the letters are addressed to Iyasu, to whom Beyyene regularly reports on affairs of the ministry. However, Iyasu evidently did not direct the government affairs very actively. But the documents do not suggest that any disorder resulted out of it, they rather suggest that the government, lead by Prime Minister Hayle Giyorgis, functioned on a very orderly basis, based on regular contacts among the ministers and government employees, and with Iyasu and his father.

Relations with foreigners and foreign powers

The documents are of greatest importance especially as they reflect Ethiopia's position during World War I. Ethiopia, in fact, never officially participated in the war, which is perfectly confirmed by this documentation. Through its foreign ministry, Ethiopia maintained both formal and cordial relations to all diplomats present at Addis Abeba. Through the reports on specific events, one can sense the tensions in the region, and the efforts of the Ethiopian government to reduce such tensions to a minimum, not to endanger its relations with its neighbours. And, above all, there is not the slightest sign for a formal or informal alliance with the German or Ottoman government, through their envoys, neither any evidence for a formal conversion of *Lïj* Iyasu to Islam.

To start with the latter: The Ottoman consul, who is indeed one of the active correspondents of the ministry, himself sends a congratulation message to the Christian Christmas celebrations to Iyasu (no. 270, 29 Tahsas 1908). All the other letters written by him to Iyasu or to the ministry treat matters of diplomacy (e.g., his condoleances for the death of *Nïgus* Mika'él's grandson Hayle Maryam, no. 93) or administrative matters concerning Ottoman subjects (e.g., no. 291 an exchange of notes concerning an arrested Ottoman citizen, or no. 275, debts left by the Turkish citizen Sarkis Terzian, an Armenian, no. 275). Only in one context World War I appears: Armenians, often regarded as Ottoman citizens, are mentioned as enlisting themselves as volunteers (no. 92).

Cross-border raids and conflicts were a problem for the maintenance of peace in the situation of a world war. The Ethiopian government tried to diminish effects of a great raid undertaken by a Tïgrayan local governor near the Tekkeze river. That noble had destroyed a bridge connecting Ethiopia with Eritrea, collected taxes in Eritrea and killed many locals during his raid. The government strongly warned him having damaged the good relations between "the two countries", and simultaneously let the Italian side know of the friendly intentions of the Ethiopian government (no. 286,

order to add one more point to their catalogue of deadly sins), but rather with an idea of a smooth transition of power when the best moment presented itself, both pragmatically and symbolically.

similar no. 217, 218). Other cross-border raids are mentioned with similar concern, like over the "French border" (into today's Djibouti, no. 223), and the killing of a Sudanese guard in Gallabat, against which the British minister protested (no. 286). There is also a British consul in Boorana (no. 279). The problem of ʿAfar territory annexed by France is discussed (no. 219). An Ethiopian consul is established in Asmera, Eritrea, who had to both maintain good relations with the Italian government and deal with problems relating to Italian subjects (no. 121, 204) - thus continuing the tradition of Ethiopian consuls established in Asmera since the time of Mïnilïk II. His reports to the Foreign Ministry are written in a secret code (no. 245). The culmination of cross-border relations in the positive sense is the official visit of *Lïj* Iyasu of Djibouti, followed by the decoration of the French governor by Iyasu (no. 274). Even if details of discussions with the foreign counterparts can often only be detected indirectly, one can conclude that the greatest efforts of the ministry lied on the (a) protection of Ethiopian interests (both economic and questions related to Ethiopian sovereignty), (b) the maintenance of good relations with all the countries involved in the region.

International treaties are mentioned on several occasions (e.g. no. 171). A great preoccupation of the ministry is the maintenance of treaties, both economic and political, and their respect by the European powers. The British minister is reminded, that the Ethiopian government possesses a monopoly in telegram services and is asked to explain himself why he established his own telegram services without prior permission by the Ethiopian government (no. 295). Discussing a treaty with France, the Ethiopian ministry underlines that the Ethiopian government fully owns the salt in the country (no. 258, the salt monopoly of the Ethiopian government is also mentioned in no. 21).

A delicate aspect was the delivery of weapons, which is to be seen in the context of World War I. Weapons trade is repeatedly mentioned in the letters. The French weapons trader Savouré ("*Musé* Saburé") has organised the delivery of Russian weapons to Ethiopia (no. 292), but there are many complaints about the quality of the "Moskob" guns. The Russian chargé d'affaires is even asked to explain the great percentage of non-working guns (no. 151, 157). Even if weapons, therefore, play a role in the correspondences, there is not the slightest hint to their planned use in the war. No conclusion, that a direct participation in the war was prepared, can be drawn from these documents.

A great part of the ministry's correspondence deals with the issuing of passports and pass permits. The ministry discusses with foreign legations to introduce standardized passports, following the European system (no. 146). There is already a degree of standardisation introduced in the course of the work - a pass permit contains detailed descriptions of the travelling persons (no. 300). The documentation is a rich source for the journeys undertaken by foreigners in Ethiopia; especially "postmen" of the foreign legations were regularly sent to the border, with gunmen accompanying them. The

British Legation often sends messengers to Moyale in Boorana. The person issuing these pass permits is the Minister of Justice and Interior T'ïlahun; every time when a pass permit for a foreigner (or an Ethiopian working for a legation) is needed, the Minister of Foreign Affairs writes to him, asking for issuing the permit (e.g., no. 302, 306). It is interesting, that neither the German nor the Ottoman legation were sending such messengers - both legations being isolated from the contact with their respective governments because of the war; the surrounding territories were controlled by the allies. It is also interesting to note, that the case of the pass permits illustrates well two typical features of the government of that period: (a) Even if the proceedings were not very formalized and detailed (no bureaucratic forms to be filled in!), one has to note (b) that the ministry was routinely doing its work, assuming the normal functions of a ministry responsible for contacts with foreigners and foreign diplomats.

Nïgus Mika'él - a virtual co-regent

A historically interesting result of these documents' analysis is *Nïgus* Mika'él's central position in the state as a de facto co-regent. Officially, as we know, *Lïj* Iyasu refused to appoint a new regent in 1911, after the regent's death, *Ras* Tesemma, who also was his personal tutor (cp. Marcus 1987:11-21; Marcus 1995:270). This was often interpreted as a sign for his unwillingness to accept anyone above himself, and a lack of maturity. These documents, however, show that *Nïgus* Mika'él had assumed an important role in the administration of the government. It might, therefore, be appropriate to partially change the vision of Iyasu's refusal of 1911. In case he had accepted another regent (not foreseen by Mïnilïk) this would also have meant the reduction of his own father's influence in government affairs.

The then *Ras* Mika'él could not officially claim the regency for himself, given his marginal position as a converted Muslim and leader of Wello of Oromo origin. The refusal to nominate a new regent therefore would mean an increase in his influence, and even more, give him the possibility to act as a "hidden" regent where deemed necessary by him. This is confirmed by the upgrading of Mika'él's rank from *Ras* to *Nïgus* ('king') a few months only after Emperor Mïnilïk's death, in May 1914 in Desé, Wello. His new rank was accompanied by the formal transmission of the supreme power over Tïgray (with the title of king of "Tsïyon" = 'Zion' = Aksum Tsïyon, i.e. the religious centre of the Empire and simultaneously standing for the government of Ethiopia itself),[9] the transfer of the imperial crown to Desé and, probably later (see Rubinkowska - Smidt 2007), the inclusion of Gojjam and Gonder (Begémdïr) into his title.[10]

9 The symbolic reference of the title "king of Zion" was understandable for the Ethiopian public in that time - only one generation before, *Atsé* Yohannïs IV had called himself "king of S'ïyon" (a title inscribed on his seals), when he first claimed the government of Ethiopia.

10 A detailed discussion of this coronation and its implications see in Smidt (2007-2008); see also Smidt, 2001.

The documents of *Qeñazmach* Beyyene do not show any trace of a formal nomination of Mika'él as a regent. This was evidently not necessary, given his formal power over his son as his "natural" tutor while he was still a minor.[11] The most clear confirmation of *Nïgus* Mika'él's position lies in the fact, that Beyyene shortly after his nomination insisted that Mika'él's formal approval of his nomination as Foreign Minister be sent to him (document no. 5, dated 25 Tahsas 1907): This letter is addressed to hakim Werqïneh (also known as "Dr. Martin"), and Beyyene asks him to let him know by telegram when he could expect the formal approval of his nomination by *Nïgus* Mika'él.

The titles used to address Mika'él in these documents are regularly *Nïgus*, but also sometimes *Nïguse Tsïyon* ('king of Zion', no. 117, to be printed in gold: no. 147) and *Nïguse Wello weTïgré* ('king of Wello and Tïgray', no. 22). This shows, that he did not claim formal jurisdiction over Gojjam and Gonder still in 1915.

Qeñazmach Beyyene reports to him, not as regularly as to Iyasu himself, but still on a constant basis. Apart from the other ministers and government employees, foreign diplomats and Iyasu he is the only addressee of the letters not falling into the former categories (no letter is addressed to any other grand noble of the Empire who is not directly involved in the government - except one to Teferi, concerning a great affair in which he seemingly refused obeyance to the government).[12] In a few cases Mika'él's decision is required - or at least his involvement - in delicate political affairs. This is the case in the highly sensitive affair of Friedrich Hall (alias *Ato* Solomon), a half-cast Ethio-German envoy and spy sent by the German government to Ethiopia during World War I in 1915. Hall, who perfectly spoke Arabic, German, Amharic and other languages, was sent by the German government to transport messages and money to the Ethiopian government, with the aim to win Ethiopia over to the German side in World War I. Hall, however, got arrested in Eritrea and never reached Ethiopia. Document no. 180 (18 Meggabit 1907) mentions that the letter which he wishes to be sent to the Ethiopian leadership, should be delivered to *Nïgus* Mika'él.

Other letters shows, that Mika'él could use the services of the Ethiopian government. The Minister of Post Tesemma Ïsheté is, for example, involved in the delivery of a letter of him (no. 76). In the whole, one can sense his high position as a power behind the official ruler, Iyasu, even if the documents do not contain information on political decisions taken by him. This is a general feature of these documents: They often rather contain formalities, formal details, the real decisions being discussed orally. The approach to decipher Mika'él's position through his formal

11 A photograph of 1914/15 shows Iyasu in a symbolic position which is underlining this relationship, with his head on the knees of his father, and Mïnilïk's crown besides them, Pankhurst - Gérard (1996).

12 This concerned the conflict between the Ethiopian government official Ydlibi in Harer and Dirré Dawa and Europeans (cp. Ydlibi, 2006), Teferi siding with the Europeans; because of the implication of Europeans, the foreign ministry was involved (no. 240, 241).

appearance in the letters, as a repeated addressee, as co-responsible for the Minister's nomination, as "king of Zion", however, allows to detect his central role in the state.

Bibliography

Aby Demissie, 1964, *Lij Iyasu: A Perspective Study of His Short Reign*, B.A. thesis, History Department, Haile Sellassie I University, Addis Ababa.

Bahru Zewde, 1991, *A History of Modern Ethiopia 1855-1974*, Addis Ababa.

Bahru Zewde, 2007, "Iyasu", in Siegbert Uhlig (ed.), *Encyclopaedia Aethiopica*, Vol. 3, Wiesbaden, Harrassowitz.

Bartnicki, Andrzej – Mantel-Niećko, Joanna, 1978, *Geschichte Äthiopiens* (ed.), by Renate Richter, tr. by Waldemar Hein, Berlin.

Berhanou Abebe, 1998, *Histoire de l'Ethiopie d'Axoum à la révolution*, Paris, Maisonneuve & Larose.

Berhanou Abebe, 2001, "Le Coup d'Etat du 2 septembre 1916", *Annales d'Ethiopie*, 17, 322-325.

Ficquet, Eloi, 2002, Du barbare au mystique: Anthropologie historique des recompositions identitaires et religieuses dans le Wello (Ethiopie centrale), Ph.D. thesis, EHESS, Paris.

Ficquet, Eloi, 2007, "Mammädočč dynasty", in: Siegbert Uhlig, ed., *Encyclopaedia Aethiopica*, Vol. 3, Wiesbaden, Harrassowitz.

Finke, Detlef, 2007, "Mazhar bey, Ahmed", in Siegbert Uhlig, ed., *Encyclopaedia Aethiopica*, Vol. 3, Wiesbaden, Harrassowitz.

Fusella, Luigi, 1987, "Le Biografie del blattengeta Heruy Walda Sellase (= *yehïywet tarik*, Addis Abeba 1915 A.M. = 1922/23)", *Rassegna di Studi Etiopici XXX, 1984-1986*, published 1987, 15-52.

Gebre-Igziabiher Elyas & Molvaer, Reidulf (transl., ed.), 1994, *Prowess, Piety and Politics: The Chronicle of Abeto Iyasu and Empress Zewditu of Ethiopia (1909-1930)*, Köln, Rüdiger Köppe Verlag (*Studien zur Kulturkunde*, 104)

Gobezé T'afet'e (Gobezé Taffete), 1996, *Abba T'éna Iyasu*, Addis-Abeba, Maison des Etudes Ethiopiennes.

Haile Sellassie I, 1976, *The Autobiography of Emperor Haile Sellassie: 'My Life and Ethiopia's Progress', 1892-1937*, transl., annot. by Edward Ullendorff, Oxford, Oxford University Press.

Kebbede Tesemma, 1969-70, *Yetarik mastawesha* ('Historical Memoirs'), Addis Abeba 1962 A.M. [1969/70 A.D.].

Leslau, Wolf, 1987, *Comparative Dictionary of Geez: Geez - English, English – Geez*, Wiesbaden, Harrassowitz.

Marcus, Harold, 1995, *The Life and Times of Menelik II, Ethiopia 1844-1913*, 2nd ed., Lawrenceville, NJ.

Marcus, Harold, 1987, *Haile Sellassie I, the Formative Years, 1892–1936*, Berkeley, CA.

Mersé Hazen Wolde Qirqos, 2004, *Of What I Saw and Heard: the Last Years of Emperor Menelik II & the Brief Rule of Iyassu*, Addis Abeba, CFEE.

Morin, Didier, 1999, *Le texte légitime, Pratiques littéraires orales traditionnelles en Afrique du nord-est*, Paris, Peeters (Langues et cultures africaines, 25), 260 (cf. translation pp. 78-79)

Nosseir Abdul-Halim Elias, 1928, *Ityopya, Les Richesses de l'Ethiopie*, Nancy, 235-40.

Pankhurst, Richard & Gérard, Denis, 1996, *Ethiopia photographed, historic photographs of the country and its people taken between 1867 and 1935*, London / New York, Kegan Paul International

Prouty, Chris, 1996, *Empress Taytu and Menilek II. Ethiopia 1883-1910*, London – Trenton NJ.

Rubinkowska, Hanna, 2005, "Coup d'état 1916", In Siegbert Uhlig (ed.), *Encyclopaedia Aethiopica*, Vol. 2, Wiesbaden: Harrassowitz, 1081 [Corrigendum of vol. 1].

Rubinkowska, Hanna – Smidt, Wolbert G.C., 2007, "Mika'el Ali", in Siegbert Uhlig (ed.), *Encyclopaedia Aethiopica*, Wiesbaden, Harrassowitz.

Smidt, Wolbert G.C., 2001, "The coronation of negus Mikael in Desse in May 1914: A photograph from the Nachlass Jensen and its historical background", *Annales d'Éthiopie*, 17, 359-371.

Smidt, Wolbert G.C., 2005a, "Gaš'", in Siegbert Uhlig (ed.), *Encyclopaedia Aethiopica*, vol. 2 (D-Ha), Wiesbaden, Harrassowitz Verlag, 710-12.

Smidt, Wolbert G.C., 2005b, *Ethiopia and Germany, 100 Years Diplomatic relations - Äthiopien und Deutschland, 100 Jahre diplomatische Beziehungen*, Addis Abeba, Goethe-Institut Addis Abeba – Deutsche Botschaft Addis Abeba.

Smidt, Wolbert G.C., 2007a, "Menilek Iyasu", in Siegbert Uhlig (ed.), *Encyclopaedia Aethiopica*, vol. 3, Wiesbaden, Harrassowitz.

Smidt, Wolbert G.C., 2007b, "Ein erster Beleg für den Titel le'ul unter leǧ Iyasu", *Aethiopica*, 10, 194-98.

Smidt, Wolbert G.C., 2007-2008, "The coronation of negus Mikael, king of Wollo and Tigray, in May 1914: New findings", *Annales d'Éthiopie*, 23, 413-34.

T'elahun Berhane Sellase, 2003-04, *Ye20ñaw kïfle zemen Ityop'ya, andeña mes'hafu (1900 ïske 1966 A.M.)* ('Ethiopia in the 20th century, vol. 1: From 1900 to 1966 Ethiopian Calendar'), Addis Abeba 1996 `A.M. [= 2003/04 A.D.].

Tornay, Serge & Sohier, Estelle, 2007, *Empreintes du temps, Les sceaux des dignitaires éthiopiens du règne de Téwodros à la régence de Teferi Mäkonnen*. Addis Abeba, CFEE.

Tornay, Serge, 2006, "A Hundred and One Pictures of Ethiopian Royal and Noblemen's Seals Collected by the French Consul Boucoiran: A New Document in Sigillography from the Time of Tewodros to the 1920s", in Siegbert Uhlig (ed.), *Proceedings of the XVth International Conference of Ethiopian Studies Hamburg July 20-25*, 2003, Wiesbaden, Harrassowitz, 496-506.

Ydlibi, May, 2006, *With Ethiopian Rulers: a Biography of Hasib Ydlibi*, ed. by Bahru Zewde, Addis Ababa.

Zewde Retta, 2004-05, *Teferi Mek^{w}ennïn režïmu yešïlṭan guzo beMïnilïk be'iyasunna bezewditu zemen 1884-1922* ('Teferi Mek^{w}ennïn, the long journey to power, from the periods of Mïnilïk, Iyasu to Zewditu, 1884-1922'), Addis Abeba 1997 A.M. [2004/05 A.D.].

Lïj Iyasu, the Austro-Hungarian Honorary Consul in Addis Abeba and the Cannon Deal of 1914

Rudolf Agstner

From Austro-Hungarian – Ethiopian Treaty of 1905 to I & R Austro-Hungarian Consulate Addis Abeba 1912

On 7 March 1905, an extraordinary Imperial German Mission to Abyssinia, headed by Friedrich Rosen[1], concluded a German-Ethiopian Treaty of Friendship and Commerce, establishing diplomatic relations between the two states.[2]

Two weeks later, on 21 March, it was the turn of Austria-Hungary. Ludwig Ritter von Höhnel, captain of HMS Panther, a small cruiser, had been dispatched with an official mission to Ethiopia. In order to assure its success, Emperor Franz Joseph on 30 December 1904 had resolved to bestow upon Emperor Mïnilïk II the Grand Cross of the Order of St. Stephen, whereas *Ras* Mekonnïn was to receive the Order of the Iron Crown 1st Class, and Alfred Ilg the Grand Cross of the Order of Franz-Joseph. The delegation came with numerous gifts – which clearly indicate the intention to promote exports of war material to Ethiopia - to be presented to Emperor Mïnilïk II and Empress T'aytu[3], among them a mountain cannon M.99 with ammunition and a book with illustrations of Austro-Hungarian troops. *Ras* Mekonnïn was inter alia to receive 12 Mannlicher rifles with 5000 rounds of ammunition.[4]

After several technical delays, the Austro-Hungarian mission arrived in Addis Abeba, where on 21 March 1905 a "Treaty of Friendship and Commerce" was signed by Emperor Mïnilïk II and Captain Höhnel.[5]

---

1 See Rosen (1907).

2 See Gehring-Münzel (2007).

3 Bieber (1948) showing a photo of a steamroller, "a present of Emperor Franz Joseph I to Mïnilïk II, opposite p. 90, suggests that the presents included the first steamroller in Ethiopia. This version has to be regarded as fairy tale, as the files make no mention of any steamroller. The first steamroller had at around the same time been imported by two Armenian businessmen; the streamroller was repaired by Saxon Willy Hentze, who had set up the Austrian minting machine in Emperor Mïnilïk's mint. This probably led to the impression that Austria-Hungary had somehing to do with the steamroller.

4 For a complete list of presents see Agstner (2004).

5 *Imperial Legal Gazette* (*Reichsgesetzblatt / RGBl.*), 206/1910 of 26 November 1910.

Fig. 1: Presentation of the M.99 cannon to Emperor Mïnïlk II

Fig. 2: M.99 cannon in front of Adwa district administration office

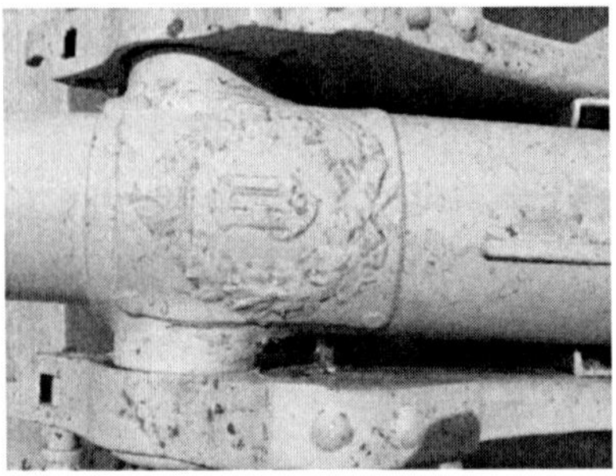

Fig. 3: M.99 cannon in front of Adwa district administration office; detail showing the plaque with the Austrian imperial crown and initials "FJI"

On 19 March 1905, a demonstration of the Austrian cannon took place outside Addis Abeba in the presence of Emperor Mïnilïk II and his court. Höhnel had the cannon fire at a cliff in 2 to 3 kms distance. Three shots of shrapnel were fired, and the emperor was not impressed and rather disappointed, as a shrapnel explodes in the air, a kind of precursor to modern cluster bombs. Höhnel then had the cannon fire on a tree 2500 m distant; using different ammunition, and the tree vanished after three shots. When Höhnel asked Emperor Mïnilïk for new instructions where to fire, the emperor flatly rejected – he wanted to keep the remaining precious ammunition (Höhnel 1926: 283-284).

Hopes that Ethiopia would buy M.99 mountain cannons did not materialize. Nine years later, Ethiopia's ruler *Lïj* Iyasu, however, opted for another type of Austrian cannon.

The M.99 cannon later was taken to ʿAdwa and placed in a little park in front of the ʿAdwa Woreda (district) Administrative Office, a few meters from a monument to Awʿalom, a warrior who played a leading role in the battle of ʿAdwa, where it still stands, although regrettably in a rather dilapidated state. Left and right Italian cannons are placed. The Austrian cannon, painted in grey, bears the following inscription: "k.u.k. Artill. 7 FAR // 231 // Art. Arsenal Wien", and the following technical specifications: "7 cm M.99 No. 79 1902 115". A plaque "FJI", reading "Franz Joseph I" or "Franciscus Josephus

Imperator", with the imperial Austrian crown, can be seen on the gun barrel.[6] Starting in 1902, the mountain cannon M.99 was delivered to the Austro-Hungarian artillery. By then, the cannon was already outdated. The M.99 cannons were mainly produced in the artillery-arsenal of Vienna, as the gun-barrelfoundry was specialized in the production of "steel-bronze" made barrels system "Uchatius".[7] At the start of World War I the M.99 mountain cannon was totally obsolete; it was replaced by the mountain cannon M.15.

It is not clear why this imperial present is now displayed in ʿAdwa, as it obviously has nothing to do with the 1896 Battle of ʿAdwa.

Unfortunately the Austrian part of the Monarchy had forgotten to inform the Hungarian part of the Monarchy and obtain Budapest's approval of the "Treaty of Friendship and Commerce", which led to a considerable delay in the process of ratification. It was on 24 May 1909 only that the treaty was ratified by Emperor Franz Joseph. Vienna was in no hurry to inform the Ethiopian side thereof. In February 1910 only, the Italian minister in Addis Abeba, who looked after the Austro-Hungarian interests in Ethiopia, forwarded the Austro-Hungarian instrument of ratification to Ethiopian Foreign Minister *Neggadras* Yïggezu. More than five years and four months after its conclusion, the treaty finally entered into force on 4 August 1910. By then, Austrian and Hungarian business circles had almost lost interest in trade relations with Ethiopia. Valuable time had been wasted, and the fact that Italy continued to take care of Austro-Hungarian interests in Ethiopia was not too helpful to promote trade relations between Ethiopia and Austria-Hungary.

Article III of the treaty of 21 March 1905 had opened the possibility to establish an Austro-Hungarian consulate in Addis Abeba. The idea to appoint a civil servant as Imperial & Royal consul became victim of the usual disagreement between Vienna and Budapest concerning the budget of the two common ministries, i.e. foreign affairs and war. In 1906 Alphons Baron Mylius[8] applied for the post of Austro-Hungarian honorary consul in Addis Abeba. The Foreign Ministry, "in view of our commercial interests in Ethiopia"[9], was in favour, and the Imperial Austrian and the Royal Hungarian trade ministries gave their consent. Yet nothing happened.

In 1907, Emperor Mïnilïk II dispatched a mission to Berlin and Vienna to reciprocate the German and the Austro-Hungarian missions of 1905. As far as Austria-

6 The author, following information by Professor emeritus Dr. Wolfgang Hahn, Institute of Numismatics, University of Vienna, and accompanied by Ato Grebremedhin Kidane, saw the cannon on 17 April 2009.

7 Franz Baron Uchatius, * Theresienfeld/Lower Austria 20 October 1811, † Vienna 4 June 1881 (suicide); Fieldmarshal-Lieutenant; in 1874 invented the "Uchatius-steelbronze" for cannons.

8 * Unterhaus (Styria, Austria) 4 May 1875, † Stochod (Russia) 18 August 1916 (killed in action); participated in the Höhnel mission of 1905.

9 HHStA, Administrative Registry (AR), Dept. 8, Box 60, Addis Abeba, Foreign Ministry 1837/1906 of 18 January 1906 to Austrian and Hungarian trade ministries.

Hungary was concerned, the mission yielded no result apart from several gifts to Emperor Franz Joseph, which found their way into Vienna's Museum of Ethnology.

In 1910 Friedrich Julius Bieber, who in 1909 again had travelled in Ethiopia, regretted that:

> *"Austria-Hungary is the only European major power neither represented diplomatically nor even by a consul. This is all the more regrettable, as the leading circles in Addis Abeba view Austria as an altruistic friend, who does not endanger the Ethiopian sphere of power by her colonial aspirations. On the contrary, Austria would, in the view of the court of Addis Abeba, be called upon to assist Ethiopia in political and economic fields[...] Germany, which entered into relations with Ethiopia far later than we, has already for a long time surpassed us. It is once again the old story"* (Bieber 1910: 438-40).

By letter of 21 January 1911 Louis Francis Kaden[10] suggested establishing an Austro-Hungarian consulate in Harer and applied for the post of I.&R. honorary consul. Kaden was the representative in Harer of the Vienna-based firm Alois Schweiger & Co[11]:

> *"Harrar, seat of a governor of princely blood, unites the elite of the most important merchants. The most important European, Indian and Arabic firms have their headquarters in Harrar. As an Austrian, I am on excellent terms with the Abyssinian dignitaries and am well respected. In general, the Austrian enjoys more confidence than other nations, the reason being, that it is known that Austria only has commercial interests [...]"*[12]

Kaden's application was not taken into consideration by Vienna. In 1911, and again in 1912 the idea to appoint Erich Weinzinger I.&R. honorary consul in Ethiopia came up. Weinzinger had studied Amharic languages at the Ecole des Langues Orientales in Paris, with a subsidy from the Austro-Hungarian Foreign Ministry, and later spent some time in Harer, where he taught French to *Ras* Teferi Mekonnïn. The idea was not followed up either. Instead, a third candidate of dubious qualifications but with excellent connections to *Lïj* Iyasu, successor to the throne, appeared.

---

10 * Vienna 1866, † Harar 1929, Turkish Honorary Consul in Harrar 1910-1912 (communication by Ambassador Can Altan) and German Honorary Consul in Harrar 1912-1917 (*Verzeichnis der kaiserlich deutschen Konsulate*, Berlin, Mai 1913, p. 3; communication by Dr. Ludwig Biewer, Political Archive, German Foreign Office, Berlin)

11 Alois Schweiger & Co., Import–Export, Vienna IX, Berggasse 7; "Export to India, China, and Japan, Import of „natural products"; branch offices in Hamburg, Milan, Manchester, Bombay, Bangkok, Calcutta, Kurachee and Shanghai.

12 HHStA, AR, Dept. 8, Box 136, letter Kaden, Harrar of 21 January 1911.

Karl Schwimmer - businessman and I. & R. Honorary Austro – Hungarian Consul

In September of 1912, Karl Schwimmer[13], a Hungarian citizen, self-styled "head of the press office of the Foreign Office in Addis Abeba", arrived in Vienna to hand over a letter by *Lïj* Iyasu as well as gifts to Emperor Franz Joseph. He was received on 26 September 1912 at 10 a.m. in Schönbrunn Palace by the Emperor.[14]

The gifts, about which the Viennese press reported extensively, included a lion, "a golden ceremonial shield" and "two silver lancets". The shield, which was presented by Mr. Schwimmer, "*is made of pure gold and shows the characteristic Abyssinian ornaments in filigree work. The lancets are wound with silver wire and show several ornaments in elaborate silver.*[15] *The lion, which was visited by the Emperor on the morning of 24 September in the Schönbrunn Zoo, is nine month old and has been caught by Shankalla negroes* (sic !) *in Wollega in Western Abyssinia and brought to Addis Abeba. The donation of a lion is a particular honour which so far was only bestowed upon the Tsar of Russia and the King of Italy* [...]"[16]

On 11 October 1912 Karl Schwimmer formally applied for the post of I.&R. Austro-Hungarian honorary consul in Addis Abeba:

> *"My experience in the Ethiopian Empire is based on a stay of close to three years in Addis Abeba.... My connections to the government and its leading personalities made it possible to negotiate and conclude contracts with the government in a big way. As proof of this I merely mention, that I recently succeeded to conclude and successfully carry through a major arms deal on behalf of the German government* [...]" [17]

The Ethiopian gifts, presently kept in the depot of the Museum of Ethnology in Vienna, called for a gift in return. Prince *Lïj* Iyasu was, by Imperial resolution of 7 November 1912, to receive a "*mountain cannon*[18] *with harnessing for mules and ammunition, a gift which would be particularly appreciated by the successor to the throne*", and the Grand Cross of the Austrian Order of St. Leopold. The Ethiopian minister for Foreign Affairs and Trade, *Neggadras* Hayle Giyorgis[19] was to be decorated by the Grand Cross of the Order of Franz Joseph, while Schwimmer was awarded the Order of the Iron Crown IIIrd Class.[20]

---

13 * Ujvidék/Neusatz/Novi Sad 1 February 1879, † ?; lived in Vienna from 1917 to 1939, moved to Budapest on 28 March 1939; son of Jakob Schwimmer, a contractor who supplied horses to the Austro-Hungarian army's cavalry. In 1906 he married in Stuttgart the daughter of German merchant Karl Stock.

14 HHStA, Neue Zeremonialakten, Box 311, R XIV, Audienzen etc. 1911–1912, 26. Sept. 1912.

15 See Plankensteiner (2006).

16 Reichspost, 27 September 1912.

17 HHStA, AR, Dept. 8, Box 60, Schwimmer to Foreign Ministry, Vienna 10 November 1912.

18 Kriegsarchiv (KA / War Archive), Register 1913, A., 7 Ak-7/3; "mountain cannon for successor to the throne of Abyssinia"; the cannon in question was a 7 cm M 99 mountain cannon.

19 Hayle Giyorgis Welde Mikael, de facto prime minister under *Lïj* Iyasu, married to *Lïj* Iyasu's sister Sïhin Mikaél.

20 HHStA, Kabinettskanzlei, Nr. 2669 of 14 October 1912; Imperial resolvit of 7 November 1912.

On 29 November 1912 the Austro-Hungarian Foreign Minister Count Berchtold submitted to Emperor Franz Joseph the proposal to establish an I.&R. honorary consulate in Addis Abeba:

> *"Already for a long time it was intended to establish, in Addis Abeba, capital of the Abyssinian Empire, a consular representation. Its task would be on the one hand to protect our local interests, and on the other hand to promote our already existing commercial relations with this country, which are capable of development. The implementation of this project, to which both trade ministries have already agreed, has so far failed because of the difficulties in filling this position"* [21].

These difficulties no longer existed due to Schwimmer's application. He was considered the right man for the post, and as the emperor had already awarded him the order of the Iron Crown it would have been difficult not to view him as the appropriate candidate. On 5 December 1912, Emperor Franz Joseph gave his approval to establish an I.&R. honorary consulate in Addis Abeba and appointed Schwimmer honorary consul. The consular district of the new office, which was – a rare exception to the rules - put under direct control of the Foreign Ministry, was to include all of Ethiopia. The I.&R. Austro-Hungarian honorary consulate started its activities on 19 April 1913 (Agstner 2004: 425), as can be seen on the document below.

Endergefertigter meldet Ser.
Exzellenz gehorsamst seinen Dienst-
Antritt vom 19.Diesed.
Der K.u.k. Konsul

Fig. 4: HStA, Admin. Reg., Dept. 8, box 60, report Cons. Addis Ababa No. 1/13 of 26 April

On 30 April 1913, Karl Schwimmer paid an official visit to the Ethiopian Minister for Foreign Affairs and Trade, *Neggadras* Hayle Giyorgis, and presented him "the Grand Cross of the Order of Francis Joseph", which H.M. the Emperor and King had most graciously resolved to bestow upon him. The Ethiopian Foreign Minister viewed the "*presence of our consular mission [...] as an extraordinarily important counterweight to the aspirations of the border powers*"[22] – a reference to Italy and Great Britain – and wanted the consul to promote Austro-Hungarian trade with Ethiopia.

Apart from informing Vienna on developments in Ethiopia and her relations to other countries – e.g. that "*on 20 April the newly appointed Imperial German minister Herr von Syburg had – for roughly twenty minutes - been received by H.I.H.* Lïj *Iyasu, successor to the throne*"[23].

---

21 HHStA, Kabinettskanzlei, Nr. 2865/1912 of 29 November 1912, Imperial resolvit of 5 December 1912.

22 HHStA, Political Archive (PA) XXXVIII, Box 358, Addis Abeba 1913, Consulate (C) Addis Abeba J. No. 17/13 of 1 May 1913.

23 HHStA, PA XXXVIII, Box 358, Addis Abeba 1913, C. Addis Abeba, J. No. 19/13 of 3 May 1913.

Schwimmer's only noteworthy activity was to broker a major arms deal between the Austro-Hungarian War Ministry and Ethiopia.

Consul Schwimmer and the Cannon Deal

On 23 August 1913 consul Schwimmer sent a confidential report to Vienna:

> *"The Abyssinian Government asked me confidentially, whether our government would have surplus rifles and carbines with ammunition at its disposal and be willing to sell them? The amount in question is 100 to 150.000 weapons and 20 million rounds of ammunition. In the affirmative the Abyssinian Government requests 5 samples each with 1000 cartridges. The Abyssinian government is awaiting information on modalities of payment. Delivery would have to be at Djibouti... 20 rifles per box, ammunition 1000 cartridges per box. A representative of the Imperial Ethiopian Government would take delivery in Djibouti. The whole transaction would be based on a contract.*
>
> *As the proposal to get rid of our old weapons does not seem to me to be without interest, I take the liberty to submit it to your Excellency's consideration, humbly requesting speedy action. According to my information we would obtain many commercial advantages if there is a possibility to accommodate the Ethiopian Government in the matter in question"*[24].

Even before Schwimmer's report had arrived in Vienna, a ciphered telegram dated 28 August 1913 – indicating the urgency of the matter - contained further details:

> *"Local Government asks confidentially, if our Government would sell 100.000 to 150.000 surplus rifles and carbines and 21 million cartridges. I suggested Werndl-rifles. Government requests quote of price and conditions of payment. Matter urgent. Request answer by cable to cable address 'Austung' ".*

On 2 September 1913 the Foreign Ministry, in a ciphered cable, informed Schwimmer that:

> *"War Ministry ready to sell 150.000 Werndl rifles fully fit for war use as well as requested number of cartridges under the following conditions: Price per rifle, including bayonet and sheath, without rifle sling, loco magazine 10 Kronen (K)"* [25]. *Cartridges including packaging per 1000 40 Kronen (K). Payment: 50% on delivery, 50% within up to one year at the discretion of Ethiopian Government. Delivery in loco to agent of Abyssinian government. In view of other requests, War Ministry expects written or telegraphic offer at the earliest convenience; carbines not in store".*

As the Ethiopian Government was offered "almost new German Mauser M. 88 – by

---

24 HHStA, PA XXXVIII, Box 358, Addis Abeba 1913, C. Addis Abeba, No. 152/13 of 23 August 1914, Confidential.

25 1 Austrian Krone (crown) of 1913 corresponds to the purchasing power of 3.50 € in 2005.

dealers at 10 Mark" and as "exporters in Antwerp and Hamburg[26] offer Werndl rifles with bayonet for 2 1/2 K, packed, fob Antwerp or Hamburg" the purchase of Austrian rifles was not followed up. Instead, as Schwimmer reported on 6 September 1913, "*the Abyssinian government furthermore requested me to inquire, whether our government would be willing to sell 70 surplus mountain cannons and 30 fortress cannons with 200 shrapnel each... Incidentally, as the Abyssinian Government does not have a single Piaster of national debt, it is without any risk to advance it this amount against her promissory notes. A concession from our side might result in obtaining commercial advantages here.*"[27].

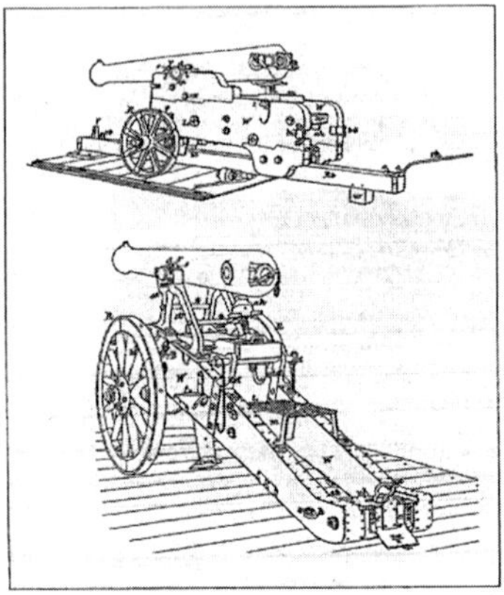

Fig. 5: M.61 Cannon, in Dolleczek 1887: 524.

It was a lucky coincidence, that major stocks of fortress cannons M.1861 were still stored in artillery depots in Vienna, Wöllersdorf (Lower Austria) and Komorn (Komarom), the Hungarian fortress town on the Danube and headquarters of the I. & R. Fortress Artillery Regiment No.6. The cannon M.1861 had originally been developed by Baron Wahrendorff in Sweden, and had been introduced into the Prussian army in 1858. After Austria had in 1859 lost its war against Sardinia and France at Solferino, Prussia left the design of the cannons to Austria, where it was introduced into artillery service two years later under the name M.1861 (Dolleczek 1887: 562).

The M.1861 was the first rifled Austrian cannon, produced in calibres 120, 150 and 180 mm, the gun barrel was of cast iron. It was used as fortress cannon, for coastal defence and by the navy. The loss of Lombardy to the new Kingdom of Italy in 1859 necessitated building a string of fortresses and fortifications along Austria's southern border with Italy. The new fortresses like Riva or Lago di Garda, Strino, Larino or Danzolino were originally equipped with these M.61 cannons. After 1880 the M.61 cannon was gradually replaced by the new cannon M.1880.

On 31 December 1913 Schwimmer informed the Austro-Hungarian Foreign Ministry by cable that "*local Government no longer interested in rifles and cartridges, buying instead 50 cannons cal. 12 cm and 50 cannons cal. 15 cm with 200 shrapnel each* [...] *one half to be paid when mission takes delivery, remainder after arrival of shipment in Djibouti. Mission*[28] *accompanied by me will depart next week*".

26 The arms dealer in Hamburg was almost certainly Benny Spiro, who in April of 1914 sold 20.000 Mannlicher rifles to the Ulster Volunteer Force and was no stranger to clandestine arms dealings (see De Wiel 2008).

27 HHStA, PA XXXVIII, Box 358, Addis Abeba 1913, C Addis Abeba, No. 165/13 of 6 September 1913 Confidential.

28 According to a hand-written note the mission was made up of H.H. Prince Belay (Belay Ali, a 19 year old

An official of the I. & R. Foreign Ministry noted on the file, that the I. & R. War Ministry was prepared to sell the abovementioned 100 fortress cannons to the Ethiopian mission.

On 16 January 1914 Schwimmer sent another ciphered telegram: "*Abessynian Government has concluded deal as indicated in telegram of 31 December of last year. I will depart today with the mission. Will in time inform about arrival of steamer*", which he did by telegram from Aden on 30 January 1914:

> "*Abyssinian mission travelling together with me on Austrian Lloyd steamer 'Koerber'*[29] *will depart 4 February from here to Trieste. I request that Lloyd will see to it that captain will very warmly receive and treat them on board.*"

Under normal circumstances anybody brokering a major arms deal would be interested to keep the matter secret. Instead, Schwimmer saw to it that his dealings were the talk of the town. On 21 January 1914, the German minister to Ethiopia, Friedrich-Wilhelm von Syburg, reported to Berlin that:

> "*weeks ago Mr. Schwimmer had informed me under the seal of secrecy of an Abyssinian 'mission to render homage' headed by him. He promised me to immediately inform me, when the mission would be ready to leave, in order to enable me to inform Berlin. The secrecy requested was unnecessary, as all of Addis Abeba learned of the mission, doing Mr. Schwimmer the favour to rack their brains over the question what he would do with this mission in Vienna, a mission made up of very low-ranking people from the entourage of the successor to the throne. The mission has been trained in European manners, especially in dining, in Mr. Schwimmer's house a few weeks before its departure.*
>
> *Mr. Schwimmer has kept the real purpose of the mission as his secret. If I were to believe him, the mission was to express the gratitude of the Abyssinian successor to the throne to H.M. Emperor Franz Joseph for gifts received. Mr. Schwimmer has started this enterprise mainly in majorem suam gloriam, to make propaganda for himself, combining it with useful deals, such as the sale of Austrian cannons and rifles to the Abyssinian government* [...]"[30]

In the meantime, Great Britain – certainly alarmed by reports from Aden - had discovered that an arms deal was in the making between Austria-Hungary and Ethiopia, and H.M. Embassy in Vienna on 10 February 1914 addressed the following memorandum to the Austro-Hungarian Foreign Ministry, which even today sounds rather relevant given the situation in Somalia:

---

nephew of *Lïj* Iyasu), H.E.Court and Palace Chief *Qeññazmach* Tesemma as well as Princes *Lïj* Abbebe Weldé and *Lïj* Teferi Chernet.

29 Austrian Lloyd Steamer, no.201; 5325 BRT; built 1903, in service until 1914, when it was confiscated after the outbreak of WW I by Great Britain in Bombay harbour; named after Ernest von Koerber (* Trient, Tyrol / Trento, Italy 6 November 1850, † Baden, Lower Austria 4 March 1919; Prime Minister of Austria 1900-1904, 1916).

30 Politisches Archiv, Auswärtiges Amt Berlin (PAAA) R 14907, Imp. German Legation, J.Nr.122, Confidential, Addis Abeba 21 January 1914.

"Large quantities of arms have in recent years been introduced into Abyssinia by irregular means and have in many cases subsequently found their way into the hands of the adherents of the Somali Mullah[31] *and other natives of the surrounding territories. This has a disturbing effect on the peace of British Somaliland and the other neighbouring British possessions.*

The French Government have recently expressed their intention of introducing new regulations governing the importation of arms and ammunition through Jibuti, and it is hoped that when these regulations have been brought into operation it will be found possible to control the sources from which the disorderly elements of the East African populations draw their supplies of arms.

A report has however reached the ears of His Majesty's Government that Mr. Schwimmer, the Austro-Hungarian Honorary Consul in Addis Abeba, is endeavouring to obtain a concession from the Abyssinian Government for the rearming of their army with Mannlicher rifles, and for supplying them with quick-firing guns.

His Majesty's Government is naturally interested in such a scheme and would be glad to receive any information on the subject which the Austro-Hungarian Government may be in a position to give them".

In the meantime the Ethiopian delegation, made up of *Lïj* Belay Ali, Court- and Palace Chief General Tesemma Ïsheté and Princes *Lïj* Teferi Chernet and *Lïj* Abbebe Weldé had on 16 February 1914 arrived in Vienna, where they resided in Hotel The audience with the emperor had however to be postponed, as the Foreign Ministry had overlooked an important detail. Erzherzog Carl.[32] The party was to be received by the Emperor on 22 February 1914.[33]

The Ethiopian delegation had not come empty-handed. Emperor Franz-Joseph and Successor to the Throne Franz Ferdinand were to receive valuable garments and a horse harness, a complete state dress consisting of green velvet trousers, a striped, long silk shirt and a valuable cape of red velvet with splendid golden embroidery, as well as a precious horse harness with saddle, a saddle blanket, a bridle fitted with gold and coloured glass beads and silver horse ornaments, a state shield and a sword with sheath covered in velvet and gilded silver ornamental fittings (Plankensteiner 2006: 164).

Three lions and two mountain zebras had already been sent in advance to the Imperial Zoo, while the other Ethiopian gifts, like those of 1907 and 1912, found their way into Vienna's Museum of Ethnology.

On 23 February 1914 Foreign Minister Count Berchtold humbly submitted to his sovereign a report on bestowing various decorations to the members of the Ethiopian

---

31 British concerns were all the more obvious, as *Lïj* Iyasu had *"sent a caravan of arms and ammunition to the perennial Somali rebel, Sayid Mohammed Abdille Hassan, the 'Mad Mullah' of Somaliland..."* (Henze 2000: 194).

32 Vienna I, Kärntner Strasse 31.

33 For an Ethiopian view of the arms deal see Merse Hazen (2004: chapter 220). The dispatch of a delegation to Austria, Merse Hazen (2004: 145-148), where Schwimmer is misspelled as Monsieur Chemir.

delegation; he suggested to award H.H. *Lïj* Belay the Grand Cross of the Order of Franz Joseph, to Court – and Palace Chief General Tessema the Commander's Cross with star, and to princes Teferi Chernet and Abbebe Weldé the Knight's Cross of this order. In view of the young age of *Lïj* Belay the Grand Cross of the Oder of Franz Joseph, and as the two princes had no rank in government or court, these grades seemed sufficient. The Emperor gave his approval on 24 February[34]. The following day, the members of the delegation visited the Spanish Riding School, and on 26 February at 4:45 p.m. they were received by the Emperor. His Majesty had deigned to give instructions that the guards at the Imperial Palace salute the delegation like an ambassador.

Prince Belay delivered a handwritten letter by *Lïj* Iyasu, dated 1 T'ïr 1906, i.e. 9 January 1914, and handed over to the Emperor typical Ethiopian products. During the stay of the delegation, the sale of 120 cannons M.1861 for 300.000 Kronen[35] was finalized. The German ambassador in Vienna, Heinrich von Tschirschky, informed Berlin on 28 February:

> *"that Italy again had become nervous, as it believed that the mission would request Austrian instructors for the Abyssinian army, which Rome would not admit. Count Berchtold confirmed this information I obtained from the Duke of Avarna and remarked, that until now no request for instructors had been addressed to him. He would not grant such a request in view of Italian sensitivities on the one hand, and as it would serve no purpose to send 2 or 3 Austrian officers to Abyssinia, which would not have been of any tangible advantage either to Abyssinia nor to Austro-Hungarian interests, on the other hand..."*[36]

The British embassy in Vienna was informed on 7 March 1914 "*that the Abyssinian government had neither acquired Mannlicher-rifles nor rapid-fire cannons in Austria-Hungary*". The cannons were sent from artillery depots in Vienna, Wöllersdorf / Lower Austria, Komorn (Komarom) and Pola to Trieste, wherefrom a steamer of the "Austrian Lloyd" transported them to Djibouti. In the meantime, newspapers took up the story. The "Berliner Tageblatt" of 12 June 1914 carried an article on "Abyssinia orders cannons in Austria".

As soon as the cannons had been dispatched, problems arose, as officials in Vienna had overlooked an increase in cargo tariffs which had taken effect on 1 January 1914. Suddenly, the I. & R. Ministry for Foreign Affairs, the I. & R. War Ministry, the Imperial Austrian Trade Ministry and the Imperial Austrian Railway Ministry were studying cargo tariffs. The latter ministry intervened with the Southern Railways to prevent that Ethiopia be charged the higher tariffs:

---

34 HHStA, AR, Dept. 2, Box 31, Hofnachrichten Staaten A 1880–1918, Abessinien, Vortrag Berchtold vom 24. Feb. 1914 (no ref.).

35 Corresponds to roughly 1,075.000 €.

36 PAAA, R 14907, Imp. German Embassy Vienna No. 58 of 28 February 1914.

> *"In view of the friendly relations existing between Austria-Hungary and Abyssinia and in view of the fact that the Abyssinian mission has promised further purchases of decommissioned weapons from the I. & R. military administration, it would be desirable to the I. & R. War Ministry if such an impression could be countered by refunding the Ethiopian Government part of the freight expenses paid* [...]. *The I. & R. Foreign Ministry too is interested in a favourable solution of this question, motivated by the intention that the commercial relations between the Monarchy and Abyssinia, which have been established by the busy activities of the I. & R. consulate in Addis Abeba, and which give rise to great hopes, are not exposed to the danger of an undesirable and possibly irreparable set-back* [...]"[37]

On 27 July 1914 Schwimmer cabled to Vienna:

> "*Money has been paid middle of June... Confidential. Successor to the Throne and Foreign Minister asked me whether it is correct that 26 Austro-Hungarian officers with 12.000 Mannlicher rifles and 6 million rounds of ammunition are leaving Trieste for Ethiopia. The inquiry by the government is a result of information from the local Italian minister, who submitted to the successor to the throne a photo of a fully assembled cannon M. 61.*"

It is not clear whether all cannons actually arrived in Ethiopia. Bairu Tafla (1994: 136) maintains that French authorities in Djibouti might have hampered transit of these weapons to Ethiopia. It is however rather doubtful whether the French authorities, who were certainly aware that the Austrian M.61 cannons were of little military value in 1914, would have confiscated any of them.

Wolbert Smidt, on the other hand, in his publication on German-Ethiopian relations reproduces a photo of *Lïj* Iyasu and Tesemma Ïshete[38] showing both with several Austrian cannons in 1914 (Smidt 2005: 69). It is obvious that the Italian services and Italian diplomacy were fully informed of the cannon deal and that they apparently were very much disturbed by the wrong information that I. & R. officers were on their way to Ethiopia.

Fig. 6: Lïj *Iyasu, Dejjazmach Tesemma Ïsheté and the Austrian M. 61 cannons near Dïrré Dawa, photo taken probably in the summer of 1914.*

37 HHStA, AR, Dept. 94, Box 14, k. k. Handelsministerium Z. 13.201 ex 1914 an k. k. Eisenbahnministerium of 4 June 1914.

38 Grandfather of Addis Abeba businessman Tadele Y. Tessema.

An official of the I. & R. Foreign Ministry noted on Schwimmer's cable of 27 July "*that the money has arrived last week and that the cannons and ammunition bought by Abyssinia were now fully paid.*" The following day, 28 July, Austria-Hungary declared war on Serbia.

It would however be wrong to see this sale of cannons to Ethiopia in the context of strengthening Ethiopian military capabilities with a view to open a second front against Italy – in early 1914 nobody in the Austro-Hungarian general staff could have known that Austria-Hungary and Italy, then allies, would be at war in May of 1915. The idea that Austria - Hungary would have wanted to weaken Italy may seem tempting, however, it is as wrong as an Italian description of Count Colli's role facing "*piu pressanti iniziativi austriache da parte del nuovo console Schwimmer, tendenti ad influenzare il giovane, dissoluto e bellicoso successore Iyasu (ligg Iasu) con forniture di armi e con una politica di penetrazione economica in funzione evidentemente antiitaliana nella provincia di Aussa.*"[39]

Schwimmer left Addis Abeba on 25 October 1914 for Austria[40], having been guaranteed safe passage via Djibouti, Aden and the Suez Canal to Genoa by the ministers of France and Great Britain. Before leaving he entrusted the protection of interests to the Italian minister Conte Colli,[41] not without having made sure to burn "the code, the code book, political files, secret files and in particular those concerning the arms deal", which explains that some aspects of the deal will forever remain shrouded in mystery. He handed over the other "harmless files" as well as the coat of arms of the I. & R. Austro-Hungarian consulate to Conte Colli.[42] Four Austrians and Hungarians liable for military service remained in Ethiopia – the Austro-Hungarian colony cannot have been very large. It was the end of an Austro-Hungarian presence in Ethiopia.

Although Schwimmer, his wife and child were in a hurry to reach Djibouti, his stay in Dïrré Dawa took longer than planned, as he was already expected there. Upon orders of the Ethiopian government he was compelled to organize, for the local Ethiopian chiefs, a demonstration of the Austrian cannons which had barely arrived there three months earlier. According to Schwimmer those powers which were

39 *Dizionario Biografico Degli Italiani*, vol. 27, Rome, 1982, p. 41. The Sultanate of Awsa is situated to the West of today's Djibouti; the first European to travel there in 1931 was Wilfred Thesiger. Austrian-Hungary had no interests at all in this region.

40 *Egyptian Gazette*, 18 November 1914, Personal and Social: "Herr Schwimmer, Austro-Hungarian Consul at Addis Abeba, has been passing through Port Said on his way home from Abyssinia".

41 Giuseppe Colli Ricci (Marchese di Feliziano), * Saluzzo 9 September 1870 † Rapallo 12 September 1937; Officer, since 1896 in Eritrea, border delimitation Eritrea-Sudan-Ethiopia (Talbot-Colli Convention of 16 April 1901); diplomatic service, Secretary of Legation Italian Legation Addis Abeba 1902-1904, Florence 1904-1907, Chargé d'Affaires Addis Abeba 1907-1919, Counsellor 1908, designed and built Italian Legation 1909-1911, Minister plen. in Stockholm 1920-1921, in Buenos Aires 1921-1924, special mission in Addis Abeba 1924. *Dizionario Biografico Degli Italiani*, vol. 27, Rome, 1982, p. 39-43.

42 HHStA, AR, Dept. 8, Box 60, Schwimmer to Foreign Ministry, Vienna 15 December 1914.

enemies of the Austro-Hungarian monarchy had instigated this demand of the Ethiopian side, hoping to prove that these old cannons were not working. Although the target practice under Schwimmer's command took place without any trained military personnel, the old cannons were fully operational – to the dismay of numerous onlookers.

After this intermezzo Schwimmer continued his trip to Djibouti, where he was forced to take the French steamer "Caledonien" to Port Said. From there he took the Italian steamer "Maria C." to Genes; the "Maria C" was intercepted off Calabria by a French auxiliary cruiser "La Provence", and Schwimmer taken off board. He later was set ashore in Messina, from where he proceeded to Rome and Vienna. On 15 December 1914 he left for Nagyvarad[43] to serve in the headquarters of the 39th Hungarian Honved Division.

On 3 May 1915 Italy, in the London Treaty, agreed to declare war on its ally Austria-Hungary, having been promised rich compensation by Great Britain and Francen, among others the German speaking South Tyrol, the Trentino, Trieste, a large part of what was to become Yugoslavia as well as German colonies in Africa. Italy's declaration of war followed on 23 May. Apart from South Tyrol, Trentino, Trieste and Istria, Fiume and Zara, it took Italy a little longer to receive a tiny part of what it was generously promised by London and Paris, at least as far as Germany's African territories were concerned. On 15 July 1924 Great Britain, in implementation of the London Treaty of 1915, ceded to Italy the area south of the Juba River with the port of Kisimayo until the present border of Kenya. That territory known as Jubaland was annexed by Italy to its colony Somalia on 20 January 1926.

Fig. 7: A M.61 cannon near Dirré Dawa in 1935 in Martin Rikli's movie "Modernes Abessinien".

The last news and views of the 120 Austrian cannons date from 1935, when Martin Rikli[44], the Swiss photographer and producer of documentary films with clearly manifested Nazi inclinations, then in Ethiopia to produce the UFA documentary "Modernes Abessinien" saw "*in Dire Dawa 40 very old Austrian cannons, which already completely useless in 1866, had been sold to Emperor Menelik for good money[...] Without ever having fired a single shot, they stood there in the open field, silent witnesses of a purchase, which even after 70 years was considered a national disgrace.*" (Rikli 1948: 146)

43 Grosswardein/Nagyvarad, today Oradea, Romania.

44 * Zürich 19 January 1889 † Zürich 7 April 1969. Rikli worked for German UFA Studios.

The cannons also figure in Martin Rikli's movie “Modernes Abessinien”.[45]

As not a single cannon M.61 has survived in Austria, it would be interesting to learn whether one of these old Austrian cannons still exists in Ethiopia. In the same year 1935 France saw – after two decades - fit to implement part of her promises made in the London Treaty of 1915. In order to divert Mussolini from attacking Ethiopia, it ceded the 100 miles wide Aouzou - Strip in Northern Chad to the then Italian colony of Libya and a 950 square km piece of land of its French Somali Coast to the Italian colony of Eritrea, which included 20 kilometers of Red Sea Coast with the by now well known Ras Doumera and the island of Doumera, occupied by Eritrea since June 2008.

Bibliography

Ahmed Hassen Omer, 1997, “State and Ethnic Relations in Northeastern Shawa (Ethiopia), 1912-1935”, in *Ethiopia in Broader Perspective* (Proceedings of the 12th International Conference of Ethiopian Studies), Kyoto, vol. 1: 138-150.

Ahmed Hassen Omer, 1997, *Islam, commerce et politique dans l'Ifat (Éthiopie centrale) au XIXe siècle : l'émergence d'une ville carrefour, Aleyu Amba*, Thèse de doctorat d'histoire, Université de Paris I, Panthéon-Sorbonne.

Bairu Tafla, 1994, *Ethiopia and Austria*, Wiesbaden, Harrassowitz Vlg.

Berhanou Abebe, 2001, “Le coup d'État du 26 septembre 1916 ou le dénouement d'une crise”, *Annales d'Ethiopie*, 17, pp. 307-357.

Bieber, Friedrich Julius, 1910, “Durch Meneliks Reich nach dem Sudan”, *Österreichische Illustrierte Zeitung*, 19 (17), 2 January 1910.

Bieber, Otto, 1948, *Geheimnisvolles Kaffa- Im Reich der Kaiser-Götter*, Wien, Universum.

De Wiel, Jérôme aan, 2008, *The Irish Factor 1899-1919 – Ireland's Strategic and Diplomatic Importance for Foreign Powers*, Dublin, Irish Academic Press.

Dolleczek, Anton, 1887, *Geschichte der österreichischen Artillerie von de frühesten Zeiten bis zur Gegenwart: Nach authentischen und grösstentheils officiellen Quellen verfasst*, W. Kreisel & Gröger.

Fontrier, Marc, 2003, *Abou-Bakr Ibrahim, Pacha de Zeyla-Marchand d'esclaves. Commerce et diplomatie dans le golfe de Tadjourah 1845-1885*, Paris, L'Harmattan.

Gebre-Igziabiher Eliyas, 1994, *Prowess, Piety and Politics. The Chronicle of Abeto Iyasu and Empress Zewditu of Ethiopia (1909-1930)*, ed. by R. K. Molvaer, Köln, Rüdiger Köppe Verlag.

Gehring-Münzel, Ursula, 2007, “100 Jahre deutsch-äthiopische diplomatische Beziehungen”, *Orbis Aethopicus*, 10, pp. 67-101.

45 The sequence comes at minutes 0.21.49 to 0.22.03 of the movie.

Hagos G. Yohannes, 2003, *Political History of Tigray: Rivalry for Power (1910-1935)*, M. A. Thesis in History, Addis Ababa University.

Henze, Paul B., 2000, *Layers of Time – A History of Ethiopia*, Addis Abeba, Shama Books.

Hussein Ahmed, 2001, *Islam in Nineteenth-Century Wallo, Ethiopia. Revival, Reform and Reaction*. Leiden, Brill.

Höhnel, Ludwig Ritter von, 1926, *Mein Leben zur See, auf Forschungsreisen und bei Hofe*, Berlin, Hobbing.

Juniac, Gontran de 2001, *Le dernier Roi des Rois. L'Ethiopie de Haïlé-Sellassié*, Paris, L'Harmattan.

Labrousse, Henri, 1992, "La neutralité éthiopienne pendant la Première Guerre mondiale", in *Récits de la mer Rouge et de l'Océan Indien*, Paris, Economica.

Lupi, Luca, 2009, *Dancalia. L'esplorazione dell'Afar, un avventura italiana*, vol. 2, Firenze, Istituto Geographico Militare.

McCann, James, 1987, *From Poverty to Famine in Northeastern Ethiopia. A Rural History 1900-1935*, University of Pennsylvania Press.

Mersé Hazen Wolde Qirqos, 2004, *Of what I saw and heard. The last years of Emperor Menelik II & The Brief rule of Iyassu*, Addis Ababa, CFEE.

Mersï'é Hazen Welde Qirqos, 2007, *Ye-hayagnaw kïfle zemen mebacha ye-zemen tarik tïzzïtayé kayehut ïnna kesemahut 1896-1922*, Addis Abeba, Addis Abeba University Press.

Plankensteiner, Barbara, 2006, "Geschenke und Gegengeschenke: Menelik und die Insignien der Macht auf dem Weg nach Europa", in K. Volker-Saad & A. Cleve (eds), *Äthiopien und Deutschland – Sehnsucht nach der Ferne,* München, Deutscher Kunstverlag, pp. 159-167.

Rikli, (Dr.) Martin, 1948, *Seltsames Abessinien. Als Filmberichterstatter am Hof d. Negus*, Zürich, Interverl.

Rosen, Felix, 1907, *Eine deutsche Gesandtschaft in Abessinien*, Leipzig, Veit.

Rouaud, Alain, 1991, *Afä-Wärq, un intellectuel éthiopien, témoin de son temps 1868-1974*, Paris, Editions du CNRS.

Smidt, Wolbert, 2005, *Ethiopia and Germany – 100 Years Diplomatic Relations*, Addis Abeba.

Teshele Tibebu, 1995, *The Making of Modern Ethiopia 1896-1974*, Lawrenceville & Asmara, The Red Sea Press.

Van Gelder de Pineda, Rosanna, 1995, *Le chemin de fer de Djibouti à Addis Abeba*, Paris, L'Harmattan.

"Who is Menelik Eyasu?", 1974, *The Ethiopian Herald*, 30 October, pp. 1-3.

Young, John, 1997, *Peasant Revolution in Ethiopia, The Tigray People's Liberation Front, 1975-1991*, Cambridge, CUP

A Visit of *Lïj* Iyasu to the Railway facilities in Dïrré Dawa in 1915

Hugues Fontaine

The *Contrôle Technique des Travaux Public* [Technical Inspection of Civil Engineering] of Dïrré Dawa, in its monthly report of February 1915, relates a visit made by the Abyssinian government. The ruling prince Iyasu accompanied by Hayle Giyorgis, the minister of Finance and Contrôleur du Chemin de fer, the *Dejjazmach* Meshasha Yïggezu and "a rather important retinue of chiefs", left the Mojo River on 27 February 1915, to go on the Awash and then reach Dïrré Dawa. This report was found in the French national archives of overseas territories.[1] It is supplemented by a collection of a dozen of photographs (B&W; 10x13 cm; no author) found in the personal archives of Jacques Auriol (who was director of the Franco-Ethiopian Railway until 1963).[2]

At the Awash, everybody poses in front of the newly built bridge. During the trip, a "minor" derailing occurs at the km point 390, at Finka Hare. The tender placed in front of the train comes off the rails. A more important derailing had already taken place the day before "*in the region where the tracks were newly laid but not ballasted*", causing the death of the train chief. The Abyssinian dignitaries were made aware of this incident upon their arrival at km 440, adds the chief controlling engineer, the author of the report, "*but the impression produced was not strong enough to stop them from continuing their trip*". Brice, the French ambassador in Addis Abeba, is onboard, as well as Hallot, the Representative of the Company. The occasion is perfect to draw the attention of the prince and of his entourage to current problems: the establishment of the station of Addis Abeba, the necessity of "*very strict law enforcement*" to avoid accidents, the consequence of repeated thefts of join bars and telegraph wire "*for which a punishment has not yet been decided upon*".

In Dïrré Dawa, where the passenger building is still under construction, the prince takes place in a track motor car and visits the facilities. The revolving plate that is manoeuvred to shunt wagons seems to please him a lot. Crowds gather. In the unfinished passenger building, a toast is served.

---

1 Archives nationales d'outre-mer, Aix-en-Provence: FR ANOM 93COL89.

2 Auriol's archives are kept by his daughter, Catherine Paoli, whom we thank.

01

02

Captions

Picture 01: *Lïj* Iyasu and his entourage pose in front of the Awash bridge, ca. 28 February 1915.

Picture 02: *Lïj* Iyasu's men in arms, forming a line along the railroad.

Picture 03: *Lïj* Iyasu (the only to remain seated) having a toast with French and Ethiopian officials in the lobby of the railway station of Dïrré Dawa, still under construction, in the beginning of March 1915.

Picture 04: The prince visits the railway facilities on board a track motor car.

Six more pictures from this collection published in:

Fontaine, Hugues, 2012, *Un train en Afrique. Djibouti-Ethiopie. African Train,* Addis Abeba, Centre français des études éthiopiennes, Shama Books.

From Wello to Harer: *Lïj* Iyasu, the Ottomans, and the Somali *Sayyid*[*]

Haggai Erlich

As emperor Mïnilïk II was deteriorating physically and mentally, he decreed in 1909 that his grandson *Lïj* Iyasu, his only male descendant, would inherit his throne. Iyasu was the son of *Ras* Mika'él, formerly *Imām* Muḥammad ᶜAlī, the leader of the Wello Muslims, who had been Christianized by Yoḥannïs IV in 1878. The story of Iyasu as Ethiopia's head of state was one of the more controversial issues in modern Ethiopian history. Here we shall confine ourselves to his relations with the *Sayyid* and with the Ottomans, until his deposition by the Christian-Shewan establishment on 27 September 1916.[1]

From our vantage point, Iyasu's reign can be divided into two phases: prior to the outbreak of the war and after this point. In the first phase, Iyasu tried to solidify his authority by playing only on the Ethiopian field. Young, inexperienced and ambitious, he worked to build new coalitions in defiance of the already entrenched "Shewan nobility" created by his grandfather. Seeking new local allies, mostly in Ethiopia's periphery, Iyasu also flirted with Islam, as if returning to the faith of his father and ancestors in Wello. Wello's Islam, flexible and moderate, had co-existed for centuries with Ethiopian Christian political culture and rulers. Iyasu's new connections and behavior irritated the leading elite, but did not yet cause an open crisis. On his part, he avoided being officially crowned as a Christian emperor, and rather symbolized his being a king of kings by having his father crowned (in May 1914) king of Wello and Tïgray. Significantly, inscribed on *Nïgus* Mika'él's new seal was the fact that he had been a Muslim leader.[2]

The outbreak of WWI and the Ottoman *jihād* proclaimed against Britain, France and Russia changed Iyasu's perspective on Islam. No longer merely the religion of his ancestors and a useful card in rebuilding his Ethiopian powerbase, Islam, as it radiated

---

* This paper is based on a section in my book, *Islam and Christianity in the Horn of Africa -- Somalia, Ethiopian, Sudan*, Lynne Rienner Publishers, Boulder, 2010.

1 For a detailed and more general analysis, see Marcus 1975: ch. IX.

2 See on this in detail in Smidt, 2007-2008.

from the Middle East, was now a political ideology fighting for victory. As can be concluded from the story that would unfold up to his deposition, Iyasu, mixing caution with miscalculation, gambled on an Ottoman victory. In preparing for it, he worked to build an alliance with the Somali *Sayyid* and Islamic holy warrior, Muḥammad bin ᶜAbdallah Ḥasan, hoping to have the Somalis included in his future empire. Iyasu apparently visualized a new order emerging after the war, under him, centered on Ḥarer and stretching over the entire Horn of Africa, a wing of a renewed, Ottoman-oriented Land of Islam.

From Ethiopian Islam to Militant Islam

Iyasu's main connection to the Ottomans was their consul in Ethiopia, Maẓhar bey. During the 1911-1912 Italian-Ottoman war over Libya, the "Young Turks" resumed their interest in Ethiopia. In April 1912, they sent a permanent consul to Ḥarer, and replaced him on 7 April 1913 with a consul to Addis Abeba, Aḥmad Maẓhar, former head of the Translation Department of the Ottoman government. The new, energetic consul had studied the Turkish language book *A Voyage to Ethiopia*, published in 1905 by the Ottoman envoy to Mïnilïk, Ṣadiq al-ᶜAzm, and was influenced by his descriptions of Ethiopia's military ability and its 1896 victory over the Italians. Maẓhar was no less impressed by al-ᶜAzm's presentation of Ethiopia as a land of good Christian-Islamic relations and of the centrality of Ḥarer as capital of Islam of Ethiopia and the Horn. In November 1913, he sent a report to Istanbul detailing how the Ottomans should help Ethiopia against the colonialist powers and win it to their side by encouraging the Muslims while avoiding undermining Christian hegemony (Orhonlu 1974: 166). Posted to Addis Abeba, Maẓhar's first action was to move his office and residence to Ḥarer. From there, he developed intimate relations with *Lïj* Iyasu as well as with the Somali clans in the Ogaden. Maẓhar also became very close to ᶜAbdallah al-Ṣadiq, the *Ra'īs al-muslimīn* in Ḥarer, who had been in contact with Istanbul since 1904. Al-Ṣadiq had been in constant touch with the Somali *Sayyid*, and was already close to Iyasu. The new Ethiopian emperor tended to seal his local alliances by marrying women, among them daughters of Muslims, including one of ᶜAbdallah al-Ṣadiq's daughters.[3] Iyasu essentially viewed the Ḥareri scholar as his guide on his road back to Islam. The connection between Iyasu, Maẓhar, ᶜAbdallah al-Ṣadiq and the Somali *Sayyid* would, after the outbreak of the war, develop into an axis around which the Islamic-Christian struggle of 1914-1916 over the future of Ethiopia and the Somalis revolved.

Ḥarer was naturally the hub of this connection. However, when the war broke out, it was governed by *Dejjazmach* Teferi, who was already emerging as the leader of

3 FO 371/2228, Thesiger to Grey, 31 March 1915. See a list of Iyasu's four wives in Haile Sellassie I 1966: 48.

Ethiopia's Christian establishment. To undermine Teferi's power, in early December 1914, Iyasu appointed ᶜAbdallah al-Ṣadiq as sub-governor of the Ogaden. That same month, the appointment was interpreted by the British as part of Iyasu's new master plan to invite the *Sayyid* to extend his sway over the whole of the Ogaden country in the confines of Ethiopia itself, once the ground had been prepared by ᶜAbdallah al-Ṣadiq, in return for which he would undoubtedly render valuable assistance to Abyssinia when an emergency arose.[4]

To further tighten his control, Iyasu appointed a Christian Ottoman subject of Syrian origin, a friend of Maẓhar and resident of Ḥarer, Hasib Ydlibi, as *Neggadras*—the official in charge of commerce and taxation—of the town and the region.[5] Teferi had little choice but to swallow his pride. For the next year and a half, he would pretend to be unaware of the activities in and stemming from Ḥarer on behalf of the future victory of Islam,[6] or share desperate observations with the British Consul.[7] He had long detested ᶜAbdallah al-Ṣadiq who, for his part, was quickly changing from a Muslim, loyal to Christian Ethiopia—like he had been in the heyday of Mïnilïk—into a busy agent of *jihād*. Al-Ṣadiq was now overseeing sending arms to Ogaden clans loyal to the *Sayyid*, sending missions from Iyasu to the *Sayyid*'s headquarters in Taleh, and spreading among Somalis and Ethiopians the word of Ottoman Holy War in leaflets prepared by Maẓhar.

On 19 December 1914, Maẓhar wrote to his superiors in the Ottoman Foreign Ministry:

> "*It is possible to get the Ethiopians on our side if we manage some compromise with them. By using this situation, we can profit in Sudan and in Somali.... I sent the missionaries to Somali and to the Sudan with the declarations. I even published the fatwas. I sent these fatwas to Yemen for translation purposes which will be published in India, Aden and Hadarmaut. The Mawla has rebelled in Somali. I am trying to involve the other tribes. With all Muslims, we are praying for the Sultan.*"[8]

Maẓhar, as is apparent from his other messages as well, envisioned an all-Islamic holy war in the Horn, which, after victory, would lead to an Islamic Ethiopian-Somali empire. He overlooked the reproduction in Arabic and spread, in the Ogaden and beyond, of the fatwa of *jihād* issued in Istanbul. The fatwa, phrased like questions from the Ottoman government to the *Shaykh al-Islam* of the Ottoman Empire, included the following:

---

4 CO 535/36 Archer to CO 19 December 1914.

5 FO 371/2227 Intelligence Report for January 1915.

6 371/2228, Thesiger to Grey, 31 March 1915: "There is no chance that Dejaz Taffari will be strong minded enough to follow this course [arresting Iyasu when he was in Harar in February 1915 and acted like a Muslim]."

7 FO 371/2595 Dodds to Thesiger, 14 February 1916.

8 Turkey, UH 120, Maẓhar to Ministry, 19 December 1914.

"If several enemies unite against Islam, if the countries of Islam are sacked, if the Moslem populations are massacred or taken captive; and if in this case, the Padishah [namely, the Sultan] in conformity with the sacred words of the Koran proclaims the Holy War, is participation in this war a duty for all Moslems, old and young, cavalry and infantry? Must the Muslims of all countries of Islam hasten with their bodies and possessions to the Jihad. Answer: Yes. … Those who at a time when all Muslims are summoned to fight, avoid the struggle and refuse to join in the Holy War, are they exposed to the wrath of God, to great misfortunes, and to the deserved punishment? Answer: Yes. … If the Muslim subjects of the [enemy] countries should take up arms against the government of Islam, would they commit an unpardonable sin, even if they had been driven to war by threats of extermination uttered against themselves and their families? Answer: Yes."(Horne 1923).

In early February 1915, Iyasu visited Ḥarer and was reported to have prayed for three hours with ᶜAbdallah al-Ṣadiq in a mosque.[9] Maẓhar, following conversations with Iyasu, wrote to Istanbul on 13 February:

"The Ethiopians want to have a harbor.… If the British are thrown out of Ottoman Somali, it might work to give Ethiopia part of the coast between Zeila and Bulkar and the territory between the coast and the eastern border of Ḥarer."[10]

In order to throw out the British, Maẓhar thought, the *Sayyid* should be armed by Iyasu. The same message continued:

"According to our information, the Mullah sent an army of 12,000 men against the tribe of Warsangeli, the tribe most loyal to Great Britain. On the coast, this army burnt some villages. At present, the army is still busy destroying. The only problem he [the Mullah] has is arms and ammunition. If an agreement is reached with the Ethiopians, this need can be covered from here. The Mullah is ready to conquer whatever the Sublime Porte orders, and his power is enough. He only applied for our help in ammunition for next year".

According to Cengiz Orhonlu, Maẓhar envisioned a united Ethiopian-Somali-Sudanese army joining the Ottoman cause and marching on Egypt. In early March 1915, he asked his superiors "*for the authority to work for a treaty of friendship if the situation allows, and to officially negotiate with the Ethiopian government*," and was in fact authorized to do so by Enver Pasha, the Ottoman Minister of War (Orhonlu 1974: 171). In mid-March 1915, Maẓhar decided to move from Ḥarer to Addis Abeba, closer to Iyasu.[11] He and ᶜAbdallah al-Ṣadiq went together to the capital and at first were quite successful in promoting contact between Iyasu and the *Sayyid*. On the 12th (or 27th) of May, Maẓhar reported to Istanbul:

9 FO 371/2228, Thesiger to Grey, 7 and 31 March 1915.

10 Turkey UH 120, Maẓhar to Ministry, 13 February 1915.

11 Turkey UH 120, Maẓhar to Ministry, 7 April 1915.

"Lij Yasu sent an imperial letter to the Mullah of Somali, by means of one of my servants. This man carried 10,000 cartridges too with this letter. The text of the letter refers to cooperation with Germany and with our government. This imperial letter has been adorned with the word of witness for Islam [the shahada]. In this letter, Lij Yasu advised the Mullah to push on against the Italians and the British. For this purpose, he will help the Mullah in any case. I have sent more statements [the fatwas of jihād – HE] to the Mullah and to the other tribes. Our attempts are going well, with the help of Allah. Lij Yasu supports us whole-heartedly. He will give the imperial orders soon. I am waiting for your answers, which will increase his efforts and encourage him in our favor."[12]

Assessing the situation, the British Minister in Addis Abeba, Wilfred Thesiger, wrote in June 1915:

"Every week offers fresh evidence of Lij Iyasu's sympathy with the Mahomedan religion and with the Moslems whom he goes out of his way to propitiate, even at the expense of the customary politeness to Abyssinian Christians of far higher standing.

... I am coming to the opinion that the heir of the throne of Solomon is at heart a Moslem and is entertaining dreams of one day putting himself at a head of the Mahomedan Abyssinians, who considerably outnumber the Abyssinian Christians, and of proclaiming a Moslem kingdom which will stretch far beyond the frontiers of his present empire.... This intention is being probably strengthened by the conviction of an ultimate Turco-German victory."[13]

However, in the middle of 1915, Iyasu was in no position to commit himself to such a cause. Defying both Ethiopia's Christian establishment and the surrounding European allies while the war in the Middle East was in its initial stages was too risky. Iyasu's policy was to evade Maẓhar's pressure to enter the war (in June, the impatient Ottoman consul suggested that his government send two planes as a gift to Iyasu). Iyasu preferred to wait while preparing for eventual cooperation with the *Sayyid*.

Opting for this wait-and-see policy, Iyasu left the capital in June 1915 and did not return until April 1916. He wandered between Wello, eastern Shewa, and the fringes of the Ogaden, and enabled ᶜAbdallah al-Ṣadiq to impose in Ḥarer what the British consul called "*a reign of intrigue*", further undermining Teferi by building a new police force in Ḥarer based on "*a collection of undesirable Arabs*."[14] At the same time, Iyasu allowed both al-Ṣadiq and Maẓhar to cultivate the connection with the *Sayyid*. In late June 1915, it was reported that Iyasu had invited the *Sayyid* to move his headquarters to the Ogaden in Ethiopian territory,[15] but the *Sayyid* declined. In August, an

---

12 Turkey UH 120, A supplement to Maẓhar's letters of 12, 27 May 1915.

13 FO 371/ 2228 Thesiger to Grey, 16 June 1915.

14 FO 371/2595 Dodds to Thesiger, 14 February 1916.

15 FO 371/2228 Somaliland Report, 30 June 1915.

Ethiopian mission, handpicked by al-Ṣadiq, was sent to the *Sayyid* in Taleh. It was said to be an official imperial mission, headed by Muhammad Matiba, an Ethiopian of Somali origin who had received some Turkish education; Farah Haji, the commander of al-Ṣadiq's armed followers; and ᶜAbdi Sarur, al-Ṣadiq's confidant. They brought presents from Iyasu to the *Sayyid* and camels loaded with arms. More camel caravans from Ḥarer to Taleh were reported in the following months. The Ethiopian-Islamic mission remained with the *Sayyid* during the coming months and in January 1916, ᶜAbdi Sarur, a member of the mission, returned to Ḥarer, bringing a gift from the *Sayyid* to Iyasu: a Maxim gun that had been captured from the British in 1904.[16] The British, for their part, could barely swallow the provocation.[17] Indeed, the *Sayyid* went on to provoke them and raid their loyal clansmen in the Berbera area and the coast. His confidence grew to the extent that he paternalistically wrote to the British suggesting that he would mediate between them and the Ottomans if the British recognized his rule over all the Somalis. In practice, however, the *Sayyid* was in a position to bother the British but not to collide with them,[18] as Maẓhar hoped. In February 1916, another mission from Ethiopia "*apparently presented the Mullah with a Turkish flag,*" but the *Sayyid* was said to have promised "*to fly this* [flag] ... *when the Turkish troops land there to join hands with him and march on Berbera.*"[19]

Expecting a Turkish victory in the spring of 1916 was not unrealistic. Though the Turks had failed to storm Egypt in February, they were preparing new forces in Palestine. They had also failed to capture Aden from Yemen, and the Libyan Sanusis, under the flags of *jihād*, were driven back from Egypt in March. But major victories were scored against the British in two main arenas. In January 1916, the British campaign in Galipoli that aimed to capture the Dardanelles ended with heavy British losses and their bare escape. The British advance in Mesopotamia (future Iraq), was stopped in late 1915, and an entire British army came under a long Turkish siege in Kut al-Amara, finally surrendering on 29 April 1916.

Iyasu was biding his time. On one hand, in October 1915, he told Maẓhar that he and his father would soon enter the war;[20] on the other hand, his men told the Italian Minister in March 1916 that Iyasu was trying to avoid the Ottoman intrigues, and that he knew that Ethiopia's interest was never to fight its European neighbors.[21] But in April 1916, Iyasu seemed to have decided to throw his lot in with the Ottomans and draw even closer to the *Sayyid*. Around the middle of the month, Muhammad Matiba

---

16 ASMAI 65/11 Cerrina to Ministero Colonie, 7 February, 27 April 1916, Sola in Harar to legation in Addis Abeba, 9 February 1916.

17 FO 371/ 2593, Thesiger to Grey, 1 February 1916; ASMAI 65/11 Cerrina to Colonie, 17 June 1916.

18 FO 371/2228 Somaliland Report, 30 June 1915.

19 CO 535/42 Archer to CO, 1 March 1916.

20 Turkey, UH 120, Maẓhar to Ministry, "updated and sent in October 1915."

21 ASMAI 65/11 MAE to Colonie, 23 March 1916; also Colli to MAE, 25 May 1916.

returned to Ḥarer from the *Sayyid*'s camp, carrying the *Sayyid*'s letters to Iyasu and to the Ottoman Sultan. The letters were lost,[22] but whatever their message, on 27 April, Iyasu made a clear statement. He returned to Addis Abeba (together with ᶜAbdallah al-Ṣadiq, "who is the living spirit behind all of Iyasu's Islamic intrigues"[23]) to attend a gathering of the capital's leading Muslims, held in the Turkish consulate on the occasion of Sultan Reshad's birthday. At the event, Iyasu bestowed on Maẓhar the Grand Cordon of the Star of Ethiopia and an Ethiopian flag on which the *shahada* was embroidered.[24] A week later, the captured British Maxim gun, the *Sayyid*'s gift, brought from Ḥarer where it had been stored, was presented to the public of the capital at an official ceremony.[25]

In late May 1916, Maẓhar received instructions from Istanbul:

> *"We are following with interest your relations with the Mullah of Somalia. It is understood that he is ready for any action under Ottoman supremacy. A guarantee can be given that if he conquers any area from the Italians or the British, that area will be given to him. The Ottomans and their allies are defeating their enemies and shall win. The enemy has been defeated at the Dardanelles. In addition, Ottoman success is continuing in Iraq and the Caucuses. At Kut al-Amara, a British army surrendered and after that, five generals and 130,000 men were captured. Our allies also have become victorious over our enemies. Sanusis took action against the British and won a victory on the border of Egypt.... If Ethiopia takes action against our common enemies as we hope, you have permission to say that whatever they capture from Italy, Britain, and France [namely, Jibuti], we will support the Ethiopians so that they will keep these territories even in peacetime. If they want a document on this subject, you can satisfy them by saying "whatever territories the Ethiopians can take from the British, the Italians, and the French, who captured these areas from the Ottomans in the past, we will support them even in peacetime to keep their conquest." This suits the Ottomans, too."*[26]

This indicates that the Ottoman government wanted Ethiopian-Somali military cooperation, but had different ideas about their future. Ethiopia, the letter implied, should be pushed in the direction of French Jibuti and could annex other Somali areas. After victory, Ethiopia would be recognized by the Ottomans as an independent,

22 ASMAI 65/11 Cerrina to Colonie, 27 April, Martini to M. Colonie, 3 May 1916.

23 ASMAI 65/11 Colli to Colonie, 16 May 1916.

24 Tepedelen, "A Forgotten Diplomatic Front": "The fate of this flag, probably sent to Istanbul by Mazhar Bey, is being researched at present at the Topkapı Museum." Maẓhar *bey* died in Jibuti in January 1920 and was posthumously awarded by Istanbul the title of *sehit* (Arabic – *shahid*), namely a Muslim who died for his country and faith.

25 ASMAI, 37/11 Colli to MAE, 30 April, 5 May 1916; Cerrina to Colonie, 2 May 1916. Haile-Sellassie I, 1966 E.C.:. 49.

26 Turkey, UH 120, Ministry of Foreign Affairs to Maẓhar, 22 May 1916.

friendly entity. Moreover, in another letter from the Ottoman Foreign Ministry, Maẓhar was instructed to promise the Ethiopians, in return for their cooperation, the keys to Deir al-Sultan, the Jerusalem monastery whose gate was disputed with the Egyptian Copts (Haggai & Gershoni 2000: 62-64). Maẓhar, unwilling to re-emphasize Ethiopian Christianity, asked permission to tell that to the Ethiopians at a more appropriate moment, and would never make the offer). Istanbul envisioned that after victory, the *Sayyid*'s Somalia would be an Islamic entity under the Ottomans. Maẓhar was told to clarify to the German Consul that "*Molla Muhammad is in the Ottoman service and under its rule. In the land that he already occupies, he uses the Ottoman flag and actually has spread Ottoman supremacy to the harbor of Eila.*" To ensure that the *Sayyid* would be recognized as an Ottoman subject, Maẓhar was further instructed: "*The title of* sheyh al-mesheyih *will be given to the* Molla *of Somali and in addition the* [military] *rank of* Feriq *or* Mushir *can also be promised to him. Whatever he has conquered from the Italians and the British* [not the French] *will be left to him.*"[27]

Instead, Maẓhar clearly did his best to make Iyasu believe that he would be the master of the entire Horn of Africa. Iyasu, on his part, was ready to raise the stakes for this purpose. In mid-April 1916, the Italians intercepted letters from Iyasu to Somali chiefs in which he claimed to be a descendant of the Prophet and his daughter Fatima.[28] He now allowed Maẓhar to re-intensify his holy war campaign and spread harsh anti-British propaganda in this spirit. Some of the leaflets, with the apparent consent of Iyasu, were even distributed in Addis Abeba. One of the leaflets, addressing the Somalis, called on them to join the war of the *Sayyid*:

> *"Three of the Christian nations, England, France and Russia, our strongest enemies since the beginning, made an alliance in order to destroy Islam; and their intention was to destroy the temples of Mecca and Medina ... and moreover, to demolish the prestige of the Caliphate and the influence of the Koran, together with the humiliation of all believers. German and Muslim armies have already destroyed the Christian nations.... Oh Somali Moujahedin, you who are famous for your righteousness and calm temper, the present day is a day of trials you have been ordered to fight ... by the wish of our almighty God ... collect yourselves and be united under the flag of the Messenger of God; throw down the fortifications of Berbera and Zaila and Djibouti, and Bulhar.... Give up the last quarrels between yourselves.... Concentrate your forces under the command of the Said Muhammad bin Abdullah Hassan. He is now holding the standard of our [Ottoman] Caliph in the Somali countries. Consult him. Do not disobey him, follow his views....*
>
> *Oh, brethren and sympathizers, be it known that the Abyssinian Government is not with our enemies and they are not in the war against the Government of Islam. They*

27 UH 120, Ministry of Foreign Affairs to Turkish Ambassador in Berlin, 22 August 1916.

28 ASMAI 37/11, Governo Somalia to Colonie, 19 May 1916; Colli to MAE, 9 June 1916. See the genealogy and more details on Iyasu's Islam in Gori's analysis in this volume. See also Wallis Budge, 1970: 542-547; Haile-Sellassie I, 1966 E.C.: 49.

are friends and advisers of the Ottoman Government. The interests of Islam in this country concur with those of the Abyssinian Government."[29]

Similar leaflets were distributed all over. On 19 July 1916, for example, a particularly venomous three-page anti-British pamphlet was posted in Ḥarer's public places. After the British consul complained, they were removed by Teferi's men (Teferi himself was staying in the capital at that time). They would be re-distributed after 21 August 1916, when Iyasu removed Teferi from Ḥarer's government.[30]

The End of Iyasu and of the *Sayyid*

The months of June and July 1916 brought little promise to the Ottoman cause. On 5 June, the Arab Revolt broke out in Arabia and Mecca was captured from the Turks in five days. The fighters under the new Arab flag went on to expel the Ottomans and, by August, had captured the Hijaz, leaving behind a besieged Turkish garrison in Medina and an isolated army in Yemen. The impact of the Arab revolt on Horn affairs was twofold. First, the Ottomans lost all contact with the Red Sea and the Gulf of Aden theaters. From now on, Maẓhar would have to send his dispatches via Europe, as communications through Yemen were impossible. Second, the revolt helped the British to undermine the very concept of the Ottoman *jihād*. The Arab movement was led by the Hashemite family of Mecca, descendants of the Prophet, and rebelled not only in the name of Arab heritage but also, inseparably, in the name of Islam. The Hashemite princes were in a position to expose the "Young Turks" as the destroyers of the Ottoman dynasty and of the political authority of the Sultan-Caliph. In contrast, they could present themselves as fighters for the restoration of pure, authentic Islam under a renewed Arab Caliphate. The British were quick to utilize this message, and their men in Berbera spread the Hashemite word among Somali tribes.[31] No less significant from our perspective was the Ottoman failure in July-August 1916 to launch yet another attack on Egypt. Their defeat in this area ended the hope that any Turkish army would land on the shores of Somalia, and that they would have any direct leverage in the Horn of Africa.

On 13 August 1916, Iyasu decided to cross the point of no return. He removed *Dejjazmach* Teferi from the government of Ḥarer and declared it a crown province, in practice, under Muslim administration.[32] In so doing, Iyasu undertook to openly defy the Christian establishment and to turn Ḥarer into a capital of *jihād*. Assessing it retroactively, this was a miscalculated move with strange timing. Explanations should

29 CO 535/42 "Manifesto from Turkish sources in Addis Ababa," enclosure in Archer to CO, 15 June 1916; see also ASMAI 37/11 Colli to MAE, 9 June 1916.

30 ASMAI 65/11 Memorandum della Legazione Britanica in Addis Abeba, July-August 1916.

31 ASMAI 65/11 MAE to Colonie, 13 July 1916.

32 FO 371/ 2595 Thesiger to Grey, 23 August 1916.

perhaps be sought in the psychological sphere. It seems that Iyasu was carried away by his own illusions and propaganda. Just before his removal of Teferi, more pamphlets were distributed that accused the British of desecrating the Koran, aiming to enslave all Muslims, and planning to destroy the Ka'ba and steal the holy black stone, with the intention of exhibiting it in the British Museum. Iyasu was now also ready to seal his alliance with the *Sayyid*. He sent a German mechanic, Emil Kirsch, to Taleh to repair the *Sayyid*'s guns and render other technical services. In the middle of August, Iyasu sent another mission from Ḥarer to Taleh to offer marriage to one of the *Sayyid*'s daughters. Preparations for her arrival, and for the wedding in Ḥarer,[33] never materialized.

Iyasu and the *Sayyid* would never meet. The Ethiopian invited the Somali to see him in Jijiga; the *Sayyid* invited Iyasu to come to Taleh. Beyond these gestures were pointed messages. Taleh was the headquarters of a proud Somali who would take second place to no one; Jijiga was where the Ethiopians had defeated him in 1899. The *Sayyid* believed that after the victory, he would be master of all Somalis, including those of the Ogaden. Iyasu was led to believe that after the victory, the Ottomans would recognize him as the ruler of the entire Horn of Africa. Yet, in spite of these contrasting agendas, they had to cooperate. Moreover, the *Sayyid* needed the alliance with the Islamizing king of Ethiopia to prove to all Somalis that victory would be his.[34] Iyasu needed the *Sayyid*, not only for fighting the British and their allies, but also for the future war with Ethiopia's Christian establishment. Indeed, some involved observers believed that this was Iyasu's real agenda.[35]

Maẓhar, for his part, continued to push Iyasu to join the war. On 4 September, he reported to Istanbul:

> *"The prince should be careful.... He is openly in touch with Islam. He is completely inexperienced.... Our enemies probably will not recognize him in the future. His position is in our favor. If we convince him that we are the only power that will maintain his political position, he will come under our influence and we can maintain the balance of power. The German consul is hesitant about this. It is our duty to convince Germany about the personality of the prince, and she must help to maintain his kingdom."*[36]

According to Italian information, the Turks continued to spread disinformation about imagined victories in Egypt and Arabia. This was most probably the work of Maẓhar. Iyasu, in any case, was acting as if he had the wind in his sails. In early September, he dared to re-enter Ḥarer, where Teferi's loyalists and soldiers were still

33 ASMAI 65/11 Cerrina to Colonie, 17 August 1916.

34 ASMAI 65/11 Governo Somalia to Colonie, 10 September 1916.

35 ASMAI 65/11 Colli to MAE and Colonie, 1 September 1916.

36 Turkey, UH 120, Maẓhar to Ministry, 4 September 1916.

stationed. In spite of their protests, he ordered to dismantle the local police force and build a new one, based on al-Ṣadiq's armed men. He also arranged for the arrest of the British consul's translator and for sending him to Addis Abeba in chains.[37] After proclaiming that he was a descendant of the Prophet's family, Iyasu left Ḥarer for Dirre Dawa where he attended an Islamic festival, oversaw a religious parade and hoisted the Ethiopian flag with an embroidered symbol of the *shahada*.

In the second week of September, Iyasu proceeded to Jijiga, where his men had organized a gathering of Somali chiefs from the Ogaden and from the British protectorate. Iyasu gave them money and arms, swore on the Koran that he was a devout Muslim and together they performed Islamic rituals. He made speeches on Islamic unity and declared that the Ottoman Caliph had designated him to liberate the coast between Massawa and Berbera, a duty he hoped to fulfill soon.[38]

Iyasu failed in his reading of the Somalis. The *Sayyid* was apparently unhappy with Iyasu's territorial claims and was already maltreating Iyasu's gift, Emil Kirsch. None of the *Sayyid*'s men attended his meeting in Jijiga. The *Sayyid*'s Somali opponents were now less willing to fight the British. The *Sayyid*'s kind of leadership did not unite the Somalis in the risky spirit of an anti-British holy war. Already in June 1916, the British assessed that:

> *"The general loyalty of our Somali tribes may be counted on at present.... The mistake he [Iyasu] and our enemies in Abyssinia are making is that they believe that the Mullah Muhammad Abdullah Hassan is held in veneration and respect by the Somali tribes. They are exhorted ... to unite under his leadership. But this they will never do willingly."*[39]

The British, as mentioned, had been spreading anti-Turkish propaganda about the Arab revolt among the Somalis, and in August they were also in a position to prove to their chiefs that the Ottomans had been defeated in Egypt and Arabia. A group of Somali leaders was taken on a tour to see camps of Turkish prisoners in Egypt (Kakwenzire 1985). Iyasu's gamble of September 1916 to mobilize an Islamic-Somali army was heading nowhere.

Iyasu's provocation was stronger than his abilities. In gambling on Ottoman victory and relying on Somali-Ethiopian Islamic unity, he also failed to assess the Ethiopian Christian response. Turning Ḥarer into the headquarters of a *jihādi* enterprise was sure to inspire Christian reaction and energize the ever-present Aḥmad "Grañ" trauma. On 27 September 1916, at an official Christian ceremony in Addis Abeba, Iyasu was deposed. Only *Abune* Matéwos, who, on Mïnilïk's order had sworn (in May 1909) that

37 ASMAI, 65/11 Colli to MAE and to Colonie, 4 September 1916.

38 ASMAI, Colli to MAE, 11 September 1916; FO 371/2595 Thesiger to Grey, 14 September 1916.

39 CO 535/42 Archer to CO, 15 June 1916.

all Christian Ethiopians would be loyal to Iyasu,[40] was hesitant, but he had to yield to the Shewan leaders. The indictment against Iyasu, read during the ceremony, reflected the political Christian ethos of Ethiopia's elite:

> *"The Christian faith, which our fathers hitherto carefully retained by fighting for their faith against the Muslims and by shedding their blood, Ledj Iyasu exchanged for the Muslim religion and aroused a commotion in our midst. In order to exterminate us by fighting, he has converted to Islam and, therefore, we shall henceforth not submit to him; we shall not place a Muslim king on the throne of a Christian king; we have ample proof of his conversion to Islam."*

After listing ten such proofs, *Abune* Matéwos excommunicated anyone who would follow Iyasu. Mïnilïk's daughter Zewditu was proclaimed empress and Teferi, now *Ras*, was declared heir to the throne.[41] A few days later, Christian soldiers massacred some four hundred Somalis while regaining control of Ḥarer.[42] Teferi would continue to develop as the strong man of Ethiopia and, in 1930, be crowned Emperor Hayle Sïllasé I.

In his memoirs, Hayle Sïllasé described the deposition of Iyasu as the removal of a Muslim from a Christian throne. We have no reason to dispute that. Iyasu challenged Ethiopia's entrenched political ethos and provoked its old siege culture to the full. All the evidence we examined supports the assumption that Iyasu was returning to Islam, expecting an Ottoman victory and a military alliance with the *Sayyid*'s movement. His steps can not be interpreted other than as leading toward a new Ethiopia, centered on Ḥarer as the capital of an Islamic, African empire, allied with Istanbul and under his rule. However, what Iyasu did in practice was to re-enliven and re-strengthen the Christian nationalism of Ethiopia's elite. Prior to 1916, the empire of Ethiopia had gradually been adopting a more pluralist nature. If Yoḥannïs IV can be described as a crusader, Mïnilïk II led a political culture of relative openness. It combined Christian domination with Islamic autonomies and with growing participation of Muslims in the life of the empire. That a son of *Ras* Mika'él, previously the *Imam* Muḥammad ᶜAlī of Wello, was designated as Ethiopia's emperor was definitely the promise of an improved Christian-Islamic dialogue in Ethiopia. However, Iyasu's transformation into a political Muslim, his apparent striving for the victory of Islam as both religion and state, undermined the likelihood of such a dialogue for many decades.

Iyasu's history after September 1916 is beyond our scope here. In October 1916, the army of his father, *Nïgus* Mika'él, was defeated by a coalition headed by *Ras* Teferi, and Iyasu spent the next two decades in or escaping from prisons. In 1935, when Mussolini threatened Ethiopia and prepared to politicize its Islam, Hayle Sïllasé saw to the elimination of Iyasu in prison.

---

40 ASMAI 65/11 Colli to MAE and to Colonie, 4 September 1916. For *Abune* Matéwos' proclamation of 11 May 1909 and its Christian terms, see FO 371/594.

41 Haile Sellassie I, 1966 E.C.: 48-50, the quotation is from p. 48.

42 Jardine (1923: 246) wrongly described the massacre as predating the deposition of Iyasu.

Bibliography

Erlich, Haggai & Gershoni, Israel, 2000, *The Nile: Histories, Cultures, Myths* (ed.), Boulder, Lynne Rienner Publishers.

Haile Sellassie I, 1966 E.C., *My life and Ethiopia's progress, 1892-1937*, Addis Ababa.

Horne, Charles Francis, 1923, *Source Records of the Great War*, Boston, Stuart-Copley Press.

Jardine, Douglas J., 1923, *The Mad Mullah of Somaliland*, London, H. Jenkins Ltd.

Kakwenzire, Patrick K., 1985, "Sayyid Muhammad Abdille Hassan, Lij Yassu and the World War I politics", in *Transafrican Journal of History*, (14), 36-45.

Marcus, Harold, 1975, "The Abortive Reign of Lij Iyasu", in *The Life and Times of Menelik II: Ethiopia 1844-1913* (ed.), Oxford, Clarendon Press, ch. 9.

Orhonlu, Cengiz, 1974, *Habesh Eyaleti*, Istanbul, Edebiyat Fakültesi Matbaasi.

Smidt, Wolbert, 2007-2008, "The Coronation of Negus Mika'él, King of Wällo and Tegray, in May 1914: New Findings", *Annales d'Ethiopie*, 23, 413-439.

Wallis Budge, E. A., 1970 [1928], *A History of Ethiopia: Nubia and Abyssinia*, Oosterhout, Anthropological Publications.

Part IV
The Long End of His Reign

Dïrré Dawa, Harer and Jigjiga in the Weeks before and after the Overthrow of Iyasu on 27 September 1916[1]

Shiferaw Bekele

The immediate causes for the downfall of Iyasu emanated from his activities in the province of Harergé, specifically in the towns of Dïrré Dawa, Jigjiga and Harer. These towns were scenes of intense activity in the weeks before and after the announcement of the overthrow of the ruler. It is therefore very important to reconstruct his movements in these towns and along the railway in those very crucial days to place the deposition and the consequences in their proper context. This article sets out to do that.

Suddenly, on the night of 28 – 29 July 1916, Iyasu took the train, at a station not far from Addis Abeba, without informing any of the relevant authorities. His destination was also kept secret to the Court in the capital city.[2] It was one of those sudden and unannounced departures of the young ruler from Addis Abeba, which he did several times over the previous few years, and to which his entourage and the government had been accustomed. In spite of the secrecy that surrounded his departure and its apparent spontaneity, there was a purpose in his journey and he seems to have thought about it in advance.[3] He took along with him some of the disgraced lords like *Ras* Lulsegged Atnafsegged,[4] *Dejjazmach* Kebbede Mengesha,

1 The research for this article was done from May 11 to 15, 2009 in the *Centre des Archives d'Outre Mer* (Aix-en-Provence, France) on the assistance extended to me by the Research Project, *Ecrire l'Histoire de la Corne de l'Afrique*. My warm gratitude goes to Dr. Anais Wion who coordinated my travel to, and stay in, France. I am also grateful to Mr. Daniel Leblanc of the CEMAF (Paris I). My friend, Dr. Simon Imbert-Vier (specialist of the history of the boundary line between the republic of Djibouti and its neighbors) introduced me to the system of the archives in Aix and in many ways helped me during my brief stay there. I am very much indebted to him.

2 Brice to French Ministry of Foreign Affairs (MAE), 24 August 1916. This is a long report, which recounts the unfolding events as of the end of July. It offers a very useful chronicle for the political history of the country. For most of the historical figures presented in this

3 See Ïmmïru, 2002 EC. In addition to the testimony of Ïmmïru, his decision to take along with him some of the disgraced lords also demonstrates that indeed Iyasu went on this journey after some consideration.

4 *Ras* Lulsegged Atnafsegged belongs to a very powerful aristocratic family of Shewa with a long history of service to the Court. His brother Wubé was one of the empire builders of the last century and he was a provincial governor. In 1891, he was married to Zewditu. There was no issue from the marriage and it was dissolved about ten years later. The other brother Abeba was a Courtier who reached the rank of *Liqe Mekwas*. Lulsegged took part in the campaign of expansion as a commander and he was a much respected courtier of Mïnilïk. He was raised to the rank of *ras* in 1910. He was briefly married to Menen, the niece of Iyasu. Her

Fitawrari Mekonnïn Tewendbelay and *Ligaba* Beyyene Wendïm-Ageñehu. He also had with him his cronies, Tesemma Esheté and *Neggadras* Abubeker Ibrahim.[5]

When news of Iyasu's departure was heard in court circles in Addis Ababa, it created a bad impression because his concubine (a relative of T'aytu) was suffering from a serious sickness and she was expected to die.[6] He left his dying mistress in a cavalier fashion, which provided juicy stuff to the rumour mongers of Addis. There was the usual wonder where he was going this time. Teferi Mekonnïn, who was the governor of Harergé, and who had been summoned to Addis Abeba in June, was waiting for permission to return to his province. He should certainly have been informed but he was not.

This royal journey, as usual, was a clear break with tradition and protocol. Let alone kings, even members of the nobility, travelled from place to place with a considerable retinue. With kings, movements were carried out on a much grander scale; after all, monarchial peregrinations were demonstrations of power and authority. In the course of the journey, important decisions (like appointments and demotions) could also be made, which enhanced the political character of the royal movements. Iyasu does not seem to have taken the paraphernalia of royal travels as crucial political institutions.

Since the very year he started to exercise political power (end of 1911), Iyasu had been travelling from one province to another in pretty much the same way. He did not make any advance preparation; the Court was not involved; and this had a huge political implication because the important lords who were present in the city at the time ought to have accompanied him. He travelled on his own leaving behind all the leading figures in government and state. This scorn of procedure was in its fifth year and the political establishment was now used to it; but all indications showed that they did not forgive him for it. Iyasu would pay the price for this breach with tradition in the coming months.

This was not the only breach of protocol. In Dïrré Dawa, he stayed in the residence of the Syrian businessman, Hasib Ydlibi, which would definitely raise eyebrows in the country. He committed a political blunder, when on 5 August, he ordered all the disgraced lords he had brought with him to return to Addis Abeba, thus giving them

uncle decided to give her to Teferi while she was still married to the old *ras*. She was secretly taken away from the residence of the lord (he was away in his province) and given to Teferi in 1911. Lulsegged was humiliated.

5 Kebbede Mengesha was the son of *Ras Bitwedded* Mengesha Atikem and a well-connected lord. Mekonnïn Tewendbelay was an important Court official. Beyyene Wendïm-Ageñehu was a Court official who later became a provincial governor. Tesemma Ïsheté was a well-known figure in the Court. He was suspected of being a Germanophile. Abubeker belonged to the famous and influential and rich ʿAfar family of Abubeker Pasha, a powerful ʿAfar merchant, slave trader and politician in the 2nd half of the 19th century. His family continue to play leading roles in Djibouti politics right through to contemporary times. The junior Abubeker is the grandson of the senior. Abubeker was the link with the family in French Somaliland. The allies suspected him of being a Turcophile.

6 The rumour mills of the time stated that Iyasu was in love with his mistress, T'ïru Werq Aligaz; this gossip found its way into the diplomatic cofrrespondence of the three neighbouring powers. See for instance the report of Brice cited above.

the opportunity to join the conspiracy with passion and dedication! As if the blunders made so far were not enough, he continued to make them one after another! Then he made political appointments without the necessary (prior) preparations.

In the morning of 7 August 1916 at 6:00 a.m., Iyasu suddenly left Dïrré Dawa for Djibouti. He took the train to the port city incognito, without informing his own government and the colonial government. The governor of the Colony was taken by surprise.[7] The short notice of the arrival of the Ethiopian ruler and the fact that the French considered Iyasu as Turcophile and Germanophile were the reasons why the Governor did not put up a formal reception to the Ethiopian sovereign at the railway station. Moreover, he was only accompanied by Ydlibi and his daughter as well as by *Neggadras* Abubeker (except of course his guards and servants) – an extremely strange behaviour for an Ethiopian monarch. Iyasu stayed in Djibouti up to 10 August. During his stay, he saw, without the presence of his French hosts, ʿAfar and ʿIsa chiefs. The French intelligence service, which had been suspicious of the motives of the Prince all along, did not find out exactly what the discussion was all about. But Iyasu's meeting with the subjects of the colony was enough to confirm French fears that the Ethiopian ruler was up to something.[8]

He took the train back to Dïrré Dawa in the morning of 10 August. In the days after his return, he made a number of demotions of old provincial and district officials of Haragé and replaced them by new appointments. On 13 August, he removed Teferi Mekonnïn from his governorship of Harer and appointed him to the governorship of the remote province of Kefa.[9] This was regarded as a demotion in effect. When this kind of politically significant measure was taken, the king would have round him – if he was wise – as many of the leading lords as possible, who would deliberate on the matter, thus making them supporters of the decision. In this case, the move was only Iyasu's. It threw Teferi into the conspiracy against his master. For this reason, some of the observers at the time date the beginning of the plot, which eventually led to the overthrow of the ruler, to the early days of August 1916.

He sacked the old *Ato* Yoséf Zegelan, who had been Ethiopia's consul in Djibouti for over two decades, and another veteran chief, Mersha Nahusennay, governor of the ʿIsa districts from around the end of the 1880s. Their replacements were men that would certainly arouse eyebrows at the very least in Court circles and within the Christian elite: (1) *Neggadras* Abubeker was given the domain that Mersha had governed; (2) *Hajji* Abdullahi Ali Tsadïq was made the governor of Eastern Harergé.[10]

7 Telegram from Simoni, Governor of French Somaliland, to Minister of Colonies dated 7 August 1916.

8 It is hard to accept Brice's assumption that the young ruler went off to Djibouti to have some fun with the daughter of Ydlibi.

9 See Marcus 1975.

10 Abdullahi had a long history of service to the Ethiopian state under Mïnilïk; he was the son of ʿAli Tsadïq, a notable of Harer. Mïnilïk appointed him to be a member of the Mission of *Dejjazmach* Meshesha Werqé to Constantinople. On his return, he was disgraced and was even imprisoned for some time.

Our sources have not clearly stated his new office (one rumour said that he was appointed police chief and another rumour made him governor of the city of Harer); but all show that he was a man close to Iyasu. Finally, the presence of the Prince in the region enhanced Ydlibi's position and influence. These men were perceived to be Turcophiles by French, British and Italian colonial authorities and diplomats.

These moves clearly show that there was indeed a serious political purpose in the mind of Iyasu. It is therefore understandable if historians and commentators of later eras praised him. Yet, the way the demotions and appointments were done had a strong amateurish character. There was no prior consultation and deliberation with the principal politicians of the Empire. In the Ethiopian state demotions and appointments were expressions of the power and authority of the king and therefore they were subjects of discussions at least in the close circles of the monarch. In the case of Iyasu, the whole thing smacked of spontaneous acts, which in the circumstance was potentially dangerous for the decision maker. If the story is to be anticipated, some of these appointments were held up against him during the announcement of his deposition in Addis Abeba on 27 September. Certainly, they were used very much in the propaganda campaign his enemies launched following his overthrow.

But Iyasu did not seem to bother about the consequences of his actions. In fact, he continued to commit even more political blunders. He stayed in the railway town for some more days and, among other things, visited the main mosque of Dïrré Dawa and socialised with all the wrong people in terms of protocol. In the same month, his arch rival, Teferi, who enjoyed the support of a good number of the Harergé regiments and of the nobility and with whom he kept in close contact, was determined to overthrow Iyasu; he even contemplated fighting him in Harer, an idea that was abandoned upon the advice of his lieutenants.

As September came round, Iyasu went directly to Jigjiga. There, he assembled large numbers of Somalis together with their chiefs (*Ugaz*). The gathering was accompanied by considerable festivity. The political purpose of the move is not clearly stated in the sources. The colonial authorities and their diplomats in Addis Abeba made serious efforts to obtain information about the nature of the discussion and the objectives of the assembly and of the festivities. But they were not able to fathom fully the reasons. One thing was clear. The gathering at Jijiga was a large scale assembly of Somali notables. It was clear that Iyasu was building up an alliance with the Somali though it was not clear whether his intention was to put them on his side in a future confrontation with the neighbouring colonial powers in alliance with the Ottoman and German empires or to integrate them into the Ethiopian body politic or both. Later generations of historians waxed lyrical on this move, which they interpreted as Iyasu's attempt to give equality to his Muslim Somali subjects in the excessively Christian dominated polity. The problem is that the sources are not very clear.

What is certain is that he was making serious political and diplomatic blunders. The three neighbouring colonial powers were getting more and more nervous about his intentions, which increasingly convinced them that Iyasu was up against them; and and these moves "confirmed" again and again in their eyes their suspicions that he was going to join the Ottomans and the Germans in a war against them. They proceeded to put pressure on the Ethiopian government in Addis Abeba to stop these activities of the Prince. Addis Abeba in its turn was getting anxious about the movements of its master and the pressures of European powers. The plotters were also using the fears of the allies as a major reason to persuade reluctant lords and clerics to join them in one vast conspiracy.

After Jigjiga, Iyasu went up to Harer on 7 September where he was lodged in the Palace. In the meantime, the conspiracy in Addis Ababa was hardening. Parallel to this, the anxiety of the allied ambassadors reached its climax, which led them to submit an ultimatum to the Ethiopian Government on 10 September. Some of the heat in Addis Abeba started to reach him. His people in the capital informed him that some of the nobles including Teferi were hatching a plot to overthrow him. He instructed Teferi, more than once, to go to Kefa as soon as possible. On his part, Teferi repeatedly - and sweetly - requested his master to allow him to defer his trip until the rains stopped and until his *guwaz* arrived from Harer.[11] Iyasu must have felt the urgency of the matter because he went into feverish activity to win over as many of the followers of Teferi as possible to his side. He also replaced those he felt were too loyal to Teferi to be trusted. As a precautionary measure, he ordered about ten high lords – formerly powerful men like *Dejjazmach* Balcha,[12] *Dejjazmach* Habte Maryam,[13] *Afe-nïgus* T'ïlahun[14] – to be brought to Harer because he suspected them of plotting against him. They stayed in Harer under his close watch in his last days as the monarch of Ethiopia.

It is very difficult to date it precisely but it was sometime in late August or in early September that Iyasu seriously undertook the task of recruiting Somali and Oromo men to be his fighters. He armed them. This created alarm within the Christian population and, much more importantly, in court circles in Addis Ababa. Tension steadily rose in the town of Harer, which then spread out to the remote districts of the province. Christian troops increasingly got agitated as a result of this development. As the conspiracy in Addis Ababa was moving to its denouement, the tension in Harerghe between the Christian and the Moslem communities escalated to a breaking point. The Christians were cowering in fear.

After repeated delays and hesitations and doubts, d-day arrived for the conspirators on Wednesday September 27, when most of the lords in the city assembled in the

---

11 *Guwaz* means supplies and goods of people who go on long distance jouneys.

12 *Dejjazmach* Balcha Safo who is also widely known by his horse name *Abba* Safo, was one of the generals who had distinguished himself at Adwa. He was a governor of Sidamo and Harergé. He was disgraced by Iyasu.

13 *Dejjazmach* Habte-Maryam Beyyan, the maternal uncle of Empress Zewditu, was a provincial governor. He was raised to the rank of *ras* later in the 1920s.

14 *Afe-nïgus* T'ïlahun was a confidant of Iyasu for some time, which led to his appointment to the rank of *Afe-nïgus*. He was disgraced by Iyasu in 1915.

palace in the morning and declared the deposition of Iyasu. The news of the overthrow reached Dïrré Dawa and Harer by telegram and telephone in the early evening of that same day. At 7:30 p.m., the employees of the railway company in Dïrré Dawa (and from them the populace of the town) got the news from the official of the railway company in Djibouti, who, in his turn, had gotten it from Hallot, the Representative of the Railway Company in Addis Abeba. In his telegram, the Director also instructed the railway official of the Dïrré Dawa station to make sure that all Europeans were within reach and that a train should be on standby for any eventuality. In the same evening the news reached Harer, which further increased the tension – and the excitement – in the town. In the morning of the next day, the news had fanned out to the towns and villages around the province.

When he heard the news, Iyasu was totally nonplussed. His first reaction, after he recovered from the shock, was to summon some of the available lords and his own retainers and confidants to swear that he had not been converted to Islam. Sometime in the course of the evening he was able to finally collect himself and discuss measures to be taken. As of the next day (September 28), events unfolded in rapid succession. Troops loyal to Teferi, stationed in different parts of Harergé, started to go to the district of Webera, to the west of Harer, to join the garrison there, whose allegiance to Teferi was not put in doubt all along. On his part, Iyasu seems to have spent the whole of that day deliberating with his supporters and lieutenants how to organize a resistance to the coup makers.

On 29 September, he issued a new appointment of commanders over the regional army of Harergé. Old *Dejjazmach* Gebré, who had served *Ras* Mekonnïn for many years, was made the commander of the army of the province.

Dïrré Dawa, 28 September to 6 October

Among his first decisions, Iyasu sent a detachment of several hundred soldiers under the command of *Dejjazmach* Gugsa Aliyu to Dïrré Dawa, in the early morning of the next day (the 28th), to put the town, the railway station and the line under his firm control, and to ensure that peace and order were maintained.[15] Upon their arrival, the

15 *Dejjazmach* Gugsa Aleyu, also known as *Abba Jerman*, was a lord born in the province of Wello. After the defeat at Mi'éso, he and other survivors of the battle took the train back to Dïrré Dawa. Early in the morning of the next day, he followed his master into the ʿAfar lowlands, apparently in the direction of Wello. But along the way, the small force got the information that *Nïgus* Mika'él was already in northern Shewa on its way to the capital. But when they reached Ankober, they learnt that a battle was imminent between the two sides and Mika'el asked his son to stay in the town for the day. Mika'el lost and when news reached Iyasu he fled into the ʿAfar lowlands to make his way to Desé to regroup the regional army for yet another resistance. Gugsa followed his master and took part in the series of battles in Wello fought in 1917 between the partisans of Iyasu and the army of the central government. Finally, he was captured at the battle of Desé when *Fitawrari* Habte Giyorgis, the commander of imperial forces, decisively defeated Iyasu's forces. Gugsa was sent into "*gezot*" for some years. Upon his release, he was fully rehabilitated – he was given a district governorship and the hand of the maternal relative of Haile Selassie himself. He died in 1927EC (1934/5).

troops joined the town's small police force (commanded by the Ottoman citizen, Yahya Effendi) and very quickly took up positions in the city. Gugsa declared to the railway people and to the white foreigners that his men were there to protect the Europeans. Gugsa and Yahya also instructed the local railway management to inform them of the movements of trains.

There were fears, entertained widely by the expatriate population (Europeans, Indians, Arabs and Arabs), and shared by the management of the railway company, that the Muslim population of Dïrré Dawa and of the region would go out on a general outbreak of unrest in support of Iyasu, all the while looting and burning the commercial sectors of the town and the residence of the expatriate community. Hence, the management of the railway company started to work on the evacuation of women and children to Djibouti. The Director of Operations of the Company, based in Djibouti, came promptly to Dïrré Dawa. Upon his arrival on 28 September, he asked the permission of Gugsa to evacuate the expatriate population. The latter accepted the request and promised to facilitate the evacuation.

Gugsa provided an escort of ten soldiers for the train of the 29th September, which would take to Djibouti the European residents of the town. The train left Dïrré Dawa at 2:00 p.m. and arrived in Djibouti midnight. On this evacuation, a total of 207 people (94 employees of the Railway Company, 46 women and 67 children) were taken to the French colony. On the morrow 1 October, the Director of the Company set out at midday, on a special train, carrying the ailing French Consul and the remaining members of the French and foreign communities and arrived, without any incident, at Djibouti at 10:00 p.m. in the night. The last departure was on 6 October, which took 30 Greeks and 16 people belonging to different nationalities to the French colony. All in all, 600 people were taken away to the safety of the Port city. Thus, Dïrré Dawa was cleared of its European population except some Germans, Armenians and Greeks who decided to stay behind and face the consequences. The Indian and Arab communities were left behind to fend for themselves.

The Battle of Mi'éso, 8 October

Gebré[16] was instructed to march out on Webera on Monday 1 October. But Gebré gave excuses and delayed his departure. Nevertheless, preparations continued to be undertaken in his camp. Ammunition was distributed to troops. Observing that regiments from the different parts of Harergé were rallying to Teferi and concentrating in Webera, Iyasu put in place a broad envelopment plan according to which Gugsa would take the train to Mi'éso, 150 kms from Dire Dawa and from there proceed to the highlands to attack the forces in Webera in coordination with Gebré who would assault from the east; on paper this was a good plan. In practice, however, the story was

16 *Dejjazmach* Gebré was a life long retainer of *Ras* Mekonnïn, which led to his rise to the rank of *Dejjazmach*. He had been governor of sub provinces in the province of Harer.

different. Even if the plan was for Gugsa was to set out by train from Dïrré Dawa on 29 September, he took several days to complete his preparations. It was finally on 7 October that his train rolled out from Dïrré Dawa.

From the very beginning, cracks became visible in the defense wall that Iyasu was desperately trying to build. A number of chiefs from the Harer army decided to go over to the side of Teferi, together with their men. They marched to the west and concentrated in the main town of Webera *Awrajja*. Teferi immediately sent a small army to link up with this force and to strengthen it.

Iyasu ordered Gebré to march on Webera on Monday 1 October. Gebré, whose heart had all along been for Teferi, continued to drag his feet on the pretext that his troops did not answer the mobilization call on time; and therefore he did not set out on 1 October as planned. In the meantime, the forces loyal to the putschists were consolidating their hold on Webera. Gebré did not move out of the provincial capital even as late as 6 October, a long delay that allowed the putschists to re-enforce their positions very well. Finally, the reluctant old commander set out on 7 October; but, along the way, he declared that he would join the putschists concentrated in Webera, thus delivering a huge blow to the cause of Iyasu. Units of the Harer army, stationed in several parts of the province, continued to go over to Teferi's forces, which led to the swelling of their ranks.

In sharp contrast to the dilatoriness that was characteristic of the camp of Iyasu, his overthrowers in Addis Abeba were swift and decisive. They had actually sent on 28 September, right on the morrow of the coup, Tekle Hawaryat, the intellectual who had military training in a Russian academy and who was also the Ethiopian inspector of the Railway Company, to the Awash railway station to prepare for the arrival of troops from Addis Abeba and from other provinces of the south and to coordinate their movements. The coup makers also put together an army contingent to go by train to Awash under the command of *Dejjazmach* Ayyalew. Ayyalew moved out of Addis Abeba promptly on 29 September and reached Awash station with advance units in the evening of the same day; there he waited for additional troops. When these arrived, Ayyalew marched to the station of Mi'éso to offer battle to the loyalists, apparently because they had already been informed that Iyasu's forces would disembark there to move to the Chercher mountain to encircle the forces loyal to Teferi.

When Gugsa reached Mi'éso, the expeditionary force from Addis Abeba was already in place and so he was forced to offer battle on a field selected by foes (in itself a major setback in military terms) rather than marching on to the highlands as was initially planned. This meant that Gugsa had to face alone the small but well-equipped and highly motivated army from Addis Abeba. The engagement, which came to be called the Battle of Mi'éso, took place on 8 October, a Sunday. The loyalists were decisively defeated.[17] This had an immediate impact on the position of Iyasu in Harer. When

17 A detailed account of the battle from the point of a participant is given in the memoir of one of the leading participants. See Tekle Hawaryat 2004 EC: 312 - 319.

the news reached him, he was completely nonplussed. For hours, he shut himself up in his palace. Finally, he decided to flee.

In the night of the same Sunday (8 October) at 8:30 p.m., Iyasu galloped out of Harer down to Dïrré Dawa abandoning machine guns and arms in the *gïbbi* [palace]. He reached the railway city in the early hours of the next day where he rested for only a few hours and again galloped, with a few followers, into ʿAfar land. He resurfaced at Ankober, the old royal capital of Shewa, on 27 October, the day of the Battle of Segelé (where was he all this time?). He waited there for the outcome. In the evening the bad news of the defeat of his father's forces reached him when he again dashed out of the town in the direction of the ʿAfar lowlands. This time the peasants in the district made attempts to attack him. When he reached Desé (he again took time to arrive there), he set to work to regroup the remnants of his father's army for another round of struggle.

The Massacre of Harer

His enemies in Harer were also swift. On Monday, 9 October, Balcha made a triumphant entry into Harer city around mid-day. The Christian population, which had been, in the earlier days, cowering in an overwhelming fear of massacre by the Somalis, was joyed, while the Muslims got into a similar situation of terror from Christian backlash. Our informant, the Italian consul, followed developments on that day, which he reported to his minister in Addis. He informs his boss that the massacre of Somalis commenced immediately after the entry of Balcha into the old city. People were killed on the narrow, winding streets, in the houses, and even in the mosques. The killing continued into the next morning. At the end of it all, an estimated 1,300 people were murdered. Some of the victims were Muslim chiefs. On the government side, 30 soldiers died and around 360 were wounded. There is no other neutral source to countercheck all these figures.

Ïmmïru Hayle Sïllasé, who was also present in Harer, when the wanton killings were perpetrated, admits that the killing of Somalis had taken place. This is a valuable statement, coming, as it does, from someone high up on the government ladder. He also writes that the killings had happened the whole day, while the Italian consul reports that the massacre started at noon on Monday and continued into the whole of Tuesday. Given the fact that Ïmmïru belonged to the top ruling group, it would not be surprising if he tried to minimise, perhaps unconsciously, the magnitude of the killings. His figure for the dead (the total for all the dead was 400 of which the Amhara would not exceed fifty, he writes) does not at all approach the estimate of the consul. Finally, he presents the event in his account as a shoot-out between the two forces rather than as wanton killing on a large scale (Ïmmïru, 2002 EC: 71). Finally, on 11 October, the authorities established calm in the city.

Re-establishing State Authority in the Province

Re-establishing the authority of the state over the province of Harergé turned out to be easy in some of the districts and difficult in others. When troops and police in and around Dïrré Dawa saw, in the morning of 9 October, that the fate of Iyasu was sealed, they had no difficulty in switching their loyalties to the winner. The railway town easily moved from one ruler to another in spite of the widespread expectation of looting and massacre. The news was telegraphed to Djibouti by the railway office asking the refugees to return to their homes.

Teferi appointed Gebré to be the interim governor of the province and ordered Ïmmïru to go up to Addis Abeba at the head of a contingent of 6,000 well-equipped troops. Ïmmïru mobilized his contingent in a few days and went up to the capital by train; from there, he marched north on foot to join the Shewan army in time to take part in the bloody battle of Segelé on 27 October. In Harergé, Gebré quickly established government authority on the plateau. But establishing law and order in the lowlands (among the ʿAfar and the Somali, who remained restive for several weeks after the flight of Iyasu) turned out to be a tough undertaking.

The railway line was derailed by the ʿIsa a number of times throughout the month of October. It was difficult to ensure the security of the line. The train only gave service to the government but it had to be accompanied by a convoy. Finally, calm returned to the Ethio-Djibouti frontier on the railway side. The Ethiopian government assured the railway company that they would ensure security; and therefore the company decided to resume the operations of the line – passenger and cargo service - on 16 November.

In the meantime, Somali clans in other parts of Harergé were attacking Christians and administrative centres. In a telegram dated 10 November the governor of French Somaliland informs Paris that the Ethiopian government crashed an "important" group of rebel Somalis at Babilé, a place on the way from Harar to Jigjiga. This clash seems to have been tantamount to a battle, which involved sizeable forces on both sides. This is confirmed by Ïmmïru in his memoirs, who in fact recalls two major engagements – one at Babilé and another at Jigjiga.

To Jigjiga was sent the old and sickly *Fitawrari* Benté at the head of a big contingent to bring under control the clans who threatened to attack the town. Ïmmïru writes that Benté overcame the rebels with "great difficulty". To counter the Somali force concentrated at Babilé, another contingent drawn from various divisions of the Harergé army (notably from the Gondaré division) was deployed under the command of *Fitawrari* Sïleshi. In the fierce battle, government troops sustained heavy losses, which included the death of some senior officers; in the confusion, the commander fled assuming that his contingent had lost. In actual fact, the rebels had sustained heavier losses than the army, and had retreated (Ïmmïru, 2002 EC: 81).

Even if the rebels were defeated, the restiveness of Somalis continued in the Ogaden. There was a brief report from the French legation that stated that on 13 November at 5:40 p.m. fighting took place between Somalis and government troops. The report states that government troops suffered heavy losses but figures are not given. By the end of the month, however, calm was restored throughout the ʿAfar and Somali territories of Harergé. Thus, it took the government about a month to re-establish its authority in the region.

Reflections by way of conclusion

Developments in Harer in the months of October and November 1916 clearly show that the change of government was more than a simple putsch. The events that unfolded elsewhere in Ethiopia, particularly in the provinces of Wello, Arsi and Balé demonstrate that, underlying the coup, there were fundamental issues that affected the people of the country in a significant way. In these four provinces inhabited by a majority Muslim population, there was large scale participation of people in the fightings for the cause of Iyasu.[18] A study on the situation in Arsi and Bale in the first four decades of the 20th century brought to light very serious attempt by some of the *ulama* and chiefs of Arsi to organize support for Iyasu. Folk couplets and poems from Arsi demonstrate the popularity of the ruler among the people. When news of his downfall reached Arsi, some of the leading Islamic clerics and local chiefs organised themselves to support him. They sent a delegation to Harer to coordinate their attacks, which however was too late, but all the same they attacked *neft'eña* villages and burnt down a number of churches. The central government had to dispatch a contingent to crush the movement. In a similar fashion, two popular revolts broke out in Balé in support of the hapless prince – one in Ginnir and the other at a place called Dallo, but was suppressed by government forces (Abbas Haji 1990: 251-53). The civil war that raged in Wello from late 1916 to August 1917 has been well-studied.

On the other hand, his foes had worked hard, before they seized power, to bring onto their side as many of the provincial governors, courtiers and ecclesiastical figures as possible. A large number of lords (from the Shewan governors of the marcher provinces of the south and west to Ras Haylu of Gojjam) marched to fight against loyalist forces in northern Shewa and in Wello. As we have seen above, the Harer army had also opted from the very beginning to fight - very largely - for Teferi. Hence, in the documents they issued for the occasion, the conspirators presented themselves as "the people".

18 The movements in the four provinces were radically different from the resistance to the coup put up by high level Christian lords. The defiance of *Dejjazmach* Mekonnïn Demsïw, governor of some districts in eastern Wellega (Arjo, Horo, Gudru and the neighbouring districts) refused to accept the new rulers. They sent a contingent against him, which led to the battle of ...resulting in the defeat of Mekonnïn. Later, he was rehabilitated; he died during the war agains the Italians in 1936 bearing the high title of *Bitwedded*. Unlike Mekonnïn's defiance, the movements in Wello, Harargé, Arsi and Bale mass-based and Muslim-based.

For this reason, it is legitimate to ask whether the term coup d'état fully captures all the events following the deposition of the young ruler. Since big social forces were involved and since there were some powerful ideas articulated, however vaguely, by the Iyasu side, it is possible to argue that the events that unfolded as of September 1916 should be regarded as more than a "coup d'état" reactions against it. The deposition displayed characteristics of a veritable insurrection because it was the result of of a vast conspiracy that involved a large number of nobles who at the same time were commanders and officers of the many regiments of the imperial army called the Mahal Sefari. That is why the conspirators referred to themselves as "we the army and the people." This expression was not pure propaganda. It reflected the reality of a large scale participation in the movement to overthrow Iyasu. Unlike many insurrections in history that were unleased by popular forces, i.e. by forces from below, this one was rather a noble insurrection, i.e. by forces from above. That is why I argue that terms like insurrection or putsch better express the situation rather than a coup d'état, which is a sudden seizure of power organized secretly by a few people without any mass participation.

Iyasu's actions and movements in Harergé had subversive implications to the socio-political system even if they were crushed at an inchoate stage. The deposition smacked of a "conservative" backlash, which took the form of a coup to seize power and to quash the movement unleashed by the prince before it cristalized. It is important, however, to point out in what sense the term "conservative backlash" is used. One of the leaders of the anti-Iyasu insurrection was Teferi, who would emerge in the decades sthat follow, as Ethiopia's first systematic modernizer comparable in many ways to Muḥammad ʿAli of Egypt (reign: 1805-1848) and other modernizers in Asia. Actually, Iyasu's tenure on the throne showed that the young ruler did not develop clear, consistent and coherent ideas of modernization in sharp contrast to his archfoe, Teferi. Therefore, the term "conservative backlash" should not be construed as being "anti-modernization" as it is often understood in Ethiopia. It is used here in the sense of retaining the social and political structure of the country.

Bibliography

Abbas Haji Gnamo, 1990, *Les Oromo-Arsi, continuité et évolutions des institutions d'une societé éthiopienne*, Ph.D. thesis, Paris I Pantheon-Sorbonne.

Bahru Zewde, 2007, "Iyasu", S. Uhlig, ed., *Encyclopaedia Aethiopica*, vol. 3: 253-256.

Bairu Tafla, 2003, " ʿAbdullāhi ʿAlī Ṣādiq", S. Uhlig, ed., *Encyclopaedia Aethiopica*, vol. 1: 38.

Bairu Tafla, 2003, "Balča Safo", S. Uhlig, ed., *Encyclopaedia Aethiopica*, vol. 1: 457.

Ïmmïru: *Le'ul Ras* Ïmmïru Hayle Sïllasé, 2002 EC [2009-2010], *Kayyehut ke-mastwsew* [Amharic: From what I saw and heard], Addis Abeba: Addis Ababa University Press.

Marcus, Harold G., 1975, *The Life and Times of Menilek*, Oxford: Clarendon Press.

Pankhurst, Richard, 2005, "Ǝmməru Haylä Səllase", S. Uhlig, ed., *Encyclopaedia Aethiopica*, vol. 2: 276-277.

Rubinkowska, Hanna, 2007, "Ləʿul Sägäd", S. Uhlig, ed., *Encyclopaedia Aethiopica*, vol. 3: 557.

Sohier, Estelle, 2007, "Käbbädä Mängäša Atikäm", S. Uhlig, ed., *Encyclopaedia Aethiopica*, vol. 2: 314-315.

Tekle Hawaryat Tekle Maryam, 2004 EC [2011-2012], *(Ye-Hïyweté Tarik)* [*Amharic: Autobiography*], Addis Ababa: Addis Ababa University Press, 3rd reprint.

Zabolotskikh, Maxim, 2010, "Täsämma Ǝšäte", S. Uhlig, ed., *Encyclopaedia Aethiopica*, vol. 4: 864-866.

Lïj Iyasu and the ʿAfar

Aramis Houmed Soulé

Lïj Iyasu's relationship, as a sovereign, with the ʿAfar, the attitude of the latter at the time of his impeachment and subsequent escape and refuge in Awsa remain largely unknown. This episode traced the contours of an unusual alliance between an Abyssinian sovereign and the ʿAfar people. We shall begin by broadly describing the situation of contemporary Ethiopia and of the ʿAfar as a backdrop to the rise to power of this young sovereign. We shall then consider the policies of the latter during his short reign toward the ʿAfar, especially those living in the foothills of the highlands of Shewa and Wello. We shall see what the attitude of the ʿAfar was at the time of his overthrow and subsequent exile in Awsa but also the consequences incurred by the ʿAfar for their foray into this struggle for power at the centre. We shall also evoke the support they gave him at the time of his departure for Tïgray, where he was to be arrested and turned over to the central government. We shall conclude by briefly evoking the story of Mïnilïk III, a character through whom the memory of *Lïj* Iyasu was long preserved among the ʿAfar.

The situation of Ethiopia and of the ʿAfar in particular

Ethiopia had enjoyed partial sovereignty since 1906, when the European colonial powers set up on the shores of the Red Sea and of the Gulf of Aden (France, Great Britain and Italy) had agreed among themselves to split its territory into spheres of influence. This agreement was based on their desire to protect their investments and any capital sums that would be placed in this country. In respect to France, its interest carried upon the railway for which it saw its right to build the second leg from Dïrré Dawa to Addis Ababa, after the one from Djibouti to Dïrré Dawa itself.

The *Compagnie du Chemin de Fer* continued to finance a private militia that operated under the orders of a French adventurer called Pierre Carette-Bovet. Its official mandate was to insure the safety of the rails and of the worksites but unofficially, it participated in the uprooting and displacement campaigns aimed at removing the ʿAfar from its route. More precisely, Rosanna Van Gelder de Pineda (1995:253) thinks that during the lifetime of ras Makonnen, the governor of the province of Harar who died in 1906, the influential position of Pierre Carrette-Bovet at his side was due to his power as a "warlord amongst the Issa". In effect, a strategic military alliance had been cemented between the French, the Abyssinians and the nomadic ʿIsa all along the railway line. This explains why, in 1906, engineer Ozil, the leader of a mission sent by the minister of colonies to undertake the feasibility studies of the second part of the track, between Dïrré Dawa and Addis Abeba, rejected the ʿAfar as possible labour for the works (Rosanna Van Gelder de Pineda, 1995 :13).

The young prince was inheriting an empire of which the territorial limits were more or less tangible only on paper with the real integration of these different elements into the state leaving much to be desired and without effective authority. When it came to the ʿAfar political entities, King of kings Mïnilïk II had managed, by playing off the rivalries of the European colonisers against one and other, to have his sovereignty recognised over a large part of the ʿAfar territories situated between the coast and the highlands of Abyssinia. However, he had not sought to directly administrate the inhabitants of these lands nor to integrate the sultans and the chiefs of the territorial federations into the system of feudal privileges. His decision could be explained by the continued existence of an attitude characterized by what could be called the "Adal syndrome" that Hussein Ahmed (2001: 9) describes for the medieval period in these terms:

> "*The threat of raids into the territories of the Christian kingdom by the nomads of the lowlands remained a perennial source of anxiety for the medieval rulers. It also influenced the evolution of provincial administration and frontier defence policies and strategies.*"

We should replace "nomads of the lowlands" by "ʿAfar nomads of the lowlands", for it was indeed the ʿAfar who were referred to for having been the vanguard of the Muslim conquest of Abyssinia in the 16th century. The perusal of the Chronicle of the Wars of Amde Tsïyon, from the 14th century, brought an historical confirmation to this suspicion.

Awsa, the main ʿAfar sultanate, both economically and militarily, had been weakened by more than a decade of a fratricidal succession war. It had been divided into two distinct parts each ruled by an autonomous sovereign. The ʿAfar were perceived on the Christian highlands not as fellow citizens, but as latent enemies. They continued to designate them as Adal, in order to perpetuate towards them an enmity that stretched back to the Middle Ages. This negative image of the ʿAfar explains the organisation by *Lïj* Iyasu, soon after his direct accession to power following the death of his tutor of several military expeditions against those of them who lived in the Abyssinian foothills. The one of March 1912, undertaken at the request of the Oromo Warra Jillee,[1] was not only particularly deadly, as the attack took place by surprise and caused much human loss of life but also weakened them economically as their cattle was seized. Marcus (1995: 260) remarks that two years later, on the 14th of March 1914, another expedition was led against the ʿAfar populations.

1 It is one of the four branches of the Oromo Karayyu, also known as Jillee Suuba.

While at Zïqʷala, Iyasu was informed of the massacre of 300 Karayyu Oromos by the ʿAfar at the village of Sadimalka on the Awash River. By the time that he reached the scene, the raiders had fled. There upon Iyasu decided on a general chastisement of the ʿAfar, and en route to Ankober he devastated the land and killed many people, sparking off a general uprising among the population. Much booty was acquired and divided among the men when they reached Ankober.

Lïj Iyasu and his new policy towards the ʿAfar

After the death of emperor Mïnilïk, which occurred on 13 December 1913, *Lïj* Iyasu initiated a new policy towards the ʿAfar and other populations living on the margins of the empire and which sought to facilitate their integration into the Ethiopian State. This was in direct opposition to the policies of his grandfather Mïnilïk II and of his predecessors.

One of his first gestures took the guise of the creation, in ʿAfar land in northern Shewa, of a royal town bearing the evocative name of Weyna Hara.[2] During his first visit to this site, located to the south east of the village of Rassa, he came in the company of a reduced entourage. It was a great surprise to the ʿAfar, who would have then forgiven him his recent military expeditions against themselves. The impact of the young sovereign's act was emphasized by the court chronicler in these terms:

"None of the old Negarit, nor the large army (Ch'ifra),

He came into Weyne-Hara with just ten men;

He did not fight against them [ʿAfar] for he felt sorry for them."[3]

Soon after, *Lïj* Iyasu undertook a second visit to Wayna Hara and its region, this time with several objectives in mind. He wanted to reassure the ʿAfar about his desire to integrate them into the imperial political system. He recognised their claim to the neighbouring lands that the Oromo Warra Jillee were contesting them and gave their chiefs to right to oversee these localities with all the attributes of power.

Another objective of this visit had the pacification of interethnic relations in mind. To this effect, *Lïj* Iyasu personally took part in the negotiation process of their conflicts. He announced his project of establishing a town on the site of the actual Senbeté which had been the main area at the heart of the conflict between them in 1912. He named the site T'énayé, after his own war name.[4] This town was to be mainly inhabited by his Muslim Argobba, Oromo and ʿAfar subjects and as such was to become an important symbol of his new policy of cementing good relations between nations.

2 An ʿAfar expression that literally means: "The forum that we have been missing".

3 Quoted by Ahmed Hassen Omer, 1997: 140.

4 T'éna was the name of his horse.

Lïj Iyasu also used his stay in the region to extend to the ʿAfar the old arranged marriage policy in order to establish blood ties with the important families. He took wives in two of the large confederations of this region (Dokʿa[5]), Modayto and Debne (Berhanou Abebe 2001: 320). He had two daughters[6] with the Modayto women. Another child of *Lïj* Iyasu, Melake Tsehay, who was to be crowned emperor on 2 September 1937 by a group resisting the Italian occupation was also born in the region of the lowlands of Yïfat. Mïnilïk Iyasu evokes in an interview Melake Tsehay "[a] *half-sister of mine from an Adali woman who was said to have died while fighting with patriot forces led by* Ras *Abebe Aregai*" (*The Ethiopian Herald*, 30 October 1974: 3).

In the course of the exchange, Mïnilïk Iyasu spoke in ʿAfar and the translation from Amharic to ʿAfar and vice-versa was undertaken by one of his distant cousins, Alwan Abdulkader. This mistake about the gender of Melake Tsehay could come from either the interpreter or the journalist. Some of the genealogies of the imperial family that we have consulted on the internet give the Muslim name of his mother: Momina. We could be here in the presence of the women from the Debne federation.

Later, probably in 1915, *Lïj* Iyasu wed a third ʿAfar women, Fatuma Abubakar. Issued from a rich family of traders, harking from the north cost of the Gulf of Tajurah, that had dominated throughout the 19th century the intermediary trade between Abyssinia and the shores of the Red Sea and of the Gulf of Aden, she was not an unknown entity. Her father was the *Neggadras* Abubakar Maḥammad, the governor of the commercial town of Channo[7] which had taken Alïyyu Amba's place after that locality's decline. Her grandfather was the *Neggadras* Maḥammad Abubakar, the governor in the last quarter of the 19th century of the commercial town of Alïyyu Amba, then the representative of the interests of Mïnilïk II on the coast and in the new port town of Djibouti that he would have granted, following certain sources, in 1888, to France (Dubois 1997:55). Her great grandfather was no other than the famous Abubakar Ibrahim Shehem, *Pasha* of Zeylaʿ (Fontrier 2003). From the end of the 19th century, the members of the family lost their role as obligatory intermediaries in favour of European traders supported by their respective states. However, one of them, the *Neggadras* Maḥammad Abubakar, continued to enjoy the trust of Mïnilïk, who was unwilling to rely solely on the Europeans. Ahmed Hassen Omer (2007: 396) insists upon his exceptional role "*as he combined the management of the commercial and diplomatic affairs* [of Ethiopia] *with those of the interests of his family and of his enduring loyalty to Menilek*".

Lïj Iyasu made the acquaintance of Fatuma upon the occasion of a reception that *Neggadras* Abubakar had organised in his honour in his home, some say in Addis

5 This geographical term designates here the escarpment of the highlands of Shewa inhabited by the ʿAfar.

6 One of them, named Fatuma, was later wed by Nasra ʿUndé [ʿUndé (son of) Nasra, the name of the mother], a great ʿAfar chief from the escarpment of north Shewa. Cf. Ahmed Hassen Omer 1997: 141.

7 Situated 40 km to the east of Debre Bïrhan, on the plateau's escarpment.

Abeba and others, in Channo. It is said that he immediately asked for her hand in marriage and a ceremony was later organised to celebrate their union. Fatuma became his favourite. It is for her that he asked when in 1922, after his arrest and imprisonment in Fïché, he had obtained the authorisation to have by his side the women of his choice (Gebre-Igziabiher 1994: 417). Fatuma Abubakar[8] was to give *Lïj* Iyasu a heir named Mïnilïk[9], about whom we shall hear more later.

If today, most agree that these marriages of *Lïj* Iyasu had as objective to consolidate his empire in its marginal regions, they were perceived at the time by Shewan Amhara as a long term threat to their interests. The young sovereign's words to the contrary did not assuage their suspicion as it continued to be exteriorised as in the following couplets by an anonymous author:

"Listen, Iyasu Abba Tena; only one word,
Your intimacies are with the Galla [the Oromo]
and Your marriage with the Adal [the ʿAfar]*!"* (Ahmed Hassen Omer 1997:142.)

Lïj Iyasu was not the first Ethiopian sovereign to wed one, or even several, ʿAfar women. Without seeking too far, he had an illustrious precedent in the person of the Emperor Yoḥannïs IV. The latter had wed Halima Sirra ʿAli,[10] the sister of Yakumi Sirra ʿAli, the chief of the Herto country in the oriental escarpment of the highlands of Tïgray. Rebaptised T'ïbebe Sïllasé, she died soon after having given birth to just one son: Ar'aya Sïllasé. The emperor himself had ʿAfar blood by his great grandfather in the maternal line, the *Shum* Weldu of ʿAgame. From this stems his family's closeness with the ʿAfar, which is emphasised by certain authors (Young 1997). Yoḥannïs IV had, in similar fashion to his predecessors, had recourse to kidnapping to realise his marriage as the parents of a Muslim cannot give their consent to an union with a Christian. The fact that *Lïj* Iyasu had been granted an exception to this rule fired the suspicion held towards him by the Christians inhabitants of the highlands. However, in the case of Fatuma Abubakar, Gontran de Juniac (2001: 63) asserts that:

"*On the eve of her wedding with Yassou although a fervent Muslim, she had had herself baptised in secret in the Abo church behind the French legation in Addis Ababa and had insured herself that her baptism was inscribed in the parochial register in order, if the need arose, to dispose of a document she could avail herself of.*"

---

8 She was the second cousin of ʿAli ʿAref Burhan who was the vice-president then the president of the Conseil de gouvernement du Territoire français des Afars et des Issas (June 1960-17 July 1976).

9 An interview with Béchir ʿAbdo in Addis Ababa the 7th of Decembre 2009 and the interview of Mïnilïk, "Who is Menelik Eyasu?" *The Ethiopian Herald of the 30th of October 1974, pp. 1, 3.*

10 His name is quoted by Teshele Tibebu (1995 :172) to illustrate how by arranged interethnic marriages, the Ethiopian political system tried to prevent ethnicity from becoming the base of political supremacy : This policy was sometimes pushed to extremes. For example, Muslims were forcibly baptized and brought into political and matrimonial bonds. Emperor Yoh'annïs IV's wife, Halima, an ʿAfar, and *Nïgus* Mika'él of Wello, are cases in point. This information is confirmed by the interview of the author of these line with the commander Mussa Yasin Mahammoda, an ex marine officer, diplomat and minister in the Derg regime. Addis Ababa, 15th of August 2006.

Lïj Iyasu frequently sojourned in ʿAfar country in the foothills of Shewa and regularly showed himself beside its chiefs. For example, in one of these photographs, he is shown dressed in similar fashion to them, bearing the famous cutlass in his belt. Prayer beads in hand, he entered many times the compound of existing mosques and undertook the construction of new ones as elsewhere in Muslim lands.

These gestures are now perceived in hindsight as resulting from the young sovereign's intention to give his Muslim subjects the right to see themselves as being full members of the Ethiopian unity and hence favour Islamic-Christian relations. For the Amhara of Shewa, the initiatives of the young sovereign formed another worrying trend. They insinuated that he was simulating being a Christian but secretly remained in reality a Muslim. For example, a rather banal fact, the Arabic inscription on his *Nïgus'* sceptre stoked the suspicion of Shewan Christianity against him. This was however a common practise in the north of Ethiopia.

As related above, during the lifetime of Mïnilïk, *Neggadras* Maḥammad Abubakar and his son *Neggadras* Abubakar continued to gravitate in the imperial entourage, even if their influence was diminished. While the father mostly lived on the coast, the son, himself, had his high quarters close to the imperial palace, more precisely in Arat Kilo, on the plot now occupied by the building of the ministry of national education, which was then called *Neggadras* Abubaker *sefer*. His status evolved with the marriage of his daughter to *Lïj* Iyasu and be became an influent unofficial adviser to the latter. In July 1916, he was part of a small group of personalities who accompanied *Lïj* Iyasu on his visit to Djibouti, considered unexpected and somehow unwelcome by the colonial administration. Upon this occasion, the presence in this port town of the ʿAfar chiefs from the north of the Gulf of Tadjourah, with whom the young sovereign would have held talks lets one think that the *Neggadras* Abubakar and his father had made preparations in advance for this trip. Upon their return, he was nominated as chief of the surveillance police of the railway between the frontier of the French colony and the Awash, in effect replacing *Ato* Mïrch'a, an Ethiopian from the Christian highlands.

Abubakar officially took his post in Dïrré Dawa but very quickly returned to Addis Abeba where the political fault lines lay, leaving his brother Adbulkader to represent him. This decision of the young sovereign was judged by De Mazérieux, an administrator of the Cie, as being very menacing to the railway.

> "*Ato Marcha had held for many years, the function of chief of police between the border and Aouache, and his replacement by Abou Baker, a Danakil long aligned with Abyssinian policies. With Ato Marcha who was conversant with the customs and methods of the Cie, and to which he was especially completely devoted, difficulties were quickly ironed out. Abou Baker is very well known in Abyssinia and in the Cie so that the same will not be expected from him*" (Van Gelder de Pineda 1995: 590).

The nomination of Abubakar in Dïrré Dawa was concomitant with the removal of *Dejjazmach* Teferi Mekonnïn from the oriental province of Harer that the latter considered as being his family fiefdom. It menaced a tacit agreement that prevailed between the French administration represented by the railway company and *Ras* Mekonnïn Welde Mika'él and his family which was detrimental to the ʿAfar of the region. On a symbolic level, it signified the return to affairs of the descendants of the *Pasha* Abubakar Ibrahim Shehem in what could be called oriental Ethiopia.

Impeachment of *Lïj* Iyasu and support of the ʿAfar

The young sovereign is overthrown on 27 September 1916, on the day of an important Christian feast, that of the the finding of the true cross, by the Shewan aristocracy, after having obtained his excommunication by the patriarch of the Orthodox Church, the *Abune* Matéwos.

Upon this occasion, the authors of the coup d'état explained their motivations as being *Lïj* Iyasu's apostasy and conversion to Islam, the religion of his paternal ancestors. Hence, they had the Christians believe that by this fact, the cat had been released among the pigeons.[11]

The neighbouring colonial powers (France, Great Britain and Italy) [12] had corroborated, or even abated these accusations. They held against the young sovereign his rapprochement with Turkey, in the context of the First World War in which the latter had aligned itself with Germany, his opposition to their policy of spheres of interest, and finally his anticolonial politics expressed on the ground by his support to Muḥammad ʿAbdille Ḥassan (the "Mad-Mullah" of British colonial historiography) at war against the British in the north of Somalia and the shored up relations with the ʿAfar chiefs. The latter were perceived by the French and the British as potential enemies as they had taken from them the trade with the Ethiopian highlands. At the time of his deposition, *Lïj* Iyasu was in Harer. After having attempted in vain to deny the accusations levelled against him, especially the accusation of apostasy, he regrouped his partisans in the region of the ʿAfar in the escarpment of the Harer plateau and led them from Dïrré Dawa on 11 October with the intention of marching on the capital. The confrontation with the Shewan forces sent to capture him took place at Mi'éso, a railway station, in the east of the country. The forces of the fallen emperor were routed but he managed, with the help of the ʿAfar, to escape his enemies and make it to Weyne Hara on the Shewan escarpment. There, he kept himself busy recruiting the ʿAfar from the region to recreate his escorting army, greatly reduced by the numerous defections under the menace of *Abune* Matéwos' excommunication. He had in mind to continue this activity in other parts of the region, especially amongst the Oromo. He

---

11 A poem of Afe-Werq Gebre Yesus dated from 9 December 1916 bears witness to the parallel established between *Lïj* Iyasu and *Imam* Ahmad Grañ. Cf. Rouaud, 1991: 265.

12 One can read the document "Manifest of the princes and people of Ethiopia'" published as an annex of Berhanou Abebe 2001.

thought they would support him come what may. For he had forged close relationships with their chiefs, who had been his "*protégés*" since his accession to the throne. On the road to Ankober he learnt of his father's defeat in Segelé on 27 October at the hands of the Shewan forces led by *Fitawrari* Habte Giyorgis Dinagdé[13] and *Dejjach* Balcha Safo[14], both Oromo.

This evolution pushed him to undertake attacks against the partisans of his Shewan rivals in the highlands, but apart from the ʿAfar, he did not find the support he had counted upon in the region. The disappointment stemmed from the attitude of the Oromo chiefs, who not only turned their backs on him but reinforced with their men the ranks of the adversaries that were attempting to seize him.

The only places still loyal to *Lïj* Iyassu and which continued to defend themselves to the end were the ʿAfar inhabited districts around his town of Weyne-Hara and it would be via Rassa and Weyne-Hara that he finally succeeded to evade the hot pursuit of the enemies. *Lïj* Iyasu's attempt to call the local Oromo to his support was not as successful as with the ʿAfar. He tried to mobilize a large force from the Fursi, Arbawayyu, and Jille Oromo through their traditional chiefs like Abba Darra Wane, Gunjo Alle, Omar Alisha Jarso, *Fitawrari* Dingo Omer and *Ato* Muhicho Arbiyyi, all of whom had been closely associated with him in the years 1912-1916. They now abandoned him in the days of his great need. (Ahmed Hassen 1997: 143-144).

This situation forced *Lïj* Iyasu to leave this region with the help of the ʿAfar for the fortress of Meqdela in north Wello, by way of Desé. Upon his arrival in this family fiefdom, a battle opposed his forces with those of *Ras* Abate. Beaten, *Lïj* Iyasu managed to escape.

On 27 August 1917, another battle took place in Wello between the deposed sovereign and *Fitawrari* Habte Giyorgis, the minister of war. The latter prevailed. *Lïj* Iyasu again fled and took refuge with a small escorting group and servitors in the sultanate of Awsa at the side of the *Sultan* Yayyo Maḥammad aka Data Yayyo[15] (r. 1910-1927). The latter gave him a reception worthy of his rank and had him benefit from the right of hospitality which is sacred among the ʿAfar. He set himself up in one of his camps, that of Gassissan, situated on a hill in the vicinity of Aysaʿyta and protected by seven walls of dry joined stone. The Ethiopians called it Iyasu Gora which

13 Born in Shewa, a common soldier in the troops of *ras* Gobana Dachi, a famous Oromo auxiliary of Menelik II, noticed at the battle of Adwa against the Italians by the latter who elevated him to the rank of *Fitawrari*, then minister of war in 1908, a charge he held until his death in 1926.

14 Raised to the rank of *Dejjazmach* after the battle of Adwa in 1896, he was named governor of Sidamo that he went on to lead for 30 years. After the death of Yilma Mekonnïn, the elder brother of Teferi Mekonnïn (the future Hayle Sïllasé), he replaced him at the head of Harar from 1907 to 1910 during which the young Tafari took his place in Sidamo. After 1916, he was reassigned to Sidamo and remained there until 1928, year in which he was arrested after a conflict with the government. Following this, he was allowed to go and live in his village of Agemja, in Gurageland. There he remained until his death in 1936 in an attack on Addis Ababa, which had just been occupied by the Italians.

15 Yayyo the Black.

translates literally from Amharic as "Iyasu's hill". *Lïj* Iyasu's choice of refuge alongside *Sultan* Yayyo in Awsa can be explained by the fact that he thought that he was the only one who could offer him protection at this difficult time. At the time of his escape, it had been less than a year that the *Sultan* Yayyo had definitely imposed himself as the unique authority of the sultanate of Awsa at the end of a bloody succession war during which he had managed to put to flight his half brother, Ḥanfaré Maḥammad Ḥanfaré. The latter had ruled over a part of the country, after a power sharing agreement had been brokered in 1910 by *Ras* Mika'él of whom he was the favourite. The few scraps of information that we have about *Lïj* Iyasu's sojourn in Awsa confirm that he lived as a Christian. He drank the alcohol that his servitors prepared for him from sorghum.

The consequences for the ʿAfar of their support to *Lïj* Iyasu

The ʿAfar paid an extremely dear price for their incursion into the central power struggle in which they supported *Lïj* Iyasu. The first reprisals were aimed at those of them who lived along the railway line, from Dïrré Dawa to Afdem. In October 1916, the Ethiopian forces victorious over *Lïj* Iyasu seized their houses (Mersé Hazen 2007: 114). The possessions of the family of the *Neggadras* Abubakar Maḥammad Abubakar in Addis Abeba and in other parts of Ethiopia were also seized.

The *Neggadras* himself took refuge in Tadjourah, then a French protectorate. There, it seems he attempted to raise troops to come to his son in law's help. In April 1917, the Ethiopian government requested from the French the permission to seize him by any means available. Permission was first granted orally by the minister of France in Ethiopia, Maurice de Coppet, to the regent *Ras* Teferi Mekonnïn and to the minister for foreign affairs, *Dejjach* Mulugéta, then confirmed by him in his letter of 14 June expressed in these terms:

> *"To this letter [letter of the 10th of April from the Ethiopian minister of foreign affairs], I answered two days latter that I would telegraph Monsieur Fillon and the 20th of April at the Guebbi, I had made known to Your Excellency and to His Imperial Highness, the Ras Raffari, that we had, the governor of Djibouti and myself, no objection to Ethiopian troops seeking to seize, even upon French soil, a man who is both an enemy of us and of yourself"* (Labrousse 1992: 239).

The Empress Zewditu Mïnilïk (1917-1930) and the *Ras* Teferi Mekonnïn, heir to the throne and plenipotentiary regent repeatedly asked *Sultan* Yayyo Mahammad Ḥanfaré to deliver *Lïj* Iyasu to them and had him summoned to Addis Abeba. But the sultan denied the *Lïj*'s presence by his side and refused to answer to the summons, invoking his incapacity to ride a horse because of his age. Some of our informers have him reply to the Zawditu-Teferi tandem that he does not recognise their authority.[16] Their declarations are given credence by his questioning of the tribute payment.

16 See also Kinfe-Regb Zeleke, 1982 :14.

In order to punish the ʿAfar of Awsa and their chief, the Ethiopian government sent, on 30 March 1919, important forces, estimated in oral sources as being several tens of thousand strong.[17] Some came from Wello and the others, from Shewa and from Harer. They were placed under the command of *Ras* Kebbede Mengesha Atikem,[18] who had been recently named governor of Wello. He replaced at this post *Ras* Kassa Haylu, relieved of his post for not having been able to capture *Lïj* Iyasu and for not submitting the neighbouring ʿAfar country to the *pax Amharica*. The forces coming from Shewa were commanded by *Azzazh* Meshesha from Ankober and were accompanied by Alo, the son of the previous *Sultan* Maḥammad Aydaḥis and the second by the deposed *Sultan* Ḥanfaré Maḥammad Ḥanfaré aka Rokkiyah Ḥanfaré.

Forewarned of the movement of the Abyssinian troops, sultan Yayyo avoided confrontation and retreated with his host and all of his possessions to the region of Balho, a locality near the north east border of the current Djibouti Republic where he was not pursued. The Ethiopian forces established their base at Dale, in the oasis of Awsa, from where they forayed out as far as the vicinity of Harissa, to the west of Lake Abhe. On their way, they seized cattle, killed men and set fire to huts and *tukul-s*. Some of our informers declare that on this occasion many precious manuscript books produced by the local *ʿuléma* and dedicated to the praises of the prophet and his followers, to treatises on the *hadith-s*, but certainly also fragments of the chronicles of the region were reduced to ashes.[19] Very quickly, the Ethiopian forces faced illnesses of which dysentery, which provoked many deaths within their ranks. Seeing this, *Ras* Kebbede took the decision to retreat on 19 May, leaving behind Rokkiyah Ḥanfaré (Ḥanfaré son of Rokkiya) who once again proclaimed himself *Sultan*. On their way home, the troops of *Ras* Kebbede continued their attacks against the ʿAfar and their cattle rustling. Italian sources give the following summary of the expedition:

> "*The Abyssinians arrived in Aussa as an army of ants, preying on all that they found; killing many enemies and creating terror among the population. The troops of Ras Chebbedè raided about four hundred camels, 10,000 cattle and little less than 3,000 sheep. About 600 Danakil were killed and 200 captured. The Abyssinians killed in combat and in the raid were only 120 but the deaths caused by disease were 700, almost all victims of dysentery and heat stroke. If we exclude the booty, from the point of view of human casualties, this Abyssinian raid over Danakil was more penalizing for the people of the plateau.*" (Luppi 2009, vol. 2: 956-957)

17 The Italian sources talk of 6 000 men. Cf. Luca Lupi, 2009: 954.

18 The son of *Ras Bitwedded* Mengesha Atikem. This faithful ally of Teferi Mekonnïn (the future Hayle Sïllasé I) had been relieved of his post as governor of Wello in September 1928 in favour of the eldest son of the latter, Asfa Wesen. He died in 1940. Cf. McCann, 1987:125.

19 Interview with *Shaykh* Mahammad Abdallah. Ad-Hamaddo (Afʾambo), 11th of May 2006.

Upon hearing of the Ethiopian troops' retreat, *Sultan* Yayyo undertook without difficulty the reconquering of Awsa from where he once again chased his half brother Ḥanfaré and his followers. The latter found his death during his flight towards Shewa in an attack of the ʿAfar of Baadu. *Lïj* Iyasu and his retinue were once again reinstated in their camp of Gasisan. For traditional Ethiopian historiography, which refuses to accept the existence at this time of a sovereign ʿAfar power, capable of granting political asylum, since September 1917, *Lïj* Iyasu had been wandering the ʿAfar desert.

Departure of *Lïj* Iyasu for Tïgray and his arrest

In the course of the second semester of 1919, *Lïj* Iyasu left Awsa, of his own volition, to meet up with *Ras* Sïyyum in Tïgray.[20]

This decision, according to oral sources, followed preliminary contacts with the latter, who was married to one of his sisters. Kept secret, these contacts had been made possible by *Sultan* Yayyo, who used the services of ʿAfar chiefs from the foothills of the Tïgray highlands, familiar with the court of *Ras* Sïyyum. It is also with their help that he managed to reach the part of this province administrated by his brother in law without being intercepted en route by the men of *Ras* Gugsa Ar'aya, the grandson of Yoḥannïs IV, who himself administered the south and the south east of Tïgray. He made this trip accompanied by a small number of servitors, leaving with *Sultan* Yayyo the others of whom a certain Tesemma. The intention behind the decision to travel to Tïgray by the deposed sovereign and the attitude of the Tïgrayan *Ras* is interpreted in different ways in the existing literature. Some think that *Lïj* Iyasu was expecting support to combat the central government from his brother in law and restore him to power. This hypothesis is difficult to imagine. *Ras* Sïyyum, a prudent man, hadn't shown solidary for his family of in-laws when they were in better straits. *Lïj* Iyasu, tired by his life as an exile in ʿAfar country, rather wanted to give himself up to the central government. Towards the end of his sojourn in Awsa, he had shown signs of fatigue. For example, he had been told to mend his ways many times for having gone down to the ford and tried to accost women.

Lïj Iyasu had obtained the promise of *Ras* Sïyyum to use his good standing with the central government to negotiate the best conditions for his rendition. This hypothesis is confirmed by the Italian sources quoted by major Dodds from the British legation in his correspondence of August 1920. In the course of a long and secret conversation in

20 Following the administrative reorganisation of the empire at the end of the 1910s, Tïgray was divided into two: the western part with 'Adwa as capital was placed under the administration of *Ras* Sïyyum and the eastern part with Meqele as capital under the administration of *Ras* Gugsa Ar'aya Sïllasé. Upon the death of the latter in 1933, his son, *Dejjazmach* Hayle Sïllasé Gugsa inherited the domain from which three localities had been subtracted of which Aksum, given to his cousin and rival, *Ras* Sïyyum, who was also named military commander of all of the province of Tïgray. Hayle Sïllasé Gugsa was not authorised to inherit from his father the title of *Ras*. Because of this he harboured a strong grievance towards the emperor and collaborated with the Italians between 1936 and 1941.

Meqelé with the Italian agent in ʿAdwa, signor Polaire, *Lïj* Iyasu would have informed him of his contacts with his aunt the empress Zewditu, who desired his surrender (quoted by Hagos G/Yohannes, 2003 : 61).

The emperor Hayle Sïllasé evokes in his memoirs the attempt of *Ras* Sïyyum to reconcile *Lïj* Iyasu with empress Zewditu and himself (quoted by Hagos G/Yohannes, 2003: 66). He however omits to add that this process was probably derailed because of his opposition and of his demands of unconditional surrender.

Following this, *Lïj* Iyasu left the territory of Tïgray under the administration of *Ras* Sïyyum for the lands under the administration of *Ras* Gugsa Ar'aya, the grandson of Yoḥannïs IV. *Ras* Gugsa easily apprehended him on 28 January 1921 and delivered him on 21 May in the town of Desé to *Ras* Teferi Mekonnïn himself.

Mïnilïk III perpetuates the memory of *Lïj* Iyasu

The memory of *Lïj* Iyasu remains alive and well among the ʿAfar by way of his son Mïnilïk. He was born in 1917 in the territory of the sultanate of Tadjourah, at that time a French protectorate, where his mother had sought refuge. The latter could have called him Abubakar, from the name of her father, or Mahammad from that of her paternal grandfather, but she chose for him the name Mïnilïk. She brought him up in her family.

Mïnilïk Iyasu surfaces in colonial sources in March 1935, when on the eve of the Italian invasion, the French administration took an interest in him after the king of kings Hayle Sïllasé had asked if the French government would like to entrust the adolescent to him so that he could bring him up as a son. Having refused this request, it allotted a stipend to the young Mïnilïk who lived in the town of Tadjourah with his cousin, the sultan Hoummad Mahammad Ibrahim (r. 14 December 1928 - 21 April 1962), his elder by seven years. They put him under close surveillance, fearing that the Italians may organise his departure for Ethiopia.[21] With the advent of the Vichy state's administration at the head of the territory and the maritime blockade imposed by the allies, surveillance was relaxed and the young Mïnilïk was deprived of the stipend he had been enjoying until then. In 1941, with the help of his maternal great uncle, Dawud Abdallah, a merchant, he managed to establish connections with one of his brothers, Yohannes, who was at the head of an anti-Italian resistance group in the Gonder area. Accompanied by a small group of companions of whom his cousin Omar Ali[22], he left Tadjourah aboard a make-do vessel for 'Asab. Boarded at sea by a British warship, he gave a false identity (Mahammad Hassan), fearing that the British he knew to be allied with Hayle Sïllasé would turn him over to the latter.[23] They were brought

21 Gontran de Juniac, 2001 :135.

22 Ayla Ali Omar in the ʿAfar manner.

23 And interview with Béchir Abdo Mohamed in Addis Ababa, on 7 December 2009.

to Aden where they remained for three days, before being released and making their way to ʿAsab. And from there, they went to Bati. Once there, Mïnilïk learnt of the return of Hayle Sïllasé and of the surrender of his brother. He turned tracks. Towards the end of this same year, his maternal family negotiated his return to Ethiopia with Hayle Sïllasé, who had just recovered his throne, through the intermediary of the heir Asfa Wesen. He was accompanied by his mother who died one year later in Dïrré Dawa. He was placed under close surveillance at the palace where he lived for four years then in the Afïnch'o Ber neighbourhood where he was assigned a decent dwelling after the failed coup d'état of the Neway brothers in 1960. This event coincided – it has to be recalled – with the accession to power in the little French colony of Djibouti of his great uncle ʿAli ʿAref Burhan. Hayle Sïllasé authorised him to move to Dïrré Dawa and to Asebot in West Harergé, where five *gasha-s* of land were allotted to him as well as Oromo Ittu to cultivate it for him as sharecroppers. Mïnilïk died without bearing descendants.

Conclusion

During his short reign, *Lïj* Iyasu initiated a policy of integrating the ʿAfar into the Ethiopian state, starting with those from the foothills of the highlands of Shewa. This decision, which was contrary to the policies of his predecessors, was a source of worry to the Amhara dignitaries but also to the European colonial powers present on the coast. After his deposition, *Lïj* Iyasu was able to measure the loyalty of the ʿAfar and of the sultan of Awsa. He was certainly the first Ethiopian *Nïgus* to have understood, despite his young age and his attachment to the Christian faith, the necessity of not marginalising the populations of the lowlands because of historic or religious rivalries.

Thanks to Yves-Marie Stranger for the English translation of the French original text.

Bibliography

Omer Ahmed Hassen, 1997, "State and Ethnic Relations in Northeastern Shawa (Ethiopia), 1912-1935", *Ethiopia in Broader Perspectives: Proceedings of the 12th International Conference of Ethiopian Studies,* Vol.1, Kyoto, 138-150.

Ahmed Hassen Omer, 2007, *Islam, commerce et politique dans l'Ifat (Éthiopie centrale) au XIXe siècle : l'émergence d'une ville carrefour*, Aleyu Amba, thèse de doctorat d'histoire, Université de Paris I, Panthéon-Sorbonne.

Berhanou Abebe, 2001, "Le coup d'état du 26 septembre 1916", *Annales d'Ethiopie*, 17, 309-359.

Fontrier, Marc, 2003, *Abou-Bakr Ibrahim, Pacha de Zeyla-Marchand d'esclaves. Commerce et diplomatie dans le golfe de Tadjourah 1845-1885*, Paris, L'Harmattan.

Gebre-Igziabiher Elyas, 1994, *Prowess, Piety and Politics, The Chronicle of Abeto Iyasu and Empress Zewditu of Ethiopia (1909-1930)*, Reidulf K. Molvaer (ed.), Köln: Rüdiger Köppe Verlag.

Hagos G/Yohannes, 2003, *Political History of Tigray: Rivalry for Power (1910-1935)*, M.A. Thesis in History, Addis Ababa University.

Hussein Ahmed, 2001, *Islam in Nineteenth-Century Wallo, Ethiopia. Revival, Reform and Reaction*, Leiden, Brill.

Kinfe-Regb Zeleke, 1982, "The Episode of Eyassu Menelik (1896-1935)", A paper submitted to the 7th International Conference of Ethiopian Studies, Lund, Sweden, April 1982.

Juniac, Gontran de, 2001, *Le dernier Roi des Rois. L'Ethiopie de Haïlé-Sellassié*, Paris, L'Harmattan.

Labrousse, Henri, 1992, "La neutralité éthiopienne pendant la Première Guerre mondiale", in *Récits de la mer Rouge et de l'Océan Indien*, Paris, Economica.

Lupi, Luca, 2009, *Dancalia. L'esplorazione dell'Afar, una avventura italiana*, vol. 2, Firenze, Istituto Geographico Militare.

McCann, James, 1987, *From Poverty to Famine in Northeastern Ethiopia. A Rural History 1900-1935*, University of Pennsylvania Press.

Mersé Hazen Wolde Qirqos, 2004, *Of what I saw and heard. The last years of Emperor Menelik II & The Brief rule of Iyassu*, Addis Abeba, CFEE.

Rouaud, Alain, 1991, *Afä-Wärq, un intellectuel éthiopien, témoin de son temps 1868-1974*, Paris, Les éditions du CNRS.

Teshele Tibebu, 1995, *The Making of Modern Ethiopia 1896-1974*, Lawrenceville & Asmara, The Red Sea Press.

Van Gelder de Pineda, Rosanna, 1995, *Le chemin de fer de Djibouti à Addis Abeba*, Paris, L'Harmattan.

Young, John, 1997, *Peasant Revolution in Ethiopia. The Tigray People's Liberation Front, 1975-1991*, Cambridge, CUP.

"Who is Menelik Eyasu?", 1974, *The Ethiopian Herald* du 30 octobre, pp. 1-3.

Family Memories on the Captivity of *Lïj* Iyasu

A Personal Account

Asfa-Wossen Asserate Kassa

The history of my great-granduncle[1] has to be reconsidered. He was not just the young, flamboyant, obstinate and careless playboy, which the Western powers depicted him as, but a man with a great vision for Ethiopia. No doubt he loved life and enjoyed his royal prerogatives, but which teenager in his place would not have? As a matter of fact *Abéto Lïj* Iyasu is to be admired for a number of his values, which are indeed unusual for a person of his youthful age:

– His wisdom not to trust the British and French governments of those days, who were eager to end Ethiopia's sovereignty.

– His instance to treat Christian and Muslim Ethiopians equally, making Ethiopia a haven of tolerance in Africa.

– His refusal to accept Italian military aid whilst hiding in Awsa not willing to give up the future colonialists a reason to invade his country.

– His Pan-Africanist policies and his rigorous stand against colonial rule in Somalia by supporting the "Mad Mullah"[2]. Yes, contrary to what we learnt from Ethiopian and Western history books in the past decades, *Abéto Lïj* Iyasu was a man of convictions and a great Ethiopian Patriot.

His shortcomings were almost all due to his trust in unworthy people like *Lïʿul Ras* Haylu, who only thought of their own position and of ways to influence a man they always regarded as still a child. His Imperial Highness's fatal mistake indeed was to accept *Lïʿul Ras* Haylu's help in fleeing from *Lïʿul Ras* Kasa's fort at Fïché. However understandable it is for a prisoner to want to regain his freedom, the break-out was ill-organized and the "worst-case" factor was never handled, the "worst case" factor being the possibility of *Abeto Lïj* Iyasu falling in the hands of the Emperor Hayle Sïllasé again. *Lïʿul ras* Haylu knew that the reason the Ethiopian dignitaries decided to put the

1 *Lïj* Iyasu was the maternal uncle of the author's great-grandmother Empress Menen

2 As the British called Abdille Hasan, the quasi-sovereign Somali leader active especially in the territory of British Somaliland, who could assert his authority over an extended period of time.

young ruler in the custody of *Li'ul Ras* Kasa was because they knew that he would never deliver *Lïj* Iyasu to his greatest foe Emperor Hayle Sïllasé. *Li'ul Ras* Kasa was well-known for his astute Christian values and was, furthermore, related to both parties. And I know from my late father, *Li'ul Ras* Asraté, that my grandfather never treated *Abéto Lïj* Iyasu as a prisoner but accorded him all the respect due to a former head-of-state. Whenever he entered the room, in which *Abéto Lïj* Iyasu was held he put off his shoes and *kabba* and bowed three times before addressing his prisoner. *Li'ul ras* Kasa insisted to Empress Zewditu that a "golden" (brass) bed be brought from the palace for *Lïj* Iyasu, which she graciously did send together with fine Persian carpets. What a difference to *Lïj* Iyasu's imprisonment in Gara Muleta! The meals of the royal prisoner were prepared by my grandmother, *Li'ïlt* Tsïggé Maryam, personally, because she feared that her cooks might be bought for money and poison him. Thus, a special wooden case was made with a safe lock, in which the different *wet'* and the *ïnjera* were put in. The case was then locked and taken to *Lïj* Iyasu, who had the only other key. In other words, *Lïj* Iyasu's sojourn in Fïché was more of a comfortable house arrest than imprisonment. His departure from there and his final capture in Tïgray by *Li'ul Ras* Gugsa Ar'aya[3], then his terrible imprisonment under the harshest conditions in Gara Muleta, guaranteed his end. This is one aspect of *Lïj* Iyasu's life, which very few know about and I am sure there are many other aspects of this dashing personality, of which we are still unaware.

May I encourage all the assembled fellow éthiopisants to research the fascinating history of an Ethiopian ruler, who still awaits a fair trial and an impartial verdict of the people of Ethiopia.

3 Governor in eastern Tïgray and grandson of Emperor Yohannïs IV and thus close relative of the wife of *Nïgus* Mika'él.

Glossary of Terms and Events of the *Lïj* Iyasu Period

Controversial and Non-Controversial Facts and Interpretations

Wolbert G.C. Smidt

This glossary discusses the following terms and events crucial for *Lïj* Iyasu's period:[1] Alga Werrash – *Awsa – Captivity – Chronicle – Conversion to Islam – Coronation - Coup d'état 1910 – Coup d'état 1916 – Emperor: Was* Lïj *Iyasu an Emperor? – Genealogy – Gimirra - Government* – Léba Shay – Lï'ul Lïj – *Marriage policy – Mika'él (*Nïgus*) – Mïnilïk II's crown – Mïnilïk II's death – Mïnilïk III – Official name and title – Ottoman envoy – Photography and political iconography – Photography II: Forged photo with turban – Regency – Rulership 1910-1916 – Succession of Mïnilïk II – Teferi (*Lïj*).*

Alga Werrash

In 1909 Emperor Mïnilïk designated *Lïj* Iyasu as his *Alga Werrash*, i.e. the 'heir-to-the-throne'. The word *alga* is used in daily language in the meaning of 'bed', with, however, slightly different connotations, as the elevated *alga* was used by high-ranking nobles and lords as a place to sit while receiving guests, courtiers or retainers, and thus could acquire the meaning of 'throne' (and is still today very commonly used as a place to sit in daytime, when guests are received in a house). The designation of a heir-to-the-throne by Emperor Mïnilïk was an affair closely followed by internal and foreign observers over years and leading to numerous debates and tensions.

[1] A part of this paper was presented at the conference under the title „The alleged conversion of Lij Iyasu in the light of his politics and of family testimonies, traditions and documents"; a full discussion of the alleged conversion based on all available sources is planned for a later article. – Due to the general overview character of this glossary on *Lïj* Iyasu's period of rule, which should serve as a guide through current historiographical discussions and contributions to it in this volume, bibliographic references are largely avoided, as they are already listed in the respective chapters; instead the relevant articles in this volume are referred to.

In mid-1909 Emperor Mïnilïk, after a series of strokes, assembled his notables and courtiers in the palace, including *Abune* Matéwos, the metropolitan of the Ethiopian Orthodox Church, in order to officially announce his successor, the *Alga Werrash*; when he murmured that the "*Lïj*" would be his heir, T'aytu is said to have first suggested that this would mean her own nephew *Lïj* Gugsa, but was then corrected by Mïnilïk, who had still sufficient strength to make clear that this was *Lïj* Iyasu, his only remaining grandson. His courtiers then swore loyalty to him. If their vow would be broken, they would engender dogs, Mïnilïk warned them, a curse, which was considered very powerful (for details on the history of this nomination, see: Succession of Mïnilïk). – Nota bene: For the reasons elaborated below (see: Official name and title) in the context of *Lïj* Iyasu's reign, also the very free translation as 'emperor-designate' could seem justifiable, based on the factual use of this designation during his reign.

Fig. 1: Early official portrait of Lïj Iyasu, produced around the time of his official designation as heir-to-the-throne in 1909, on the basis of an older photo (collection of the author)

Awsa

Awsa is the name of the greatest of the several traditionally autonomous Afar sultanates of northeast Africa, centred in the fertile plains of the Awash river and bordering Djibouti; it is traditionally ruled by the Modayto dynasty (with the actual ruler being *Amoyta* Hanfadhe ʿAli Mirah) and covers a great part of today's Afar Regional State of Ethiopia. Enjoying an almost total autonomy in the early 20th century, Awsa provided political asylum to *Lïj* Iyasu after his deposition, refusing to deliver him to the putchist government. A heavy military intervention by the Ethiopian government into Awsa was in vain. The Ethiopian army managed to reach Awsa, but the sultan with his courtiers and *Lïj* Iyasu moved away; at the end, the army, exhausted, had to retreat without achieving anything, and nothing was changed by fact about the quasi-independence of the Awsa leadership, continuing to provide asylum to *Lïj* Iyasu. - After the successful coup d'état of 1916 it became public knowledge in Addis Abeba that *Lïj* Iyasu was roaming around in the country as a fugitive, without any place to stay permanently, moving with nomads and other people at the margins of the country, until captured in 1921 in Tigray (see: Captivity). With the research of the last two decades, this widespread idea, which is still found in history textbooks, cannot be taken fully serious any more. Especially the fact that during the last decades the Afar sultanate of Awsa, which had preserved a degree of autonomy even during the period of Hayle Sïllasé, became more accessible to researchers, both from within and outside, has contributed to a change of this image. Important works by the Afar historian Aramis Soulé (see in this volume) have made knowledge from Awsa accessible which until recently was virtually unknown. In a 2008 interview with *Amoyta* ʿAli Mirah Hanfadhe (the then sultan of Awsa), carried out by the two editors of this book, for example, the *Amoyta* remembered *Lïj* Iyasu from his childhood as a prominent permanent guest of the sultanate; he reported that *Lïj* Iyasu had been accorded his own territory in Gassissa, a hill above today's town of Aysa'iita in the centre of Awsa (similar to the *gult* system of the highlands), receiving economic support by the Awsa sultan Yayyo Mahammad, and that he continued to practice Christianity even as a guest of this exclusively Muslim sultanate. The stay of *Lïj* Iyasu in Awsa demands still further research. One could argue that Awsa, providing shelter to him, would recognize the sovereignty or at least suzerainty of Ethiopian rulers over Awsa, and concretely recognize *Lïj* Iyasu as their own Emperor; this interpretation is widespread, but has to be treated carefully, as the Awsa tradition insisted until the 1940s on its almost total independence – or autonomy, depending on the informant. The exile of *Lïj* Iyasu in Awsa falls into an ambiguous grey space open for different interpretations; Awsa had started to accept *Lïj* Iyasu as a partner in the power networks of wider Ethiopia, due to his politics of integration of the very different Christian and Muslim entities of the region; he recognized their existence – and thus acted beyond the official administrative map of a unified Ethiopia, which, on the ground, did not exist as claimed. In this framework, a certain recognition of Ethiopian overrule or suzerainty by Awsa in the *Lïj* Iyasu period was already understood, it seems; this would now result in the continued recognition of *Lïj* Iyasu even after his deposition. However, another aspect is more important for understanding the asylum of *Lïj* Iyasu in Awsa: There is a traditional law practiced by many Afar groups to offer asylum to highland rebels and political refugees. In some cases such refugees were integrated into the Afar society and stayed there; in other cases the exile was temporary. An example for this was *Balambaras* Kasa Mïrch'a of Tembén (the later Emperor Yohannïs IV), who got asylum in an Afar region when he rebelled in 1866/67. He then married an Afar woman, as *Lïj* Iyasu did later.

Captivity

Lïj Iyasu was captured in early 1921 and then transferred to Fiche, the strong-hold of his relative *Ras* Kasa Haylu, who was also a close relative of *Ras* Teferi (see on this captivity the family memories by Asfa-Wossen Asserate, in this volume; on his arrest see Aramis Soulé in this volume). After *Lïj* Iyasu's escape (with the help of *Ras* Haylu of Gojjam, his father-in-law) and re-arrest he was transferred to a much stricter confinement in Gara Muleta nearby Harer, a territory belonging to *Ras* Teferi himself. There his life ended under unclear circumstances after the beginning of the Italian invasion. – These few facts are almost the only ones, which are well doubtless; almost all other details are subject to controversies, popular oral traditions, rumours or legends, and conflicting reports. Oral traditions report for example that *Lïj* Iyasu was caught in 1921 in a remote church in Tigray, but there are different reports on the exact circumstances; it seems that he had hoped for protection by the Tigrayan leaders with whom his family was interlinked through marriage relations; others suggest that he was ready for a conditional surrender, but was betrayed. Sources agree that during captivity *Lïj* Iyasu continued to act as a Christian and rejected any rumour regarding his conversion to Islam. In Fiche, he was treated as an emperor in captivity, as family memories show. His escape may have been linked, different reports suggest, with Italian funding and advise; *Ras* Haylu, involved in permanent power struggles with *Ras* Teferi, the regent, trying to preserve his personal (and his province's) political and economic autonomy against centralisation, would have believed that Italian involvement would help him in his claim for power, to be supported by *Lïj* Iyasu back in government as a rather weak ruler. – Reports on *Lïj* Iyasu's captivity in Gara Muleta are especially rare and show rather the typical characteristics of rumour and legend, which still await evaluation. Sources only agree that his access to any outside communication was extremely restricted and that the confinement was almost total. In the same time he disappeared from public discourse as he was already not alive any more.

Chronicle

Chronicles, written in Gïʿïz or in Amharic, belong to the most interesting forms of secondary sources on Ethiopian history. In philological tradition they are often regarded as primary sources due to their proximity to the rulership and the events reported (which they really are for studies of the literary language of the time and for the study of dominating narratives and political culture), while they are secondary sources in the sense that they presented a highly controlled narrative of events often not witnessed by the chronicler, compiling and creating a tool of interpretation of – and for – the reign of his king. The tradition of chronicle-writing, which marked the Ethiopian highlands (and partially its direct Muslim neighbors) had started in the period of its medieval rulers and was continued until the period of *Lïj* Iyasu and his successor, the Queen of Queens Zewditu. The chronicle on the period of *Lïj* Iyasu and Zewditu, written by the courtier and traditional scholar Gebre-Ïgzi'abïhér Élyas, was almost unknown, except for very few specialists, until the 1990s, when it was re-transcribed, published and translated by Reidulf Molvaer (1994). This chronicle reports, following the traditional style, events and dates virtually without commenting. It gives the impression that its compilation had started during the *Lïj* Iyasu period, for the purpose of writing a chronicle of Iyasu, as it did not strongly follow the great anti-Iyasu narratives of the Hayle Sïllasé period, such as his alleged conversion to Islam (see below); criticisms are reported, including those proclaimed during the coup d'état of 1916, but also great events originally designed by Iyasu as success-stories; the objective tone is then kept also for the narration of events after Zewditu was crowned Empress. Today, the chronicle is a precious source on the *Lïj* Iyasu period as many of his government documents are lost. Gebre-Ïgzi'abïhér Élyas seems to have designed the chronicle as a tool to document those events considered central by Iyasu and his courtiers for the state, and less to strengthen the new narratives established by Iyasu's successors. This may have been one of the reasons why the chronicle remained unknown for so long. Other short chronicle texts are known, which add to this main chronicle, largely confirming its narrative, such as the recording of events by Mïrs'é Hazen and the short chronicle by Gobezé T'afet'é, both published in recent years.

Conversion to Islam

The alleged conversion of *Lïj* Iyasu to Islam is one of the key issues popularly linked with the history of his reign and downfall. The coup d'état of 1916 (see below) was mainly justified with this alleged conversion to Islam, which was inacceptable for a ruler of a Christian Empire, as the Ethiopian ruling elites defined it. The proofs included a forged photo showing *Lïj* Iyasu with a turban, distributed to Shewan notables (see below: Forged photo with turban); his marriage with daughters of prominent Muslims; a flag with a reference to Islam given to the Ottoman envoy. Detailed studies on all aspects of this alleged conversion are yet missing, but new sources do allow preliminary conclusions. Among them are: Papers of his government do not show any sign of conversion until 1916; when marrying daughters of Muslims, in all known cases they converted to Christianity (see the article by Augustyniak in this volume); *Lïj* Iyasu had the habit – fitting to his general pluralistic policy – to adapt to any dress according to the context in which he found himself, because of which we have his photos in traditional Christian dress, in a modern European costume, in a skirt of an Afar warrior, in Harer Muslim gear etc.; the flag given to the Ottoman envoy was a return gift after he had previously given a similar flag to *Lïj* Iyasu; even as a captive *Lïj* Iyasu claimed to be Christian and followed Christian rites. Detailed studies will provide more contextual material in the future, but at this stage of research it is safe to conclude that the known proofs – seen in their respective contexts better known today – can also be understood just as elements of a policy of integration aimed at the Muslim regions in his realm and in no way suggest a formal conversion. It seems that *Lïj* Iyasu had a very pragmatic, almost modern approach to religion – rather interacting with religions as regional and cultural phenomena than as systems of truth, which would exclude each other; in this sense he could integrate himself practically into different religious contexts without creating any inner contradictions, and without giving up his Christian identity. (For the international and regional political context of *Lïj* Iyasu's rapprochement to Islam see also: Ottoman envoy).

Coronation

Lïj Iyasu has never been crowned. Secondary sources – perhaps based on contemporary oral traditions or popular rumors – suggest that this was due to a prophecy which warned that he would loose power when he crowned himself; others suggest that he planned to crown himself only when he would not be minor any more. This shall be linked with the fact, which we know from primary sources, that during his whole reign *Lïj* Iyasu officially ruled in the name of his ailing grandfather Mïnilïk. It was only after *Lïj* Iyasu's downfall in 1916 that the death of Mïnilïk (of December 1913) was officially announced. Behind this seems to be a rational decision: To establish his own power-structures in the name of his grandfather would provide him the necessary time until the time of official transition and avoid direct challenges against him while being a minor; at the time of the official announcement of the death of Mïnilïk he would have established stable structures. Iyasu systematically worked on this, putting those people close to him in key-positions. In fact, he had organised a coronation – not his own, but the one of his father, *Nïgus* Mika'él (see below) being made king of Wello and Tigray by *Lïj* Iyasu in early 1914, only a few months after the factual, unannounced death of Mïnilïk. This was part of Iyasu's policy to create multiple sources for his legitimacy, being the "son of two crowned kings" (Mïnilïk II and Mika'él).

Fig.2: Coronation of Iyasu, church painting donated by Wag Shum Gïrmay; Debre Samu'él in Adil Badil near Korem (photo by Michael Gervers, 93-10-19).

Coup d'état 1910

In 1910 key-figures of the Shewan nobility prepared a conspiracy against the then de-facto-regent of Ethiopia, *Ïtégé* T'aytu, who had started to control the government, first in end 1909 only representing her ailing husband, Emperor Mïnilïk (sealing official government orders with his seal), then subsequently exercising power in her own name (giving government orders under her own seal). At the convened day troops occupied all the important places of Addis Abeba and took control of the Emperor's palace. T'aytu was officially deposed and told only to care for her sick husband; most followers of T'aytu who had been appointed by her to key-positions during her regency had to resign. Ras Tesemma was declared regent of Ethiopia, ruling as the tutor of the heir-to-the-throne *Lïj* Iyasu, from now on head of the Empire in the name of his ailing grandfather. The coup d'état was terminated with a great celebration and parade on Jan Meda, in front of *Lïj* Iyasu and *Ras* Tesemma, the leading notables of the country and the foreign diplomatic corps.

Fig.3: Scene after the accomplished coup d'état of 1910: During the celebration on Jan Méda, in the centre Lïj Iyasu posing as the new ruler, on his left: the regent Ras Tesemma and four European envoys (on the picture: of France, Italy, Germany); on his right: Ras Mengesha and Ras Gugsa; photo by Arnold Holtz (German newspaper photo from the author's collection)

Coup d'état 1916

In September 1916 *Lïj* Iyasu was declared deposed by the metropolitan of Ethiopia, following an initiative by leading nobles and notables of Shewa, who claimed that he had become a Muslim (see: Conversion to Islam). *Lïj* Iyasu, following the example of the itinerant kings of the past, was in Harer at that time and quickly organized a military counter-strike against the putchists. However, too many of his key-followers deserted him, and finally, after the battle of Sagalee (Segelé), *Lïj* Iyasu had to retreat and continued to control only very few marginal areas during the years to come (see on the events in detail Shiferaw Bekele in this volume; see on the civil war situation after the coup Aramis Soulé in this volume). With his deposition, a dramatic re-definition of his role as a ruler started, greatly shaping both the official and non-official 20th century historiography, making this period the most obscure of modern Ethiopian history. - In modern historiography the term "coup d'état" is by now established for the events leading to *Lïj* Iyasu's deposition. This is based on the observation that the putchists had set up an exact plan of action, involving only few key-players, and rapidly formed a new government without, in the beginning, any popular mass involvement – which, however, was quickly added as a factor while the events evolved. If we consult historical sources of the time, it is interesting to note that in diplomatic circles of Addis Abeba these events were rather labeled as a "revolution", in reference to the revolutionary movements world-wide, which at the end of World War I really changed the political systems in numerous countries. This refers to the fact that this coup was quickly supported by popular movements and small-scale uprisings, which were used to militarily suppress the resistance by *Lïj* Iyasu's and his father's troops. Because of the military character of the conflict, it may even be justified to speak of a short "civil war" from 1916 to 1917 (or 1921, as there continued to be clashes in some areas until the capture of *Lïj* Iyasu). Others suggest the term "insurrection" (or "noble insurrection from above"), such as Shiferaw Bekele (in this volume).

Emperor: Was *Lïj* Iyasu an Emperor?

Modern historiographers increasingly tend to call *Lïj* Iyasu "Emperor Iyasu", and occasionally even "Iyasu V", which are anachronistic re-constructions in a continuous, well-established process of re-writing and re-creating historiography. In a stark contrast to that approach, *Lïj* Iyasu had previously usually been depicted as just an immature "heir-of-the-throne" (i.e., even not a ruler, but just ruler-to-be!) acting irresponsibly without any structures of regency and/or government, as especially early texts of the Hayle Sïllasé period suggest. The contrast between the ways how Iyasu was depicted as a ruler or, precisely, non-ruler, in the 1990s or 1930s is extreme. We shall, in any case, note that the propagandistic approach of the 1930s cannot be taken as a basis for interpretation of his role. Iyasu was an effective ruler, not just a ruler-to-be. It seems, however, a matter of definition of the term "emperor", if Iyasu can be called emperor or not. Different from what is sometimes rumoured, he never used the designation "*nïguse negest ze-Ityop'ya*" ('king of kings of Ethiopia', usually translated in Europe as 'emperor') in any official document or seal, i.e. never claimed the title (see: Official name and title). However, when we look at his function, the term "emperor" again may seem justified if just meant to designate the supreme rulership, as he assumed the function of supreme leader and claimed the throne (being the *Alga Werrash* = 'heir-to-the-throne'). A coronation (see above), which would assure him the title of 'king of kings', did not take

Fig. 4: Photo by B.M. Boyadjian, Addis Ababa, from the collection of André Evalet, Geneva

place. However, historiography usually calls Ethiopia's leaders already emperors even before their official coronation ceremonies. *Lïj* Iyasu did not claim the title, but assumed the rank by fact – while, however, not legally claiming it as he continued to uphold the fiction of ruling in Mïnilïk's name (see above: Mïnilïk's death). If an English term is needed, it seems that for the last reason a term such as "emperor-designate and ruler" would seem the most correct (see above: *Lï'ul Lïj* = 'supreme-prince'; also see: *Alga Werrash* = 'heir-to-the-throne', i.e., in this case, emperor-designate). – A philological note: Another issue not discussed here is the question if the Ethiopian term *Nïguse Negest* ('king of kings') can be translated as "Emperor", the latter term corresponding to a different concept within the European state system; historically, the Ethiopian term is a superlative basically meaning "great king among the kings (of the world)", which does not correspond to the European concept of Emperor, but rather to an ancient concept of "great-king" widespread in the Oriental world. However, in European publications the translation "Emperor" became more and more popular in modern times, especially after Mïnilïk won the battle of ʿAdwa, with the effect that "Emperor" became the correct translation by default.

Genealogy

Genealogies are not simply a historical fact, but serve as the historical basis for the justification and establishment of networks of political and/or economic friendships and alliances. A genealogical justification of claims is powerful because of the essentialist idea that descent from specific kings would entail a potential right of claiming their heritage (in this case: rulership over Ethiopia); what was owned by the fathers would be owned by his children – in case of powerful lineages often including descendants of daughters. Heritage not only through the father's lineage, but also through maternal descent was widespread in the Ethiopian highlands. Thus, genealogies are part of a process of political construction, re-construction and invention of history, in which the "discovery" of the right lineage even through remote maternal lines could help to decide power struggles. However, genealogies alone were not sufficient, given the lack of exactly defined rules of succession; the dynamic use of genealogies linked with political wisdom and shrewdness helped to create alliances in a struggle for power. *Lïj* Iyasu's use of genealogy is an especially interesting example. Through his marriages (see: Marriage policy) he created new genealogical links, to serve as a basis for a future genealogical network of his descendants and relatives. *Lïj* Iyasu himself was part of such a network created by his predecessors, and in fact in his case belonged to quite conflicting networks of very different backgrounds, Christian and Muslim. Claims for supreme power had traditionally to be justified through descent from the Christian Solomonic dynasty (as modern historiographers call the "Israelian" line of Ethiopian rulers claiming descent from king Solomon of Israel). Through his maternal grandfather *Atsé* Mïnilïk II *Lïj* Iyasu belonged to this lineage, while through his father *Nïgus* Mika'él he descended from the "Mammedoch", the "Muhammedan dynasty" of Wello (see on this dynasty's genealogical links with ruling Christian lineages the article by Éloi Ficquet in this volume). This dynasty had only shortly before started to claim descent directly from prophet Muhammad, while its designation originally rather stemmed from a Wello ancestor called Muḥammad (see on this genealogy the article by Alessandro Gori in this volume). This claim of "Sharifian" descent, however, played an interesting role for *Lïj* Iyasu: Sources report that this descent from the most prominent of all Muslim lineages was used by *Lïj* Iyasu in his contact with the Ottoman Empire (see: Ottoman envoy) and with the Somali ruler Maḥammad ʿAbdille Ḥasan. It has to be noted that it was not new for an Ethiopian ruler to claim descent not only from the Solomonic lineage in order to justify his accession to the throne, but also from other locally influential lineages; this reflects an ancient federal-like structure of the provinces and princedoms of Ethiopia, whose support was needed. It is, however, new that such a claim included a prominent Muslim lineage. Thus, also in this case *Lïj* Iyasu showed a new approach, based on the ancient structures of genealogical politics.

Gimirra

This was a term used in the past by highlanders to designate groups of lowlanders at the margins of the Ethiopian state, often victimized through slave raids, at the borders of the ancient Kefa kingdom (which had conducted slave raids into this territory before the arrival of Christian Ethiopians). The term is imprecise and encompasses several groups, such as the Dizu (the Bench', She and Mer), the Sheko, Nayi and Ch'ara. The region was totally submitted to Ethiopian rule in the course of the southern expansion of Mïnilïk II, in 1897/98. In 1910 *Lïj* Iyasu made the then Minister of Finance, *Dejjazmach* Mulugéta (the later Minister of War *Ras* Mulugéta) Governor of Gimirra and thus removed him into one of the remotest regions, far away from the centre of power. This pattern of nominating personalities whose influence was feared and whose loyalty was put into doubt, to positions in remote regions continued throughout the whole 20th century ("inner exile").

Fig. 5: Imprisoned "Gimirra" in 1911, photo by Georges Montandon (archives of the Hiob Ludolf Centre of Ethiopian Studies, Hamburg University, "Äthiopien Landeskunde III")

- The today often praised federalist policies of *Lïj* Iyasu found their limits in the "Gimirra" region: In contrast to his politics of integration, marked by his political marriages and by his travels throughout the country, towards Oromo territories, or the Muslim Afar and Somali, or to the different Christian regions from Tigray to Shewa, *Lïj* Iyasu acted differently among the "Gimirra". Not genuinely interested in their integration, he in the contrary conducted huge "sportive" raids among them in 1912, enslaving tens of thousands and deporting many to Addis Abeba (mostly Bench' and Nayi). With these raids he stood in the tradition of slavery and enslavement of "black" peoples at the western and southwestern borders of the Ethiopian state, already strongly furthered before by Mïnilïk and his slave-trading agents. *Lïj* Iyasu is reported to have taken later "measures of integration", as they were understood in his time, by marrying them to members of other groups in Addis Abeba and giving them plots of land. A quarter nearby the Egyptian Embassy is still inhabited today by their descendants.

Government

Historical narratives of the post-1916 period tended to focus any criticism of *Lïj* Iyasu's period on himself and some individual advisors and friends, such as the former musician Tesemma Ïsheté. In a similar pattern, popular positive re-evaluations of *Lïj* Iyasu's rule of recent years tend to praise achievements of this period as his individual decisions. However, the power structures were complex and (at least partially) well institutionalized. Emperor Mïnilïk II had created government institutions in 1907, which continued to exist and be functional during Mïnilïk's fatal incapacitation and the assumption of power by *Lïj* Iyasu and his regents (see: Regency). Several ministers appointed by Emperor Mïnilïk II continued to lead their ministries, while others were appointed to new positions. The formal government super-structures also included the regent *Ras* Tesemma (in 1910/11) and later *Lïj* Iyasu's father as his tutor (see: Mika'él, Nïgus); decision-making structures were formalized, which suggests that Iyasu's politics were highly informed by the experienced ministers close to

Fig. 6: Behind Lïj *Iyasu, the minister of foreign affairs* Bitwadded *Hayle-Giyorgis, on his right, the minister of war* Fïtawrari *Habte-Giyorgis. Jan Méda, 3 Feb. 1913 (detail, from the collection of Johannes Bohnenberger).*

him. Especially important were the long-time minister of foreign affairs and de-facto prime-minister *Bitwadded* Hayle-Giyorgis, and the minister of war *Fitawrari* Habte-Giyorgis, who were both linked with each other in a system of competition and alliance. The minister Tesemma Ïsheté was an interesting addition to the government, being of humble origin (as the minister Habte Giyorgis), and having an international background, due to his German education. *Lïj* Iyasu, however, built up also his own structures of advisorship, parallel to the government; this consisted of provincial leaders – from traditional local dynasties from the Christian highlands, Oromo territories, Afar and Muslim Harer, to name but a few, and others being modernizers and sometimes even foreigners (such as the Christian Syrian Ydlibi in Dirré Dawa). Sources generally agree that these different government and administration structures were often not interconnected, and government affairs domi-nated by very different stake-holders. At the end, the weakening of the central structures in Addis Abeba – certainly together with a rising fear of direct involvement in World War I on the side of the Axis (see: Ottoman envoy) – contributed to the decision by key-government ministers, such as *Fïtawrari* Habte Giyorgis, and the then foreign minister *Qeññazmach* Beyyene Yïmer, to break with *Lïj* Iyasu and join the Coup d'état against him in September 1916.

Léba Shay

Modern historiography of the *Lïj* Iyasu period generally claims that one of his great reforms was the abolishment of the *Léba Shay* system (see the article of Ahmed Hassen Omer in this volume; see also Bahru Zewde's standard work *Modern History of Ethiopia*). This system, then widely practiced in the highlands, was a way to identify an unknown thief (*'léba'*): A person was intoxicated and then, in a state of half-consciousness, moved around until identifying the thief by going to him or holding him. In local judiciary tradition this ritual identification of a criminal was considered a real proof. *Lïj* Iyasu's government, consisting of experienced notables enrooted in the administration established by Mïnilïk, continued the Mïnilïk's gradual modernisation of the Ethiopian state system; this included the abolishment of traditional judiciary methods considered superstitious by Ethiopian modernizers and European advisors. However, a social anthropologist perspective leads to a partial correction of what political history narrates: Ethiopia was by far not a centralist state, the government notably not controlling most of the legal and judiciary traditions practiced in the different regions, even in the core area of the state, the highlands; it was only with the increasing centralisation and the establishment of bureaucratic structures even in remoter regions that such traditions really disappeared, which may have continued well into the 1950s.

Li'ul Lij

This is a specific title created by *Lïj* Iyasu for himself. Even if in modern Ethiopian historiography one speaks generally of *Lïj* Iyasu ('Prince Iyasu'), the few original primary sources, which have survived from his government, usually name him as *Lï'ul Lïj* Iyasu (from Gï'ïz *lï'ul* 'the high one', i.e. 'His Highness Prince Iyasu', but also translatable as 'Supreme-Prince Iyasu', possibly also with the connotation of 'Imperial Prince'). Occasionally he was also called *Lï'ul Abéto* Iyasu (with an almost identical meaning, reviving the old Gondarian title *Abéto*). Before Iyasu's reign the term *Lï'ul* ('High' in the sense of 'High-born') only appeared as a term of polite address for different nobles, e.g. in letters. It was only in the period of Iyasu that it appears as a fixed element of a noble title, evidently with the function to distinguish Iyasu from other young nobles with the same title *Lïj* (such as *Lïj* Teferi), who were not in a position of rulership. This example was followed later by Hayle Sïllasé I when he created new high-ranking titles for the highest nobles of his Empire.

Marriage policy

Lïj Iyasu's marriage policy was a subject of numerous historical controversies and continues to be discussed in Ethiopian historiography. Authors differ on the number of official wives, but usually ten to twelve are mentioned; all marriages were Christian marriages, some of these with daughters of Muslim notables, baptized for the occasion of the marriage. Marriages in Ethiopian political history have to be understood in the context of political interests and the need for networking. In this sense it falls into a very similar category as genealogy (see: Genealogy). While genealogy serves as the historical basis for the justification and establishment of networks of political and/or economic friendships and alliances, marriages serve as a dynamic instrument to create and re-create such networks. Marriage policy is the basis for what would become genealogy later; while genealogy is inherited and thus not changeable, marriage policies serve as an instrument to create a new genealogy. This observation leads to an important insight into the function of *Lïj* Iyasu's marriages: Usually, ruler accessed their throne already at a certain age, when younger relatives and/or sons and daughter were already "at hand" and could be married to political allies (and foes); *Lïj* Iyasu, however, had not reached such an age, therefore chose to marry himself the daughters of political allies. The function, however, was the same: The establishment of alliances through marriage, which is confirmed by the fact that in different contexts his fathers-in-law acted as *Lïj* Iyasu's allies, some even after his downfall. *Lïj* Iyasu's polygamy was not rejected by any of them, be they Christian or Muslim princes and notables. Another aspect is to be added here: If historiographers claim that *Lïj* Iyasu's special form of marriage politics was new for the country, this does not seem to be totally correct. The number of rulers who married more than once – and often had even several wives and official concubines in the same time (such as Nïgus Sahle-Sïllasé of

Shewa) – is rather high, and many of them chose their partners not only based on their "sexual appetite" but also in the framework of political alliances. (See the article by Augustyniak in this volume).

Mika'él (*Nïgus*)

The father of *Lïj* Iyasu was one of the most important key-figures of *Lïj* Iyasu's government, as a hidden co-regent behind the government, and ruler over the northern kingdoms and provinces of Ethiopia. Being his natural tutor after *Ras* Tesemma's death (the tutor assigned by *Atsé* Mïnilïk II) during *Lïj* Iyasu's years of minority, he was a key-person behind all crucial government decisions of the period. Also newly discovered government papers of 1915/16 illustrate this, as appointments of new ministers were only done with his confirmation (see the contribution by the author in this volume; see also below: Regency). - In public memory and modern oral tradition in today's Ethiopia, he is usually remembered as "*Ras* Mika'él", while he was in fact *Nïgus* ('king') at the end. Not according him the correct title in public speech implied a non-recognition of his status which was accorded to him during the "transitional" *Lïj* Iyasu period. The process of re-discovery of his role and its evaluation in early 20th century Ethiopia is not yet finalized; today he is more often called *Nïgus* Mika'él. This is significant, as it marks a turn in his historical evaluation. – It is has always been public knowledge that *Lïj* Iyasu's father was a Muslim originally (while the partial Muslim origins of the later Emperor Hayle Sïllasé through his mother remained largely unknown). - Originally, he was a leader with a double religious and political leadership, by then named *Imam* Muhammad Ali, governor of Werre Himano in Wello. This background was underlying the discourses about *Lïj* Iyasu's Muslim sympathies. – Both *Nïgus* Mika'él's important political role and the fluctuating interpretation of it in later times make it necessary to have a closer look at several details (see a recent thorough biographical study in the *Encyclopaedia Aethiopica*, vol. 3): *Imam* Muhammad was from the local Oromo Wello dynasty which called itself the Mammedoch, which had recently started to claim direct descent from Prophet Muhammad (see on this the contribution by Ficquet in this volume; see also above: Genealogy). This lineage was one of the important power brokers within Wello and mainly enrooted in Werre Himano; these local rulers assumed the religious title *Imam*, but in the same time also controlled political power. What is, however, much less known, is their multiple genealogical interrelations with the then leading Christian dynasty of Ethiopia in Gonder and other Christian families; *Ïtégé* Menen I, the mid-19th century main power broker of Gonder, was the direct aunt of *Imam* Muhammad Ali (see on this the contribution by Ficquet in this volume). Conversions and re-conversions to Christianity and to Islam were one of the key-features of this family network. It is interesting to note, that even Mïnilïk II entered into this network, when he married his wife's daughter, Man Allebesh, to *Imam* Muhammad – without demanding his conversion. In 1878 during the Council of Boru Méda, which had as the main target the political and religious unification of Ethiopia, *Imam* Muhammad converted to Christianity and was since then called *Ras* Mika'él, with *Atsé* Yohannïs as his god-father (from whom he took the name "Mika'él", as that was the Christian name of the Emperor, which he used on very rare occasions); *Ras* Mika'él then got Mïnilïk's daughter Shewa Regga as a new wife – out of which marriage *Lïj* Iyasu was born. A long history of consolidation of his power followed, with the peak after the de-facto-accession of *Lïj* Iyasu to the throne; in 1913 he was crowned king of all provinces and kingdoms of northern Ethiopia (see Coronation; below: Mïnilïk II's crown). After the downfall of *Lïj* Iyasu (see: Coup d'état of 1916), he intervened with his troops, but dramatically lost the decisive battle of Sagalee (see on this the contribution by Shiferaw Bekele in this volume). He was paraded in the streets of Addis Abeba thereafter and kept as a prisoner, while his grandson-in-law (husband of *Ïtégé* Menen II), *Ras* Teferi, gradually started to dominate all the power structures of the country.

Mïnilïk II's crown

When *Atsé* Mïnilïk II died in December 1913, this was followed by a further widening of *Ras* Mika'él's power and his accession to the highest ranks possible for him: In May 1914 his son organized his coronation in Desé in Wello, with, surprisingly, the crown of Emperor Mïnilïk used for the coronation, with a European film team present, photographers, and on which we have reports by Ethiopian chroniclers. This highly symbolic re-usage of this crown, contrary to Ethiopian traditional usage were crowns were personal, signified the shift of power from Shewa to Wello, and Mika'él politically re-taking the place of Mïnilïk as the "father of *Lïj* Iyasu". He was crowned king not only of Wello, but also of Tigray, whose traditional dynasty he confirmed in their governorship, now placed under him instead of under the central power; in 1915 *Nïgus* Mika'él was also confirmed king of Begémdïr and Gojjam, under similar conditions. Instead of meeting concern and resistance from these regions, this was received rather positively, as his rule assured their increased autonomy. Mïnilïk II's

Fig. 7: Official coronation portrait of Nïgus *Mika'él in Debre Hayq, with Mïnilïk's crown (photo by Michael Gervers)*

crown was later replaced by another crown. The impression, however, stayed: Shewa was clearly told that their domination of power was over; this should have strongly contributed to discontent, but interestingly post-1916 historical sources focus all criticism of government failures on *Lïj* Iyasu, while *Nïgus* Mika'él is spared and the history of Mïnilïk's crown obscured (perhaps to keep the direct lineage of the now-ruling *Ras* Teferi, closely related to him through marriage, free from blame, and create the impression that what was going on in the time of *Lïj* Iyasu was the failure of this individual only, instead of being part of a greater political design, involving many?).

Mïnilïk II's death

Different from what history books of modern Ethiopia – including secondary school history books – usually note, the death of Mïnilïk did not constitute any historical break, as he had ceased to rule the country already in late 1909; most books mentioning the modern rulers of Ethiopia, note mistakenly that *Lïj* Iyasu ruled only from 1913 to 1916, while all primary sources document his continuous rule from 1910-1916 (see below: Rulership 1910-1916). When Mïnilïk's death occurred in December 1913 (after his death had been reported already before occasionally), none of the power structures established by *Lïj* Iyasu's government was affected or changed in any way, no burial was organized, and no official mourning declared; officially, the death of the Emperor did not take place, and *Lïj* Iyasu continued to reign in his name, as if he was alive; foreign legations were even notified the death of Mïnilïk's favorite horse, but never Mïnilïk's own death. Archives of foreign legations, available today, show, however, that his death did not remain a total secret to high-ranking courtiers and was widely rumoured; government papers documenting the years until 1916 mention Mïnilïk still occasionally as if he was still alive, even if inactive. We were here in fact in a situation of a head of state continuing to rule virtually even years after his death. This was done, it seems, to ensure a smooth transition while Iyasu was still a minor (see above: Coronation). After the coup d'état of 1916, the death of Mïnilïk was officially announced and then fixed on the already rumoured date in December 1913; mourning was declared and *Tezkar* (memorial) ceremonies carried out by his daughter, the new Empress Zewditu. Thus, what was designed as an instrument to assure transition in favor of *Lïj* Iyasu, was efficiently used against him, helping to create a powerful legitimacy for his successors; while they should and could have simply been regarded as putchists, they managed to appear as the direct heirs of Mïnilïk, assuring his – almost broken – succession.

Mïnilïk III

One of the least known sons of *Lïj* Iyasu was Mïnilïk Iyasu or "Mïnilïk III", as he was called once in a short historical moment. Even if virtually unknown, rumours on his existence were widespread throughout the Haile-Sïllasé period. Only very recently, few short and scattered publications revealed some credible details on his life (see for example the article by the author in the *Encyclopaedia Aethiopica*, vol. 3). As he was named after *Lïj* Iyasu's grandfather, Emperor Mïnilïk II, already his name contained a strong promise and claim. He was born in exile in the French Territory of the Afar and Issa (today's state of Djibouti), several months after *Lïj* Iyasu's downfall (see: Coup d'état of 1916). His mother Fatumma, from the prominent Afar Obakarto lineage, rose him as an Afar Muslim in the Afar areas behind the traditional port of Tadjoura. The French authorities, knowing about his existence, funded his schooling in colonial schools, and tried to keep him away from any foreign contacts, while preparing to possibly use him during political turmoil in Ethiopia; but they could not control his contacts to Afar, who started to visit him in Tadjoura when he was growing up, and regarded him as the most legitimate claimant to the Ethiopian throne. When Italy occupied Ethiopia, Ethiopian exiles and refugees in Djibouti discovered him as a potentially powerful weapon in their resistance against Italy and proclaimed him as the new Emperor around 1940; this was followed by an invitation by another prominent son of *Lïj* Iyasu, *Dejjazmach* Yohannïs Iyasu, who was one of the leaders of the Ethiopian resistance against the occupation, to join him in the struggle. When Mïnilïk III (first traveling under the cover-name of Mahammad Hasan; see Aramis Soulé in this volume) arrived in Ethiopia in 1941, however, the British had already started to occupy Ethiopia, in alliance with Hayle-Sïllasé. The latter successfully negotiated with Mïnilïk, offering him to share "the palace" (i.e. power over Ethiopia) with him; but when he arrived in Addis Abeba, he was instead put under house arrest first in the palace, later in a compound nearby. He was never able to leave his compound, except for travels to his second residence in Dirre-Dawa. Afar and Somali, to whom his house was permanently open, considered him as one of their potential leaders; he remained virtually unknown to other Ethiopians. In Addis Abeba, his Somali wife bore him only a dead child, which nourished rumours of poisoning; however, as a young man in Tadjoura, he indeed had a son, shortly regarded by Afar notables as a future Muslim claimant-to-the-throne of Ethiopia. He was named Ali Mïnilïk, nephew of the sultan of Tadjoura, descendant of the Afar rulers of Zayla', while also being Emperor Mïnilïk's great-great-grandson. However, Ali died as a child in Tadjoura.

Official name and title

Usually, historiographical literature uses the simple designation "*Lïj* Iyasu", or, as in his and Zewditu's Chronicle, "*Abéto* Iyasu". When using a father's name, Iyasu made usually reference to his grandfather, Emperor Mïnilïk, which made him "Iyasu Mïnilïk", or, in Gï'ïz "*Iyasu welde le-Mïnilïk*". In the usage of the time, father's names were often an expression of a political programme, so that the politically relevant grandfather's name could also be used as a father's name. However, also other versions of his name appear in publications, such as Iyasu Mika'él, anachronistically linking the name with the father's name following today's naming standards of Ethiopia (the seal published in the standard work on seals, by Tornay & Sohier,[2] which names him as "Iyasu we[lde le] Mi Shewa", cannot be interpreted as a clear reference to Mika'él, but rather played with a double sense referring both to Mïnilïk – sometimes also spelled Minilïk – and Mika'él; especially as "Shewa" was added, this referred rather to his official father's name Mi/ïnilïk). On his seals and in official texts Iyasu chose the following Gï'ïz formula to denominate himself, the most complete formula being: *lï'ul Lïj iyasu welde le-mïnilïk nïguse negest ze-ityop'ya* ('Iyasu, supreme-prince, son of the king of kings of Ethiopia Mïnilïk', see the contribution by the author in this volume). As this formula has no comma, a certain ambiguity remains; at least at first sight, it could possibly also allow a reading such as 'His Highness Prince Iyasu son of Mïnilïk, king of kings of Ethiopia', with the imperial title somehow linked with Iyasu, not with Mïnilïk. However, any contemporary would understand this ambiguity rather as a claim for future heritage, not as an actual claim for the title (similarly, only a few decades earlier, the governor of Tigray and son of Emperor Yohannïs IV, *Ras* Mengesha, had also included the reference to his father "Yohannes, king of kings of Ethiopia" into his seal during a period when he claimed the right to ascend the throne for himself, but did not use the imperial title directly).

Fig. 8: Example for the seal of Lïj Iyasu which shows his father's name ambiguously as Mi[ka'él / nilïk]; courtesy of Dr. Girma Y. Iyassu Menelik.

[2] Tornay, Serge & Sohier, Estelle, 2007, *Empreintes du temps: Les sceaux des dignitaires éthiopiens du règne de Téwodros à la régence de Täfäri Mäkonnen*, Addis Ababa, CFEE, pp. 70-71.

Ottoman envoy

The Ottoman envoy (with the title of consul-general) to Ethiopia was an exception in the diplomatic scene of Addis Abeba. International relations of Ethiopia were, starting from the late 19th century after the Battle of ʿAdwa, almost totally dominated by Western countries. When the Ottoman Empire opened their own consulate-general in Harer in 1912, the first aim was the diplomatic protection of Ottoman citizens, many of whom were traders in Harer (or supposed Ottoman citizens such as Yemenis from British colonial territory), which was originally assured by the German legation. When in 1913 Ahmed Mazhar Bey was appointed consul-general, a most dynamic relation with Ethiopia was inaugurated. Mazhar suggested that the Ottoman Empire would send teachers and preachers to the Muslim communities of Ethiopia, aiming at Ottoman involvement in their organisation. In early 1915 – World War I had just started – he moved to Addis Abeba to be closer to the political centre. The activities of the Ottoman consulate were regarded with worries by the Allies, who rightly feared potential Ottoman involvement among Muslim communities in their colonies surrounding Ethiopia, which could mean new fronts in an increasingly complex war. It was rumoured that Mazhar Bey enjoyed a privileged access to the young Prince and attained an undue influence over him. And, indeed, there is evidence that Mazhar's involvement in the political affairs of the Horn of Africa started to bear fruits in 1916, such as a rapprochement between the Ottomans and the independent Somali leader Mahammad Abdille Hasan (called the "Mad Mullah" by the British). The latter controlled a vast territory not foreseen on the colonial map, a map, which in fact was already partially fake; the Ottoman Empire's politics in the Horn supported these developments by recognizing the Mullah as an independent leader of all territories controlled by him, under Ottoman suzerainty (on this see the contribution of Erlich in this volume). And this went hand in hand with a rapprochement of Abdille Hasan also with *Lïj* Iyasu's government, who even contributed with experts and offers of support, and who in this way already started to enter into a part of the "collateral" conflicts of World War I. Ottoman involvement in the region meant the possibility of a radical reshaping of the political map as an outcome of World War I. The relationship between *Lïj* Iyasu and the Ottoman envoy therefore became increasingly subject of hidden debates especially in the capital. - One rumour became an established fact even in serious history books later: It was told (based on facts, but leaving away one detail), that *Lïj* Iyasu gave an Ethiopian flag with the crescent and the Muslim formula of faith to Mazhar, which was interpreted by some as a sign for the submission of Ethiopia to Ottoman overrule; however, the re-reading of Ottoman archives shows that this was a part of an exchange of gifts, which reduces the scale of importance of this gesture: Before, Mazhar had given Iyasu a similar flag, which now demanded for a return gift. It was even rumoured that Ethiopia was placed "in religious dependence" of the Ottomans in 1916. Also in this case, Ottoman archives show that the facts were slightly, but significantly differing from how they were interpreted by the Allies and influential notables of Shewa. In fact, it were only the religious affairs of Muslims in Ethiopia, which were put under the authority of Ottoman religious institutions, following a pattern also practiced in other regions of the world and not implying any question of sovereignty (see, based on a re-reading of the Ottoman sources, Finke in the Encyclopaedia Aethiopica, vol. 3). All this was seen as proofs for the conversion of *Lïj* Iyasu to Islam, an interpretation which had the power to significantly change public opinion, while the truth seems much more political: Instead of speaking of a personal conversion, it would be much more correct of speaking of a political restructuring, a radical reformu-lation of regional politics: The creation of a new political role for Islam and Muslims in the political structure of the Horn of Africa. *Lïj* Iyasu was preparing an ambitious inter-alliance with Muslim groups and regions far beyond Ethiopia, aiming at a great Christian-Muslim entity unifying the Horn of Africa (under Ethiopian leadership), and thus radically defying colonial interests in the region. In this sense, true, *Lïj* Iyasu together with the Ottomans was about to work on a political revolution from above. This was about new regional power structures, not conversion.

Fig. 9: Mazhar Bey at the German Legation Addis Abeba, 1914, on the occasion of the German emperor's birthday, from the Lorenz Jensen Nachlass, collection of Wolbert Smidt.

Photography and political iconography

The importance of photography for both international and internal politics was quickly grasped by the Ethiopian leadership, especially starting from Atsé Mïnilïk II. In Europe, political leaders and other personalities had a long tradition of creating images of themselves in the public. Photography in this sense just continued the long tradition of portrait art and provided new chances of self-interpretation. In Ethiopia, photography also entered into a long-established albeit partially different iconographic tradition: Rulers and religious figures were depicted on church wall paintings and icon donations and thus imprinted their image in the public consciousness, based on idealized patterns, and less interested in naturalistic portraits. Iconography was established as an instrument to create common narratives and images, in religion as in politics. Photography could fulfill these needs perfectly: All insignia of power were shown in these new portraits, which were distributed among foreigners and Ethiopian notables. The role of photography for the creation of a public image continued with *Lïj* Iyasu, but in the same time there was a change of pattern. One aspect was added – that of playing with very diverse roles. In the case of Mïnilïk II, he let himself already photograph with different costumes on different occasions: As an army leader, or as a ruler in full regalia, perfectly fitting into the public imagination of an Emperor, but also as a daily-life ruler, without a crown but with a head-gear, in distinguished clothes. This continued with *Lïj* Iyasu, but with a considerable modification: The number of images – both photos and painted portraits – showing him in different costumes sharply increased. *Lïj* Iyasu is seen as a traditional army leader; as a ruler with some (not all) insignia of power; as a traditional Christian notable in civil gear; as an Afar nomad; as a modern official in European clothes[3]; in a Harer costume with turban, typical for the Muslim élites; as a family person, showing himself for example as a submissive son with his father, or casually in groups with family members. It is probably not a pure coincidence, but a sign for some developments typical for the time, that in this he strongly resembles the German Emperor William II, who also steadily produced photographs showing him in the most different roles, from German Emperor and Prussian king, to British admiral, to a private archaeologist in Greece, for example, playing with continuously changing identities and roles. The political background of this iconographic politics, as it may be called, was the idea that the leader had to assume, both internally and internationally, very different roles and identities to integrate the diverse political and cultural streams and interests of his Empire (see on this the article by Sohier in this volume; her standard work quoted in that chapter; and the important photo collection Ethiopia Photographed by Richard Pankhurst and Denis Gérard). The photos shown

Fig. 10: A portrait of Lïj *Iyasu, from Ernst H. Schrenzel, 1926, Land ohne Hunger, Land ohne Zeit, p. 226*

3 See the photo reproduced by Sohier in this volume, showing *Lïj* Iyasu with an unnamed European diplomat identified as "German" by Ethiopian tradition; however, as he wears a Hungarian uniform (friendly communication by Rudolf Agstner), he can only be an Austrian-Hungarian diplomat – therefore we can assume that this photo shows Karl Schwimmer, the only Austrian-Hungarian diplomat in Addis Abeba during this period. He was close to *Lïj* Iyasu and organized the well-known weapons deal at the beginning of World War I; see the contribution by Agstner in this volume.

in this glossary – some of them yet unknown – are some typical examples for how *Lïj* Iyasu presented himself. Many of these photos were produced by Armenians, pioneers of photography in Ethiopia.

Photography II: Forged photo with turban

Historiography reports that a photo showing *Lïj* Iyasu with a turban was distributed among Shewan notables in Addis Abeba (and, as some claim: also to a few foreign diplomats) in the foremath of the coup d'état of 1916, and that it was forged by the Armenian photographer in Addis Abeba, Leon Yazedjian, from whom we know several photos of *Lïj* Iyasu. It is generally believed – without final proof – by researchers that the forgery was funded or even fully initiated by the British legation, which was actively involved in the downfall of *Lïj* Iyasu (details on this, with references to witnesses of the period: Pankhurst in this volume). After the coup d'état, however, the photos seem not to have been preserved by anyone, because not one single copy of it could be found until today. Richard Pankhurst has, however, discovered a real photo showing him in Harer in complete Muslim dress with the family of his father-in-law Abdallahi (from a private collection, apparently originally not known to anyone outside Muslim circles, re-published in this volume, see the contribution by Sohier; for the context of this photo see above: Conversion to Islam; Coup d'état of 1916).

Regency

From late 1909 to 1916 we can speak of different forms and periods of regencies, with de facto and officially designated regents assuming power under an actual or designated emperor. When Emperor Mïnilïk realized that his health would soon not allow him to continue to rule, he officially declared to the court public in 1909 that *Lïj* Iyasu would be his heir-to-the-throne, with *Ras* Tesemma as his tutor. The function of "tutor" would in this context be equivalent to "regent". When Mïnilïk really became incapacitated soon thereafter in late 1909, the regency was, however, not transferred to *Lïj* Iyasu and *Ras* Tesemma, but was exercised by *Ïtégé* T'aytu, who took over control of the government, i.e. acting de facto as a regent, first using Mïnilïk's seal, then her own. She actively replaced Ethiopian officials and governors by nobles linked with her by alliances and family relations. This lead to the coup d'état of 1910 (see above), when the partially dis-empowered nobility supported *Lïj* Iyasu and *Ras* Tesemma to take over the roles assigned to them by Mïnilïk. After *Ras* Tesemma's death in 1911, no new regent was appointed, officially because *Lïj* Iyasu wanted to assume this role himself; however, being still a minor, his natural tutor was his own father, *Nïgus* Mika'él, who thus could assure that he would be involved in all government affairs, being able to act as a regent behind Iyasu (see on this the contribution by the author in this volume). This is confirmed by government papers, which show the involvement of *Nïgus* Mika'él in all crucial government affairs such as ministerial appointments. This de-facto-regency was dissolved in 1916 with the coup d'état (see: Coup d'état of 1916).

Rulership 1910-1916

When modern history books note that *Lïj* Iyasu ruled the country from 1913 (see above: Mïnilïk's death) to 1916 (see above: coup d'état), this is a post-Iyasu anachronistic invention; this was based on his successor's version of historiography aimed at shortening this period to a minimum, thus underlining the purely transitional character of *Lïj* Iyasu's reign. Iyasu ruled the country, in fact, in the name of the incapacitated Emperor from 1910 to 1916 (with a regent only in 1910-11, see above: Regency). During the coup d'état, the rationally-designed secrecy around Mïnilïk's death was subject to a most radical and successful re-interpretation: Instead of understanding this secrecy (known also from earlier historical periods) as a method to ensure transition, it was re-interpreted as a sign for disregard and disrespect for the grandfather, thus a sign for the unworthiness of the heir-to-the-throne, who broke with most fundamental traditions, and thus was not fit to continue his grandfather's heritage.

Fig. 11: Postcard of 1934, showing Lïj Iyasu as a traditional Christian Ethiopian warrior, and with an example for the years of reign accorded to him by historiography after his deposition.

Succession of Mïnilïk II

When Mïnilïk had started to reach higher age, it was first generally assumed that he would assign his younger and favorite cousin from his aunt's side, *Ras* Mekonnïn, his successor, Mekonnïn being his de-facto foreign minister, experienced with the intrigues of international powers, and an able governor; this, however, was made impossible through the latter's death in 1906. For a short time Mïnilïk thought of making his grandson Wesen-Seged his heir, who, however, was a dwarf and thus barely acceptable for Ethiopian tradition, expecting bodily strength from the supreme leader; this was made impossible by Wesen-Seged's death (see the article of Sohier in this volume). Already in 1907, however, Mïnilïk had taken the firm decision to make his remaining, then still very young grandson *Lïj* Iyasu his suc-cessor; his diplomatic envoys to Europe brought the official portrait of Iyasu to the European courts with the official announcement of Iyasu as his heir. Interestingly, this anno-uncement was not yet made to the Ethiopian nobility by then, but only in 1909; this period of transition was marked by his wife's attempts to get her nephew, *Lïj* Gugsa Walé, accepted as the future emperor, while Mïnilïk was successfully networking to win support for his own lineage to continue in power (see above: *Alga Werrash*).

Teferi (*Lïj*)

Lïj Teferi, the son of the early-deceased Ras Mekonnïn of Harer, went through most dramatic transformations during his career: Being first *Lïj* Teferi, descending from a female side-line of the Shewan kings' house, he rose to diverse, more and more prestigious governorships (even replacing his elder brother in their father's fief, Harer, and attaining the rank of dejjazmach), and finally managed to take hold of the supreme power in the country after the coup d'état of 1916, first as a seemingly rather weak compromise-figure, becoming finally Emperor Haylé Sïllasé against all probabilities. - It is useful to look at personalities of specific periods strictly in the context of that period, not anachronistically from a later perspective, based on their later accomplishments. It is difficult, certainly, for any reader of modern Ethiopian history to see *Lïj* Teferi just as *Lïj* Teferi – not as the later Emperor Hayle Sïllasé I, the long-time ruler of Ethiopia, so influential for Ethiopia's fate. But who was *Lïj* Teferi in the time of *Lïj* Iyasu? He was very far from being a future Emperor. - *Lïj* Iyasu was the Emperor's grandson and heir, while Teferi was a son of the Emperor's younger cousin *Ras* Mekonnïn, the Emperor's second degree nephew through a maternal line, thus according to genealogical politics not very close to the throne. Due to the closeness of *Ras* Mekonnïn to the court, he was, however, close to the Emperor; from 1906 he passed a part of his youth at the court. Much later, *Lïj* Iyasu, married him to his niece Menen Asfew and thus integrated him into the genealogical-political networks of the *Nïgus* Mika'él family, binding him even closer to the court. It may be that these only quite indirect relations of *Lïj* Teferi to the imperial family, together with his apparent bodily weakness (still a subject of anecdotes about him and the much stronger-built *Lïj* Iyasu), may have contributed to his underestimation by *Lïj* Iyasu. When Teferi was removed from his governorship in Harer in 1916, this was later described by him as a break of a vow between him and Iyasu: As long as Iyasu would not touch his fief, he would not touch Iyasu. The direct cause of this removal is not well-known; but contributions in this volume show several reasons – among them is Teferi's involvement in the removal of pro-Muslim announcements in favor of the Somali rebellion in British colonial territory (see on this Erlich's contribution in this volume); another factor directly leading to resistance was Teferi's indignation over the appointment of the Syrian Ydlibi (a Christian, not a Muslim, as usually believed) over Dirré Dawa, which strongly disturbed Teferi's economic activities in the region. When an insurrection from above was ripe, Teferi was ready and participated in the coup d'état of 1916 (see above) – being a compromise candidate between modernists, who saw in him a representative of the new reformist generation, and traditionalists who saw in him a defender of Shewan interests, but weak enough not to challenge them. They were surprisingly wrong. The years to follow, Teferi softly removed any obstacle to his power and re-shaped Ethiopia's political and territorial structures dramatically, not less dramatic than *Lïj* Iyasu had started it, but certainly in a totally different direction: Centralisation of the country, an establishment of absolutist-like monarchic

structures with elements of enlightenmer
local powers, in the name of modernisatior
another coup d'état, again in the name of n

World War I

See: Ottoman envoy

structures with elements of enlightenment and the appeasement or removal of any local powers, in the name of modernisation – until he himself was removed in 1974 in another coup d'état, again in the name of modernisation.

World War I

See: Ottoman envoy

Fig. 12: Lïj *Iyasu with his followers moving in Addis Ababa, with* Dejjazmach *Birru,* Ras *Tesemma, and further right* Dejjazmach *Meshesha (with European hat), photo taken by a European in the crowd, 1910/11 (collection of the author)*

Portrait of Lïj *Iyasu, with two (unidentified) children. Date and place unknown, ca. 1916. Private collection.*

List of authors

Rudolf Agstner - Historian, Austrian Ambassador to Ethiopia and Permanent Representative to the African Union, Addis Ababa (2006-2009) / Lecturer at the Institute of Contemporary History, University of Innsbruck (2001-2003), title Professor (2004)

Ahmed Hassen Omer – Historian, Director of the Institute of Ethiopian Studies of Addis Ababa University.

Aramis Houmed Soulé - Historian, independant researcher in Djibouti / Associated Researcher at the French Center of Ethiopian Studies, Addis Abeba

Asfa-Wossen Asserate - Historian, writer and political analyst / Chairman of the Board of Patrons, Orbis Aethiopicus

Zuzanna Augustyniak – Historian, Researcher at the Institute of Oriental Studies, Warsaw University

Haggai Erlich - Historian, Professor Emeritus at Tel Aviv University, Department of Middle Eastern and African History / Academic Adviser at the Open University of Israel

Éloi Ficquet - Anthropologist-Historian, Assistant Professor at the School for Advanced Studies in Social Sciences (EHESS). Paris / Director of the French Centre of Ethiopian Studies, Addis Ababa (2009-2012).

Hugues Fontaine – Photographer, independent researcher, France.

Alessandro Gori - Philologist-Historian, Department of Linguistics - University of Florence / A. von Humboldt Research Fellow at the Hiob Ludolf Centre of Ethiopian Studies, Hamburg University

Richard Pankhurst - Historian, former director of the Institute of Ethiopian Studies, Addis Ababa / Professor at Addis Ababa University

Shiferaw Bekele - Professor of Ethiopian History and Secretary General of the Academy of Ethiopian Languages and Cultures, Addis Ababa / Founding Fellow of the Ethiopian Academy of Sciences

Wolbert G.C. Smidt - Ethnohistorian, Associate Professor at the Department of History and Cultural Studies, Mekelle University / Assistant Editor of the Encyclopaedia Aethiopica, Hiob Ludolf Centre of Ethiopian Studies, Hamburg University

Estelle Sohier - Historian, Researcher at the University of Geneva, Switzerland

Valeria Semenova - PhD student of Museum of Anthropology and Ethnography of the Russian Academy of Sciences, assistant lecturer of the St. Petersburg State University, Faculty of Asian and African studies.

The Hamar of Southern Ethiopia
edited by Ivo Strecker and Jean Lydall

Ivo Strecker
Berimba's Resistance
The Life and Times of a Great Hamar Spokesman. As told by his son Aike Berinas
When Balambaras Aike Berinas, also called Baldambe, told me the story of his father, I felt very privileged to be the one to record and translate his exciting narrative, realizing it was a 'historic' moment: Spoken words were being transformed into written ones, and a text with its own distinctive features and literary style was emerging.
The drama of Berimba's Resistance was played out in the hot and rugged terrain of southern Ethiopia where, in the aftermath of the Ethiopian conquest, Berimba (ca. 1875 – 1952) was chosen by the Hamar to act as their spokesman. Baldambe relates in minute detail how Berimba dealt and negotiated with the intruders, and how he resisted their often high-handed rule until eventually he was murdered.
Bd. 4, 2013, 264 S., 19,90 €, br., ISBN 978-3-643-90343-3